## Acclaim for *The Girl Who Dared to Defy*

"Jane Little Botkin has unearthed an extraordinary story that reveals a hidden world. Her protagonist, Jane Street, was until now a mere footnote in the annals of American social history: a plucky young woman who appeared out of nowhere to organize an ahead-of-its-time labor union of domestic workers in early-twentieth-century Denver. But Botkin brings Jane Street's whole saga to life in intimate detail— her bohemian youth; her struggles in love and parenting; her battles with the elite matrons, the criminal underworld, and the hardboiled men of the Industrial Workers of the World; her pursuit by the Bureau of Investigation during the height of the Red Scare; and finally her unexpected later years as an amateur poet, a trained psychotherapist, and a doting grandmother. It is an astonishing drama full of burlesque dancers, conmen, radicals, thugs, pimps, muckraking journalists, and undercover agents. Botkin's exceptionally well researched and very readable book adds a new chapter to the histories of the American women's movement, the American labor movement, and the American West, and it will be a great resource for future historians of the early twentieth century."

—**DAVID KIRKPATRICK**, Pulitzer Prize–winning
journalist for the *New York Times*

# THE GIRL WHO DARED TO DEFY

# THE GIRL WHO DARED TO DEFY

## JANE STREET AND THE REBEL MAIDS OF DENVER

*Jane Little Botkin*

UNIVERSITY OF OKLAHOMA PRESS : NORMAN

This book is published with the generous assistance of the Kerr Foundation, Inc.

LIBRARY OF CONGRESS CATALOGING-IN-PUBLICATION DATA

Names: Botkin, Jane Little, 1952– author.

Title: The girl who dared to defy : Jane Street and the rebel maids of Denver / Jane Little Botkin.

Description: Norman : University of Oklahoma Press, [2021] | Includes bibliographical references and index. | Summary: "Biography of Jane Street, who attempted to organize Denver housemaids from Capitol Hill into an Industrial Workers of the World (IWW) union in 1916, and how her successful but short-lived efforts were undermined by male chauvinism within the IWW"—Provided by publisher.

Identifiers: LCCN 2020032981 | ISBN 978-0-8061-6849-4 (paperback)

Subjects: LCSH: Street, Jane, 1887–1966. | Industrial Workers of the World—Officials and employees—Biography. | Labor leaders—Colorado—Denver—Biography. | Women household employees—Labor unions—Colorado—Denver. | Women household employees—Colorado—Denver—Social conditions. | Labor movement—Colorado—Denver—History.

Classification: LCC HD6509.L4 B67 2021 | DDC 331.8/6092 [B]—dc23

LC record available at https://lccn.loc.gov/2020032981

The paper in this book meets the guidelines for permanence and durability of the Committee on Production Guidelines for Book Longevity of the Council on Library Resources, Inc. ∞

To my grandmother Louise Peterson,
a Colorado housemaid

And to my granddaughter Lacey Jane,
successor to a long line of independent women

The Maids' Defiance

*(Sung to the tune of "It's a Long Way to Tipperary")*

We are coming all together;
We are organized to stay.
For nigh on fifty years or more,
We've worked for little pay.
But now we've got our union,
We'll do it never more.

*Chorus:*
It's a long day for housemaid Mary;
It's a long day's hard toil.
It's a burden too hard to carry,
So our mistress's schemes we'll foil.
We'll be silent no longer.
We won't be kept down.
And we're out for a shorter day this summer,
Or we'll fix Denver town.

We've answered all your doorbells,
And we've washed your dirty kid.
For lo these many, weary years,
We've done as we were bid.
But we're goin' to fight for freedom,
And for our rights, we'll stand.
And we're goin' to stick together
In One Big Union band.

We've washed your dirty linen,
And we've cooked your daily foods.
We've eaten in your kitchens,

And we've stood your ugly moods.
But now we've joined the union,
And we're organized to stay.

You've paid the going wages.
That's what kept us on the run.
You say you've done your duty,
You cranky son-of-a-gun.
We've stood for all your crazy bunk,
And still you rave and shout
And call us inefficient
And a lazy gad-about.

                    Denver Housemaids' Union

# CONTENTS

# PREFACE

I first came across Jane Street, supposedly a housemaid who organized other domestics against mistresses on Denver's Capitol Hill,
while researching for my book *Frank Little and the IWW: The Blood
That Stained an American Family* (University of Oklahoma Press,
2017). My own Danish grandmother, product of a frontier mining envi-
ronment, had been a housemaid in an elite neighborhood in Boulder,
Colorado, at the exact time of Jane's story. She had run away, like many
young girls who became domestics, to escape a forced marriage in
Iowa and search for work. Regarding Denver's domestics, a Denver
Public Library historian later confirmed an old Scandinavian adage,
"Good girls become housemaids." Would my grandmother have heard
of Jane?

I have a habit of chasing rabbits, so I immediately paused to discover exactly who Jane was and if she was significant to Frank Little's
story. I discovered she wasn't, but he was surely essential to hers.
Frank Little indeed had met Jane, even helped her, but few specifics
completed the circumstances of their meeting. Women in the Industrial Workers of the World (IWW) are not historically well documented
apart from Elizabeth Gurley Flynn and a few other prominent activist
women. In fact, when I searched for Jane in western labor histories
and women's studies literature, she was mentioned only marginally,
though credited with starting a housemaids' union long before significant national conversations seriously discussed legislative protections
for the lowest class of women's professions, prostitution excepted.

Only one document, it seemed, existed, a 1917 letter written to
Mrs. Elmer Bruse, previously hidden in the bowels of the National
Archives Records Center. In it, Jane detailed methods that she employed
to organize maids and also provided new revelations: how IWW men
sabotaged her efforts, even assaulted her. In the age of #MeToo—
with heated national discussions and disagreements concerning

victimhood, survivorship, sexual assault, gender discrimination, and false accusations—I was intrigued. This was not just a western labor story but perhaps a narrative that might shed some light on disparate views today.

Discovering David D. Kirkpatrick's 1992 Princeton thesis, "Jane Street and Denver's Rebel Housemaids: The Gender of Radicalism in the Industrial Workers of the World," sealed my decision to research the rebel girl's story even further. Kirkpatrick, a *New York Times* international journalist, introduced me to the concept of "virile syndicalism," basically men joining together to assert their dominance in environments where they have been denied traditional male roles as husbands and fathers. He wrote that Jane's presence among the IWW seemed deliberately "almost nonexistent," an "aberration in a masculine organization in its least adulterated and most radical region [the West]." Kirkpatrick primarily used the Bruse letter, contemporary newspaper accounts, and general labor studies to discuss events of 1916 through 1917, a step toward unpeeling the layers of the Jane Street story that no other historian had ever taken. I had to find more about this story that involved core western views.

Being adept at researching old Bureau of Information files, I located a seventy-page dossier on Jane Street. Information and case histories collected between 1917 (when it was finally legal to confiscate and read suspected radicals' mail) and well into the 1920s contributed even more information. But it was my final discovery that propelled my decision to write Jane's life story. Through Ancestry.com, I located Jane's extended family. She had left a pile of writings—poems, essays, short stories—expressing her deepest sorrows and greatest joys, her regrets and hopes, her protests at societal injustices, her acceptance of aging, and her fervent desire for motherhood. Just as wonderful, her grandson, keeper of Jane's private papers, was alive and eager to talk about the grandmother he knew and adored.

By searching Denver's well-known characters, their homes, and correspondences, I was able to patch together images of Denver's Capitol Hill and flesh out residents relevant to Jane's story. Many of the mansions still exist with little change in appearance, easily helping this Denver sightseer to envision life in the late teens of the twentieth century. Sometimes I was fortunate, and a Capitol Hill mansion came on to the real estate market. The Campbell mansion's interior, in particular, is detailed in this narrative by studying marketing photos. I researched women's attire, pre–World War I language and attitudes, and historical context in order to set Jane into a narrative that, I hope, reads better than a generic nonfiction account. Finally, framing Jane's unusual life are the labor wars in the western mining camps and the first Red Scare—its leaders, villains, and victims—when Americans' xenophobic and uber-patriotic attitudes melded together to produce a troubling picture of what our nation can become again.

This book is not a purposeful study of feminism, the IWW, or domestic studies, although these subjects are surely present. Instead, the book traces the life of a woman who was not even a maid, her indoctrination into the IWW, her remarkable success organizing the "unorganizable," and her downfall due to her sex. Jane's two worlds collide—that of traditional motherhood and wife, and that of an unencumbered revolutionary, fighting for an unconventional new world. Themes involving sexual exploitation, violent assault, misogyny, and virile syndicalism permeate the narrative. In the book's periphery, western women, with their unique spirits and backgrounds, strive to bring independence to all classes of women—except for the housemaids. Thus, Jane Street, who originally supports the IWW's fight as a class war and not a gender war, evolves into an organizer for female domestics in a battle staged against some of Denver's well-known suffragists and club women, even as she fights her male counterparts along the way. Both groups betray her, and as the resulting tragedy unfolds, the reader is left with a surprising ending.

# ACKNOWLEDGMENTS

Much of my early research for this book came from researching Frank Little's biography. At that time, with this second book already in mind, I collected materials from various archives and libraries whose wonderful staffs deserve my thanks yet again, including William W. LeFevre of the Walter P. Reuther Library at Wayne State University and Verónica Reyes and other staff in Special Collections, University of Arizona. Writing *Frank Little and the IWW* provided the foundation I needed to get an early jump on Jane Street.

While I prepared for Denver research, I discovered two repositories where I was able to find a variety of primary documents on early Colorado suffragists, Denver club women, and of course, the indomitable Louise Sneed Hill and her Sacred Thirty-Six. The Stephen H. Hart Library and Research Center at History Colorado provided numerous documents belonging to Denver's early movers and shakers. Holding Susan B. Anthony's letters to Colorado suffragists in my hands was a unique experience, as was perusing Caroline Bancroft's confidential notes on the famous Sacred Thirty-Six in the Western Genealogical and Research Library (Denver Public Library). Thank you to staff members who accommodated me! I spent over a week in the two archives—mornings at the SHL and afternoons at DPL—moving my car in and out of the same parking garage slot at lunch to avoid paying high parking fees. The results of my research were worth the extra effort.

Other people deserve my thanks as well. *New York Times* journalist David D. Kirkpatrick provided his early thesis on Jane Street and tried to explain "virile syndicalism" to my stubborn brain from across the pond. MaryJoy Martin, who had helped me with Frank Little research, shared her voluminous files once again. Her book, *The Corpse on Boomerang Road*, brings Telluride's labor war into focus (as told with MaryJoy's incredible wit), so naturally, she had specific files to share regarding villain Bulkeley Wells.

Mike Anderson in Bisbee, Arizona, provided early legwork regarding the IWW's union hall; Phil Wright, Herbert R. Bumpass's step-grandson, provided photographs of the elusive con man; Melanie Rosenberg, married to a descendant of Phil Engle's family, offered insight and background on early Jewish immigration, all the way from Jerusalem herself; and Cora Cowan's nephews, Rob Huysman, Jim O'Hare, and Mark O'Hare, provided genealogical and other family information to assist me in profiling an atypical domestic. I had quite an interesting conversation over dinner in Tucson with Mark, who shared some remarkable anecdotes about his aunt. All but Mike Anderson were connections I discovered through Ancestry.com.

I want to thank Kathy and Jack Devlin, Charles Devlin's cousin, whom I also met through Ancestry.com. Their early Devlin research was absolutely invaluable. We had many early telephone conversations, met in person later in Texas when they visited family, and finally traveled together to see Jane's grandson in Arizona. My new friends and I speculated who Jack Street was—if there even was a Jack Street—while unraveling family secrets, separating truth from fiction, and analyzing Jane's relationships. As each notion was proved or dispelled, a new door opened, requiring research and more conversations.

Finally, meeting Guy Leslie, Jane's grandson, and his wife Loui was the pinnacle of my research. Guy graciously laid out all the Tuttle family photos and loaned me all Jane's private papers, including her precious writings, a researcher's dream. I am so indebted to him and hope he is pleased with this book. I encourage him to donate her papers and union photos to Denver's Stephen H. Hart Library and Research Center or the Denver Public Library so that other historians may peruse Jane's ideas through her writings.

What fun this project was, discovering who Jane Street really was—her passions, loves, and greatest disappointments. I had company on this literary journey, so much so, that I was invited to share each discovery and then contentedly bask as my friends, too, became vested in my subject. During the course of preparing the manuscript, unexpected national stories entered our passionate discussions as we analyzed and sometimes second-guessed each of Jane's decisions and how she would have resolved her issues today. To my first readers—dear friends, Debbie Font and Karen Williams—thank you. My husband, Gary, also read each draft chapter, sharing an important male perspective that often resulted in new ideas that I would later incorporate. I am especially indebted to him.

Finally, I want to thank my editor and mentor, Chuck Rankin. Only because of him, have I become a better writer. He continues to take chances on me, for whatever reason, I absolutely cannot fathom. I am surely grateful.

# ABBREVIATIONS

| | |
|---|---|
| AFL | American Federation of Labor |
| AWIU | Agricultural Workers Industrial Union (Industrial Workers of the World) |
| AWO | Agricultural Workers Organization (Industrial Workers of the World) |
| BMMWU | Butte Metal Mine Workers Union |
| C&S | Colorado and Southern Railway |
| DAR | Daughters of the American Revolution |
| DWIU | Domestic Workers Industrial Union (Industrial Workers of the World) |
| GEB | General Executive Board of the Industrial Workers of the World |
| GRU | General Recruiting Union (Industrial Workers of the World) |
| IUMMSW | International Union of Mine, Mill, and Smelter Workers (Former WFM) |
| IWW | Industrial Workers of the World |
| MMWIU | Metal Mine Workers Industrial Union (Industrial Workers of the World) |
| MOA | Mine Owners Association |
| OBU | One Big Union (Industrial Workers of the World) |
| SPA | Socialist Party of America |
| SLP | Socialist Labor Party |
| UMWA | United Mine Workers of America |
| WFM | Western Federation of Miners |
| YW | Young Women's Christian Association (Denver) |
| YWCA | Young Women's Christian Association |

# PROLOGUE

God almighty made women and the Rockefeller gang of
thieves made the ladies.

    Mary Harris Jones, *Autobiography of Mother Jones*

Marcelina Pedregone, her thin skirt partly ablaze in the early morning light, recalled running hard—sprinting northward toward a fence, then crawling into a smoky arroyo where she could lay flat in the rocky dirt, trying to become invisible from the bullets nipping around her legs and feet like a mad dog. She saw some women dodging flames to desperately help their children reach a well and then scramble inside after them, while others sought safety in a pump house, its walls being chewed by gunfire. Amid their shrieks and wails, Marcelina allowed a brief hesitation to worry about her own children she had left behind, Cloriva and Rodgerio, just four months and six years old. They had been staying with the Valdez and Costa children near Tent No. 58, one of about 150 makeshift homes for Colorado's southern coalfield miners and their families when someone shrieked, "Dynamite! Dynamite!"[1]

As militia soldiers exploded several bombs to signal their assault on the striking miners, Mrs. Costa would have rounded up the youngsters and scuttled them for safety into the deep, dirt cellar beneath the tent's wooden floorboards. Hadn't Mother Jones, who had come to Trinidad in late 1913 and early 1914, urged families to prepare for such a fight? Even then, Jones had been arrested for challenging mine operators and the Colorado National Guard, commanded by Adjutant General John Chase.[2] In fact, Ludlow Colony had been fearing violence for seven months now, after witnessing a Gatling gun discharge

147 bullets into a coal miner's tent, whose occupant survived by lying prone during the attack.[3]

Ludlow's colony of tents housed over one thousand people, including 271 children. Most tents covered shallow pits, some now filled with weeping women and babies.[4] But the Costa pit was deeply dug, its black maw waiting to swallow three women and eleven children and keep them safe from the bullet sprays. Knowing this, Marcelina could alternately crawl and run until she, too, could escape the barrage of bullets screaming from Gatling guns atop Water Tank Hill. She had no way to know that once the shooting stopped at sundown, uniformed men would begin torching the canvas tents not already aflame, many flying American flags above them.[5] She would not have seen the murder of their Greek leader Louis Tikas, who, carrying a white flag, was struck in the head with a rifle butt and then brutally shot.[6]

The next day, as survivors straggled into Trinidad, Marcelina asked with parched lips if anyone had news of her children. Not until a "dead" wagon arrived, loaded with fourteen bodies, did she find Cloriva and Rodgerio, smothered, burned, and swollen, along with others who asphyxiated in the Costa death pit. Cardelima Costa's dead, pregnant body remarkably gave birth to a stillborn baby, doctors calling it the "strangest childbirth ever given to a woman."[7]

One year later on May 2, 1915, a petite Elizabeth Gurley Flynn, the famous girl-orator recently named the "most magnetic woman in America," looked down from a dais to a scant crowd in Denver's East End Turner Hall and reminded the audience of Ludlow and the importance of organizing and cooperating with Colorado's working-class women.[8] Flynn expressed deep disappointment in Colorado's women. She expected better of them—*all* mothers, wives, and daughters should have protested in a loud voice against the Ludlow episode. In the audience, a smitten *Denver Post* reporter described her dainty but determined oration, "liquid eyes and alluring soothing voice," and her way of "lisping revolutions as if the revolution were a lullaby or a nocturne."[9] To him, Flynn was a new Joan of Arc, born to trouble of a socialist father and Fenian grandfather, who works her "spells" in any "atmosphere of strife."[10] Attributing her appeal to feminine charms, the reporter, like other men before him, underestimated Elizabeth Gurley Flynn's power and impact.

Denver's Chamber of Commerce and local newspapers did not view Flynn as innocuously and had originally suppressed word of her planned appearance, even as they had taken criticism in recent months from a new, powerful Women's Law and Order League. Led by Helen L. Grenfell and Mrs. Charles H. Jacobson, certain ladies from Denver's Capitol Hill objected to besmirching the state's National Guard as child murderers, despite an inquest corroborating the guard's crimes against civilians, and they had organized.[11] Governor Elias Ammons and some of the Capitol Hill ladies' husbands and sons, who had been among other Denver and Central City–Black Hawk mining district businessmen commissioned—and paid—by the state when the guard was called up, were now perceived as "victims of the press."[12] Even Adjutant General Chase, who employed unlawful and even unconstitutional tactics at Ludlow, was an ophthalmologist to certain Capitol Hill families.[13]

Still, other prominent women, led by Colorado state representative Alma Lafferty, Colorado state senator Helen Ring Robinson, and suffragist Dora Phelps Buell of the Women's Peace Association, had supported the miners' families with humanitarian relief while at the same time protesting the violence in coalfields to Governor Ammons and their sisters in the Law and Order League.[14] Moreover, Denver's *Rocky Mountain News*, deploring the widening of class lines, had demanded that the league's new catchphrase "law and order" include "and justice," and that it publicly endorse full enforcement "of *all* laws and obedience by *all* the people *all* of the time," challenging the Law and Order League's sole claim of righteous entitlement.[15]

Flynn was not fooled, however, that fickle public opinion temporarily railed against J. D. Rockefeller Jr. His interests, which owned the mines, sent the C&S train carrying the state militia and gunmen scurrying to Ludlow in April 1914, yet he claimed no responsibility for the crimes.[16] A new European War had ramped up, and opportunists needed workers to produce wheat, steel, and bullets. Flynn's call to working-class women, in remembrance of Ludlow's wives and mothers, was to become soldiers in the Industrial Workers of the World (IWW), an organization united in 1905 for all working-class people battling the capitalist enterprises that dominated America's industrial revolution.

The radical American labor movement had been partly borne after earlier losses in mining-labor conflicts across western states, especially the 1903–4 Colorado labor wars, propelling the Western Federation of Miners (WFM) to merge with the IWW. A recent economic panic, resulting in lost employment and wealth, combined with tyrannical corporate-owned industries, an underpaid workforce laboring in unsafe conditions, and loss of American artisanship to industrial automation, now led to enormous worker-discontent across the continent. It was not surprising that many workers questioned democratic capitalism.

With Elizabeth Gurley Flynn in mind, popular IWW bard Joe Hill famously advocated women's roles in the IWW movement, claiming the organization needed women to offset "a kind of one-legged, freakish animal of a union" that was too much of a "buck affair."[17] Naturally Flynn was inspiration for his song "The Rebel Girl," and it was dedicated to all IWW women in 1915.

> There are women of many descriptions
> In this queer world, as everyone knows.
> Some are living in beautiful mansions,
> And are wearing the finest of clothes.
> There are blue blooded queens and princesses,
> Who have charms made of diamonds and pearl;
> But the only and thoroughbred lady
> Is the Rebel Girl.
> We've had girls before, but we need some more
> In the Industrial Workers of the World.
> For it's great to fight for freedom
> With a Rebel Girl.[18]

Indeed, many women were now self-identifying as rebels, just as Elizabeth Gurley Flynn had at the tender age of sixteen in New York's Bronx neighborhood.[19]

Over a thousand miles away and almost two years after Ludlow, Flynn's leadership in western free speech fights and eastern women's industrial labor strikes had not gone unnoticed, especially to an obscure young woman—a single mother—simultaneously struggling to support her child and improve her lot. That certain ladies did not empathize with Ludlow's mothers and children personally offended her sense of feminine integrity. Her name was Jane Street, and she resolved to change the status quo.

Jane Street would orchestrate a domestic mutiny against Denver's Capitol Hill women, that is, against the powerful and elite. The housemaid rebellion would soon make national and local news. It would simultaneously herald club support for women's suffrage, improved morality, and education of the underprivileged, even as it patronized the efforts of a neglected working class. Jane would face sexist attempts at suppression, including sabotage and betrayal, arrests and abandonment. For this, she deserves more than a small piece of working women's history. Jane Street never claimed to be a victim, but her tragic life story makes one wonder why she did not.

*Part One*
# VISIONS

## Chapter One
# THE GIRL IN RED

I was told that when I was a little girl, I said that when
I grew up that I was going to marry a preacher and have
six children. I don't remember saying it.

Jane Street, "The Lost Prince"

On the evening of July 19, 1906, Luna Park's music and shrieks barely overpowered distant sounds of clanking metal, shouting policemen, and one quick-talking carnival barker near its back boundary. There stood another amusement tent, its front filled with a crowd of incensed women. Emboldened by the previous night's mass meeting at Calvary Evangelical Church, they were banging dishpans in protest over the performance within. Newburgh's village police, attempting to preserve order, were pushed back by what had become several hundred protestors intent on mob destruction. Trying to ignore the threats, the announcer found himself drowned out, and when one bully in skirts threatened him with her tin pan, a policeman came to his rescue, but only briefly. "Touch that woman and I'll break your head," threatened a bystander to the officer.[1]

Luna Park was to many Ohioans the best trolley amusement park of its kind in the United States. Modeled after Coney Island in 1905, a panoply of amusements and alcohol awaited paying guests on the thirty-five-acre grounds in Newburgh's Woodland Hills neighborhood.[2] At the park's grand entrance was a Japanese Village where visitors could experience a tea room, Geisha girls, Japanese music, and benign dancers. Other ethnic curiosities and a carnival of noise, sights, and smells interspersed among grander amusement rides, including a figure-eight roller coaster screaming with thrill-seekers, an elaborate carousel of galloping steeds, and a towering Ferris wheel, all leading to the park's "midway." There thousands of lights illuminated an area of special attractions including a casino, funhouse, pool, and merry-go-round. Inside the "Edisonia," awed guests could listen to phonographs and watch moving pictures on a kinetoscope, while outside the more adventurous in boats could "shoot the chutes" into a blue lagoon.[3] But, to Newburgh's citizens, the burlesque show at the rear of the park's grounds was not family-friendly and definitely not compatible with their moral virtues.

Soon, the entertainment inside the tent ceased, and the show's barker was momentarily reduced to silence. Recovering, he assured the pugnacious crowd, "There is no show here. Look in everybody, and see that there is nothing doing." Indeed, the evening's burlesque of "The Girl in Red" was concluded.[4] Inside the tent, behind the stage, was a dancer, more girl than woman, crouched behind a filmy, scarlet veil that barely concealed her body. Mob members could see her obvious terror and made no attempt to do the girl bodily harm, although shouts from outside offered severe ways to dispose of her.[5] Satisfied that the performance had ceased, the crowd's excitement died, and the mass of people left to strategize new measures for suppressing Newburgh's latest stain of immorality. For the production company, the plan was much simpler—the show would move on to Cincinnati. For Grace Tuttle, the "Oriental" dancer who dressed in sheer red and called herself "La Neta," the run was over.[6]

Grace had spent the previous three years aspiring toward stardom. After reflecting that she was no doubt beautiful, though "hipless and breastless," she ran away to Philadelphia, Atlantic City, and finally New York City. There she worked as an artist's model in well-known studios and performed in various small musical productions.[7] The work was nothing that she would want her "mother nor father nor Sunday School teacher" to know about, except for a handful of Atlantic City souvenir postcards she had mailed home.[8] Instead of staying home and making plans to attend business school like her little sister, she had posed for a portfolio of nude photographs, her lithe body lit up like a beacon in a sea of black.[9] In Grace's words, "I weighed ninety-six pounds . . . and like the song goes, 'they went wild, simply wild over me.'"[10] With a musical background and unburdened by what she called "bug bears," such as religion, patriotism, and respect for law and order, Grace easily transitioned to a starring role in burlesque.[11] After other dancers performed exotic cooch dances, Grace, with her boyish figure, floated on stage, "a creature in scarlet disguises of diaphanous kinds," and with twists and turns, mesmerized those in attendance.[12] Now, following a nervous breakdown and extended relapse after the Newburgh incident, her grand plans for fame dissipated.[13] Grace Tuttle, along with her secrets, traveled to her mother's home in Hot Springs, Arkansas, late 1906, where her sister—her best friend—was waiting.

Jane Tuttle stood alone on a train platform anticipating her sister's arrival. Their father, Frank Tuttle, had passed the previous year, and Mary Ann, the girls' mother, was too steeped in despondency at their home on 515 3rd Street to assist Jane in retrieving Grace.[14] The Rock Island train finally arrived, shuddering to a stop, and after a few moments, Grace emerged onto the train station's platform. Immediately, Jane recognized her mirror image. Though tinier than Grace, at five feet tall, Jane Tuttle was almost a twin to her sister, small boned with black hair and black eyes.[15] She was also as vain, and soon after Grace arrived in Hot Springs, the girls had boudoir photos taken. Jane appears to be wearing a dressing gown with her thick hair down.[16] Grace countered with a similar but more suggestive pose with her throat and shoulders exposed in her studio portrait, remarking, "A la Jane!"[17]

Jane implicitly knew that Grace was the more uninhibited performer on stage, but Jane was comfortably chatty in a regular setting and also had artistic talents.[18] The sisters' shared interests were filled with fun banter and competition, yet their differences were striking. While Grace had sought to fulfill her creative side, Jane, the pragmatist, studied stenography and honed organizational skills. She was about concrete detail; Grace, about imitation and impression. Both desired approval and acclaim. Not surprisingly, the girls' mutual relationship was constructed much like a yin-yang, their lives interconnected and interdependent long before their mother deserted the family in 1904.

Jane Tuttle, ca. 1907.
*Courtesy of Guy Leslie,*
*Jane Street Family Papers*

Grace Tuttle, "A la Jane!"
ca. 1907.
*Courtesy of Guy Leslie,*
*Jane Street Family Papers*

Mary Ann Tuttle appears to have struggled with depression, possibly due to five deaths occurring within her immediate family before she entered marriage with Frank Tuttle, a surveyor, in 1876. Averaging one bereavement every other year, another eight deaths—including brother, sister, and parents—would follow. Mary Ann lost three infant sons before giving birth to Grace on November 17, 1883.[19] After Jane was born on February 20, 1887, in Terre Haute, Indiana, Mary Ann's four-year-old daughter Anna also died.[20]

On January 3, 1904, the *Indianapolis Journal* reported that Grace, too, had succumbed, in the infamous Iroquois Theater fire in Chicago on December 30, 1903, when 587 people were burned or trampled to death.[21] Grace had arrived in the city to study at the Chicago Musical College just one week earlier. The devastated family grieved for over twenty-four hours before Frank received a telegram that the Grace Tuttle whose name was on the dead list was not his daughter.[22] Broken, Mary Ann had fled, moving to Arkansas shortly afterward, possibly seeking holistic comfort in Hot Springs' mineral waters.[23] Afterward, Frank, along with Jane, joined his wife in Arkansas while Grace modeled in New York City. Living with a mother thus distracted, it is not surprising that both Jane and Grace Tuttle sought father figures and needed the approval of men.

Jane had begun seeing a war hero, John "Jack" Street, and had photographs of him to prove it. Five feet, nine and a half inches tall with light brown hair and eyes, Jack Street presented a handsome appearance in his earliest military photograph.[24] In another photo, Jack Street sits astride a tall horse, quirt in hand and dressed as a dandy—bowler hat, suit, gleaming boots. The mount's saddle pad was even emblazoned with a shabraque, a military decoration, to further support his claim of military service. Not long afterward, Jane and Jack invited Grace and her various beaus to share in picnics and other diversions at McLeod's Happy Hollow Amusement Park in Hot Springs, the closest recreational area similar to Atlantic City and Luna Park that the Tuttle family could enjoy. Grace recorded these dates with photographs, though no photos of Jane and Jack together exist— perhaps deliberately.

The most popular tourist attraction in the area, McLeod's Happy Hollow Amusement Park was located at the head of Fountain Street,

Herbert R. Bumpass, alias John (Jack) Street, in an armed services photo, ca. 1898.
*Courtesy of Phil Wright*

just off Central Avenue, north of Hot Springs Mountain. Its center-piece, Norman McLeod's photography studio, advertised his specialty of "Wild West Combination" and "Rustic and Comic" photos, such as sitting on the back of burros ("I Don't Know Where I'm Going, but I'm on My Way"), a log shack ("Our Summer Home"), stepping up to a bar ("Arkansas Travelers' Saloon"), other humorous vignettes, and western and American Indian dress. Even Babe Ruth was captured on film, burdening a small burro with his bulk, among other professional baseball players who trained in Hot Springs and had their pictures taken on donkeys.[25]

One early McLeod photo in Hot Springs' Happy Hollow Amuse-ment Park presents a still-living and slight, white-bearded Frank Tuttle along with Jack Street astride burros, their feet inches above the street's surface, in an attempt at hillbilly humor. Since Tuttle died in late 1905, the photo dates the approximate time when Jack Street began a lifelong pattern of ingratiating himself into a vulnerable family in order to seduce its daughter, typically a much younger woman.

Jack Street was actually a silver-tongued charlatan, self-described as a "soldier of fortune" who served as General Adna Chaffee's personal orderly in the 1898 Peking Relief Campaign. Further embellishing his war story to the family, Street described his participation as a member of Queen Victoria's Imperial Light Horse Regiment.[26] Street neglected to reveal that he had returned home as a dishonorably discharged felon in irons aboard an army transport from Taku, China, on February 1901, along with the remains of sixty-one dead soldiers from the battle of Tiensin.[27]

In fact, Jack Street's real name was Herbert Ross Bumpass, and in 1905, at thirty years old, he was twelve years Jane's senior.[28] By trade, he was employed as a printer with one of his brothers at Shannahan's Printery in Hot Springs.[29] Another brother, Robert H. Bumpass, worked as an attorney and collection agent along with their father in the family firm, also in Hot Springs, making one wonder how and why the Tuttle family did not question the Street name. Clearly Street was a predator whose pattern of relationship with Jane fits a pedophile's profile, and Jane was a vulnerable eighteen-year-old. The couple continued to meet at McLeod's Happy Hollow park, where Jack stealthily groomed Jane, gaining her trust and dependence—and filling her father's void. As Street succeeded in swallowing Jane in little bites, she became totally consumed by the man who now wanted her to call him "Horse," his lifelong predilection for nicknames further masking his various personas.[30] Her personal writings reveal her complete adoration for Street. Using the pseudonym Gertrude Riske in a poem titled, "A Lover's Prayer," Jane asks for God's blessing over her lover:

> Beloved is that holy prayer,
> I shall see you standing there,
> Divinely, radiantly fair;
> And for your love so grand and rare,
> Which you devotedly declare,
> I shall kneel to God.[31]

Jane, it seems, believed Jack Street was a divine gift, and she had no intention of losing an opportunity for marriage and motherhood. Jane desired normalcy after her mother had failed miserably in domestic happiness.

Though Mary Ann Tuttle may have felt relief that her daughter had found a suitor, a war veteran at that, she would have had no idea or been too depressed to realize that Street was slowly isolating Jane from the family home, which now included Grace and Grace's new husband and printer William D. Franz.[32] Not to be outdone by Jane and her steady boyfriend, less than a year after the Newburgh incident, Grace had married Franz on June 7, 1907, about the same time Jane's relationship with Jack Street became more intimate.[33] Shortly after Grace's marriage, Jane discovered she was pregnant. That she was to become an unwed mother did not dent her absolute love for her unborn baby.

When Street orchestrated a pathway to remove Jane from her family in Hot Springs, where Mary Ann or Grace could awaken Jane to her perilous situation, Jane obliged, moving to St. Louis, Missouri. Street found new employment as a printer at the Arkansas Bank Note Company, also out of town but in Little Rock, under his Bumpass name.[34] With Jane safely stowed, he could continue his two lives as Jack Street in St. Louis and Herbert Bumpass in Little Rock as he traveled back and forth. The scheme was more cunning than even Jane knew. Jack Street had also left a young wife, Dollie, with his parents in Hot Springs, whom he had married while he was courting Jane.[35]

To confound matters more, Grace divorced her husband after only one year of marriage, soon after marrying Jack's younger brother, the attorney Robert H. Bumpass.[36] Grace surely knew Robert was Jack's brother, possibly even delighting in the fact that now the sisters shared relationships with brothers. One would assume that they questioned the difference in the brothers' surnames, but Jack had that covered too, reportedly telling an attorney, in another criminal matter, that he came to have two names after he had been adopted as a small child, taking the name of his adopted parents. He then embellished more, adding that the adoption had not been legal, thus preventing anyone from disproving his adoption claim or proving that he used an alias to hide criminal enterprises.[37] Jack Street excelled as a con man.

Jane's son by Jack Street, Josiah Mars Street, was born and died March 1, 1908.[38] Three months later, Jane was pregnant again and still unwed, indicating that having a family, no matter how unconventional, was paramount to Jane. Nevertheless, on December 21, 1908, three weeks before Jane's second baby was due, John (Jack) Street finally married Jane Tuttle in Van Buren, Carter County, Missouri.[39] On January 15, 1909, the couple named their newborn son Dawn Philander

Street and moved to 2737 Locust Street in St. Louis.[40] Aside from Street's affinity for mythological names, the verb *philander* coincidentally described the baby's father perfectly. After their marriage, Jane briefly continued her reveries about her future with Jack Street, dreaming of how the two would grow old together and once more sit together at the park and reminisce of old times. In her poem "To Her Husband," Jane asks whether she has succeeded in providing Jack's happiness.

> When we return to our lovers' seat,
> On some bright morning, cool and sweet,
> Like the one when the hours went by unheeded,
> You must tell me whether I have succeeded.[41]

Jane finally had her family, while in Hot Springs, Street fathered a child with his wife, Dollie Bumpass.

Did Jane eventually discover her Jack Street was Herbert Bumpass, already married with another child? Circumstances would indicate

At McLeod's Happy Hollow Amusement Park, late 1908. *Standing, left to right:* Robert Bumpass (with face scratched out), Grace Tuttle. *Sitting, left to right:* Jane Tuttle (Street), Mary Tuttle. *Courtesy of Guy Leslie, Jane Street Family Papers*

that she had indeed learned of his duplicity sooner than later. Not long after Dawn Street's birth, Jane untangled her relationship with Street, the man to whom she had dedicated verse. Grace evidently was also not suited for wedlock. She divorced for a second time, for whatever reason. The hostility toward her second husband is visible on his scratched-out face in yet another McLeod Happy Hollow photo featuring the couple, Robert and Grace Bumpass; Jane, her contented face full with pregnancy; and a dour-faced Mary Ann Tuttle.[42]

For Grace, opportunity lay in California where the "girl in red" hoped to find stage fame once again. The motion picture industry was barely in its infancy, but dancing and singing had evolved into major vaudeville productions since the California gold rush. Jane would join her, the disenchanted young mother and son withdrawing from any family connections left in Arkansas, while the Bumpass brothers predictably entangled themselves in criminal and legal cases in the years to come.[43] The Tuttle sisters' miscalculations and failed relationships, no doubt damaging, did not prevent them from desiring male companionship in the future. Jane would continue to carry the Street name, though Grace shed all vestiges of her marriages. Packing their family baggage with them, the sisters looked west.

## Chapter Two
# REBEL GIRL

The "queen in the parlor" has no interest in common with "the maid in the kitchen."
Elizabeth Gurley Flynn, *Solidarity*, July 15, 1915

Twenty-five-year-old Jane Street stood at her stenographer's booth, greeting some of the regulars by name, mostly men. Joining the minority women who ventured out into the business world in 1912, Jane had arrived to work at Sacramento's Golden Eagle Hotel in a tailored dress, buttoned to her throat. Her appearance was calculated to advertise professional services and not companionship.[1] Offsetting the practical attire, she had worn a broad, velvet hat, its feather drooping to one side, hinting at the feminine spirit within. With the hat put aside, other single-minded hotel guests, if they bothered to look her way, saw a petite woman, just tall enough to command her stand, wearing her heavy brunette hair parted in the middle and pinned up, extending her petite height above dangling earrings.

The ground floor of Sacramento's Golden Eagle was busy, crammed with customers, many scurrying to shop at Mark Harrison & Co., a high-end men's clothier, or to eat at the hotel's in-house café. Others strode to the hotel's Delta Club, a men's social club where hotel proprietor Kirk Harris and his backroom tables hosted illegal draw-poker games.[2] Harris had made changes recently, updating the hotel to best serve its eminent clientele, dealmakers and businessmen, running

Jane Street's appearance was calculated to advertise professional services and not companionship, ca. 1910. *Courtesy of Guy Leslie, Jane Street Family Papers*

schemes out of their rooms after advertising in the *Sacramento Bee*.[3] Jane's presence was such an upgrade. She had begun work sometime in 1912, after approaching Harris, with a three-year-old child in tow, and requesting work.[4] Harris had no idea that Jane was a divorcee, and like others, might have described her employment chances, and even her character, pejoratively. But Jane had lied, telling Kirk Harris that her husband was dead.[5]

Outside, on Sacramento's busiest corner, where K and Seventh Streets collide, stood the imposing Italianate structure that spread almost one city block, its three floors of tall arched windows hinting at luxurious accommodations within. Its commanding vertical sign above, spreading *Golden Eagle Hotel* from the top floor down to the first floor over striped canopies, proclaimed the hotel's presence. In front, on K's wide street, pedestrians dodged streetcars, Model T Fords, sundry touring cars, and horse-drawn conveyances to cross over to Sacramento's Capitol Hotel. The Capitol was currently vying with the Golden Eagle for an anticipated influx of easterners and other visitors on western tours from points across the world. Only the Golden Eagle had a reputation for being the mainstay of the Republican Party.[6]

Sacramento's hotels were now bulging to capacity, and the Golden Eagle's 150 rooms had been occupied for the last three months with more reservations booked up to three weeks in advance.[7] To meet demands for more occupancy, hotels employed hundreds of chambermaids, cooks, laundresses, busboys, dishwashers, doormen, elevator pilots (operators), and other occupations necessary for running top-notch hospitality enterprises. As the current workforce's satisfaction ebbed and flowed in relation to the flood of tourists, discontent was beginning to spread.

Initially, Jane was unaware, if not immune to labor unrest enveloping the city and within the Golden Eagle. Her new job mimicked self-employment and gave her a sense of independence. For a price, she functioned like a private secretary, taking dictation in shorthand, typing, and formatting letters, as well as performing other clerical tasks that could be accomplished at her "public stand."[8] Though Jane's life had evened out, she regretted leaving Dawn in the care of others, likely at her boarding house, a two-story Victorian at 806 U Street, ten blocks south of K Street.[9] Jane's maternal guilt is evident in a portion of an early poem:

> Mommie, Mommie,
> I'm so alone.
> Mommie, Mommie,
> Can't you feel my tiny heart-strings
> Drawin' you?
> Mommie, Mommie,
> Mommie, won't you please come home?[10]

Still, the routine was welcome, a palliative that softened the bruises from Herbert Bumpass's duplicity. Jane probably cared less that to many, her work as a stenographer categorized her as unmarriageable.

Historically, since women first entered the stenographer workforce in the late nineteenth century, eventually displacing men with their cumbersome fingers, many male employers were charged with treacherous and "perfidious" methods that degraded young women. The Anti-Stenographers' Society, first organized by women in Columbus, Ohio, cautioned parents not to permit their daughters to accept positions as stenographers.[11] It claimed employers often disgraced vulnerable girls, frequently promising marriage to them, rendering the women unfit for wifely duties.[12] And even as Remington Typewriter Company pushed ads with attractive, young, unmarried "Gibson Girls," whose nimble fingers and stylish attire offered male employers more for their money, the society claimed that only one in twenty stenographers was considered suitable for marriage anyway, having been "desexed" by paid work.[13]

Though the first Stenographers and Typewriters Union formed in 1903 in Massachusetts, advocating that sexual harassment and misconduct be expelled from the workplace, no record of Jane belonging to such a union in the Sacramento area exists.[14] In fact, the American Federation of Labor (AFL) included few women in its craft unions. Most AFL unions excluded women by "subtle" means, that is, by demanding higher fees and dues from workers who typically earned on average half of what men earned.[15] Jane did not earn twenty-five dollars per week until 1920, when she worked as a stenographer for an attorney, while her male counterparts earned near this amount as early as 1904.[16]

Theoretically, while women working in organized trades could have become affiliated with existing national labor unions in 1912, few joined. The only exceptions were those in textile industries. Because of the AFL's "multifaceted hostility" toward women workers, the proportion of women who organized into unions between 1900 and 1910 declined to just 1.5 percent.[17] Other statistics reveal more. By 1920, of female clerical workers, stenographers like Jane who made up 20 percent of all women wage earners, only 3 percent were unionized. By contrast, their sisters working in the garment industry made up 29 percent of the female workforce, and they had unionized in greater numbers, facing a patriarchy where class and gender historically benefited from their exploitation.[18]

Now IWW agitators, such as Elizabeth Gurley Flynn, were trying to help women redefine their self-identities by rejecting paternal expectations and urging them to become equal partners in labor's resistance movement. When the IWW organized in June 1905, its purpose of economic equality attracted and included all ethnicities, genders, and crafts—skilled and unskilled—a tenet the AFL had not embraced. For unemployed Americans, drowning in economic and ethnic oppression between 1910 and 1915, the organization, promoting itself as "One Big Union," promised to rescue disenfranchised men and women and give them solid footing, with the hope that a single class of workers could actually dominate all aspects of labor. An "unapologetically socialist organization," the IWW was far different from the AFL and other contemporary labor unions.[19] By 1911, IWW members called themselves Wobblies.[20]

Jane possibly could have become acquainted with the IWW through newspaper stories about the fiery rebel girl soapboxer, Elizabeth Gurley Flynn, as early as 1909. Both women were expecting babies about the same time but were preoccupied in different ways. A pregnant Flynn was thrown into a Spokane jail for one night during an ugly free speech fight. Jane could not have known that Flynn had combatted an all-male committee in order to soapbox in public. The IWW men had believed that her pregnancy should be concealed.[21] The fact that a more recent 1912 strike involved primarily women, more than likely interested Jane. News of the Lawrence, Massachusetts, textile strike came to Sacramento when the *Bee* headlined the unrest. Boldly pictured on its front page were Pearl Magill, leader of the strike, and, not surprisingly, Elizabeth Gurley Flynn, now a young mother of a son, just like Jane.[22] The Lawrence strike involved women whose wages had been reduced by two hours' pay—about thirty-two cents and the cost of five loaves of bread—to align with a new state law shortening women's workweeks.[23]

Looming immediately above New York's fashion hints on the *Bee's* editorial page that October was a photograph caption of twenty-two-year-old Flynn proclaiming her an "important figure in strike."[24] A year later, another eastern textile strike again brought Flynn into notice in Sacramento. The Paterson Silk Strike, fought for an eight-hour workday and better working conditions, highlighted Elizabeth Gurley Flynn's willingness to thrust herself into a fight, even getting herself arrested again when necessary, a novel and frightening prospect for most women readers. Readers of the *Bee*'s front page on January 25, 1913, met Flynn's somber gaze, a caption below the photo reading, "Elizabeth Flynn Who Sways Big Men with Voice."[25] Though the 1913 Paterson Silk Strike would be lost, the sum of Flynn's deeds and rhetoric of resistance and liberation helped propel working women's self-identification as a movement. It united them, not only to reject their oppressed class but also their exploited gender. Jane was probably impressed.

At the Golden Eagle and other hotels in the California Bay Area, union talk had infected workers who were following national news. The IWW organized an eastern hotel workers' union in New York City, with Elizabeth Gurley Flynn helping lead that charge as well.[26] As a result, *Solidarity*, a weekly IWW publication, put out a call to organize other hotel workers, waiters, and cooks across the country, a frightening proposition for Sacramento and San Francisco hotel proprietors now in the midst of planning accommodations for the 1915 Panama-Pacific International Exposition.[27] San Francisco, recently having won the exposition, would require more skilled hospitality staff and labor for construction. Jane certainly heard the chatter about union organizing at the Golden Eagle and witnessed an army of unemployed men, more than would be required, who had recently arrived in Sacramento to find work. Many were immigrant, impoverished, and unskilled, evoking public fear through overt racism.[28]

A tent city of homeless men began occupying the city's outskirts. Sacramento leaders immediately passed ordinances to reduce vagrancy and shut down inciteful street-corner speeches. Not knowing how to handle the deluge of humanity, city officials ordered all unemployed to board trains back to San Francisco, declaring the "Army of the Unemployed" not welcome.[29] When the men refused and dug in, state militia, special police, and vigilantes attacked them with clubs, guns, pick handles, and a high-pressure stream of water from a City of Sacramento fire truck. Reports of injuries and even deaths filled *Solidarity*.[30] The city's response was Jane's first experience observing civic opposition, as she witnessed firsthand the violence on Sacramento's streets.

Thus, Sacramento became prime territory for IWW organization. With the large unemployed-worker camp and nearby labor unrest, the IWW found fertile ground to bring attention to labor abuse and increase its membership. Sacramento IWW Local No. 71 organized and received its charter during an infamous labor strike that began in 1913. Herman D. Suhr, a feeble-minded IWW, and Blackie Ford, an IWW agitator, had been arrested during a fatal confrontation between hops pickers and county law enforcement on the Durst Ranch in nearby Wheatland, California. Both men were blamed for the deaths of four others, including Yuba County District Attorney Manwell and a deputy sheriff, during a workers' protest meeting for humane treatment. The two men had no guns and never fired shots, but the event had been sparked by "the nervous impact of the exceedingly irritating and intolerable conditions under which [those] people worked," after a law enforcement officer fired his shotgun into the air to get attention.[31]

Together, this incident, the Lawrence and Paterson textile strikes, and ongoing western free speech fights gave the IWW much-needed publicity in growing membership. By August 31, 1913, exactly 236 new locals were organized. Thirty were "mixed" locals (locals with various trades), including Sacramento's Local 71, a general recruiting union (GRU).[32] The following year was packed with more labor conflicts, some notoriously egregious including Ludlow, the deadliest labor conflict in American history, further bringing the IWW's work to the forefront in national newspapers, including Sacramento's. In spring 1914, Local 71 ordered 150 copies of *Solidarity* weekly for its members to read, indicating growing interest in the union.[33] By year's end, the number had more than doubled.[34]

The reading room at 1119 32nd Street had been twenty-five blocks east of the Golden Eagle and was not in Jane Street's path to and from work.[35] Still, in 1913 and 1914, IWW soapboxers had begun speaking on downtown Sacramento's busy street corners, hoping to draw new membership to the recently organized local. Their standard speeches included deliberate criticisms of capitalism and class conflict, often beginning with "Fellow Workers and Friends," a gender-neutral greeting. In 1914 the local began holding "successful" meetings in Plaza Park at J and 10th Streets, three blocks northeast of the Golden Eagle, sometimes featuring speaker Charles Ashleigh, who editorialized "Woman Wage Workers and Women's Suffrage" in one April edition of *Solidarity*.[36] Ashleigh noted:

There is always a surplus of middle-class girls, who failing to enter the chosen trade of marriage, must turn to some other form of activity to gain a livelihood. Modern industry, with its armies of office workers, provides a place for many of these, although the lesser paid ranks are also occupied by girls of proletarian origin. . . . She discovers that she is paid less wages than man for the same work. Hence, sex-antagonism, which, despite official suffragist protestations to the contrary, certainly seems to pervade the suffrage movement. Professional men, acutely conscious of competition in their respective fields, also either passively or actively oppose the entrance of women into the different branches of professional activity. . . . The Industrial Workers of the World, the One Big Union of the working class, makes no sex distinctions any more than it recognizes distinctions of color or race. It appeals to women to join the ranks, not as women, but as wage-earners, as members of an exploited class. In the IWW, men and women fight side by side, in perfect equality.[37]

In other words, the female wage worker was not concerned in a sex war; she was concerned in a *class* war. Evidently the IWW would not focus on sexual bias in general, but on the exploitation of women as a working class. Still, the view allowed for male domination within the IWW's ranks, just as Elizabeth Gurley Flynn had experienced in 1909. A review of IWW records indicates that Flynn and Matilda Rabinowitz (Robbins) were the only two female general organizers from the organization's inception until 1920.

Nonetheless, the IWW promoted stories about western women in labor disputes in 1914 and 1915. In May 1914, *Solidarity*'s front story led with "'Hello Girls' in the West," calling attention to a Seattle telephone operators' strike, after noting that the "girl question" of the class struggle had typically been addressed only in the East.[38] Also in 1914 Margaret Sanger, noted for pioneering birth control, edited *The Woman Rebel*, a monthly publication with the tagline, "The First Female Head Raised in America."[39] And it was Frank Little, famous IWW agitator and leader, who asked for a special women's page to be included in *Solidarity* at the 1916 convention.[40] He called on the IWW to actively recruit women and develop a separate bureau specifically for their needs, though his request never came to fruition.[41]

In spring 1914, Jane's employer, Kirk Harris, suddenly left the Golden Eagle to run the Hotel Sutter and manage the San Francisco Hotel Bureau. He began working on exposition plans, organizing 240 hotels to provide forty thousand rooms at the bureau's disposal, contracting tens of thousands more rooms within two months.[42] Grace Tuttle also had plans for the exposition. After moving to Los Angeles in 1914, she began formal voice training with Professor Enrico Giuseppe Botta, a noted Italian composer and former maestro of the Royal Academy of Rome. How Grace was able to become acquainted and accepted into training with the famous musician is unknown. One observation can certainly be made—Grace surely had talent, talent that obscured her former amateurish and even vulgar occupational endeavors. She was rewarded for her efforts when, in late 1914, Botta began training Grace for an operatic role in *Dolores*, to be performed in the twelve-thousand-seat Panama-Pacific International Exposition Auditorium in 1915. Botta claimed that Grace, a soprano, was selected for "her natural ability as a singer."[43] Plans to take the performance to Philadelphia and New York City afterward clearly elevated Grace's prospects.

After Harris and Grace departed Sacramento, Jane chose to leave the Golden Eagle, moving with her son, Dawn, to San Francisco, where she found clerical work. At her new San Francisco residence, a Queen Anne boarding house at 1822 McAllister Street, Jane pined for Bumpass.[44] About this time, Jane began the practice of submitting her writings to various magazines and newspapers in hopes of earning income. Rarely was she published. After each piece was rejected and mailed back to her, Jane pigeonholed the failure behind the few successes that were accepted, attached to their publications.

The resulting collection reveals much about her life. Among the paperclipped, yellowed sheaves—all typewritten or carbon copied—are poems, short stories, and essays that reveal a lonely woman who passionately loved her children, and later grandchildren, and who also had begun to develop a social awareness. Jane identifies several humorous pieces as "filler," similar to *Readers' Digest* vignettes. Other pieces are radical commentary couched in short stories or poems with autobiographical themes. The majority are quite intimate, revealing depression or regret at failed relationships and loss of beauty. Her oldest piece, written most certainly for Herbert Bumpass under the pseudonym Gertrude Riske, was rejected and returned to her at the McAllister Street address.[45]

By summer 1914, Jane had returned to her old boarding house on U Street in Sacramento. She remained at this address briefly, next moving downtown into a three-story building at 625 K Street, acquiring another stenographer's job, near street corners where IWW soapboxers orated and handed out materials. As her work résumé expanded within the proximity of IWW propaganda, Jane's views began to morph. She discovered she did not like working for a boss in a group setting, preferring to have independent command of her working conditions similar to her job at the Golden Eagle. Stanzas from another early poem, "Office Worker," reveal her emerging view of constraints within a stenographer pool:

> I wait, another hour,
> And it will be time to go.
> This is Wednesday,
> The week is half over.
> I look at the faces
> Of the other slaves.
> They are thinking
> What I am.
> We smile at each
> Other—sickeningly;
> Whisper puny jokes
> When the boss is out
> And strain at laughter.
> For our minds are water-logged
> With words and figures.
> We all are soggy
> With repetitions[46]

Jane's use of the word "slaves" reveals that her identity with working-class labor developed while working as a stenographer.

In fact, her social and political transformation occurred quickly. While residing in Sacramento in 1913 and San Francisco in early

Sacramento IWW Local 71 headquarters with Charles
Lambert likely standing at the entrance, ca. 1914.
*Courtesy of University of Washington Libraries, Special
Collections,* UW11394

1914, Jane had registered to vote but declined to identify a political
party.[47] This changed in late 1914 when Jane updated her voter registration and boldly proclaimed her new political affiliation, Socialist.[48]
On February 1, 1915, Jane Street became a member of Sacramento
IWW Mixed Local 71, where Charles Lindsay Lambert had become
secretary-treasurer.[49] Lambert would play a role in Jane's future as
a labor organizer. Jane's original red IWW membership card, discovered hidden under her mattress by Bureau of Investigation agents in
late 1919, records her industry as public service and her occupation,
stenographer.[50]

Around the first of July 1914, Jane began working on a letter to the
editor to be included in *Sacramento Union*'s "The People's Forum."

The resulting piece is Jane's first public voice, aside from her rejected poems. In the letter, she supports a proposed state constitutional amendment prohibiting alcohol. Her argument, available within the *Union* on July 8, 1914, is strictly from a woman's perspective. So passionate is her rhetoric, one wonders if alcohol plagued her father or Herbert Bumpass.

Jane wanted all window cards telling citizens to vote "wet" removed from storefront windows, claiming that the cards "strike at the women of the state."[51] Jane writes, "This movement against the liquor traffic is a woman's fight right from the bottom up." Obviously not intending to use a pun about a drinking toast, Jane recognizes that the "bottom" is the woman of the family. She writes that when a man gets drunk in a saloon or place of business, the "disgrace of her men-folks is her disgrace; his sorrow is her sorrow; his fine is her fine; his poverty is her poverty and the poverty of her children."[52] Affirming her continued faith in men, Jane admonishes, "If you are a man, you will stand up for her (wives and mothers), no matter what your business association or political affiliations or your appetite may dictate. You'll stand by her because you are a man."[53] Jane still trusts that man's traditional role is that of a woman's protector.

*Solidarity* continued to bring women's issues to the forefront using Elizabeth Gurley Flynn's current battle against social and economic injustices. Jane read every word of *Solidarity* and other local papers, developing an appreciation of using newspapers as tools for disseminating opinion. In early January 1915, Jane read where Flynn had plans for a national tour on various topics. Each week, Jane looked forward to seeing new front-page photos of Flynn and reading information associated with each new speaking engagement.

For Flynn, the speaking tour enabled her to pause in Salt Lake City, Utah, to visit IWW songwriter Joe Hill as he awaited the results of an eleventh-hour appeal on death row. They had exchanged letters but had never met face-to-face.[54] He had begun composing the lyrics to "The Rebel Girl," and finished the song soon after their visit. The song instantly propelled Elizabeth Gurley Flynn into labor lore, and sheet music helped popularize Hill's "The Rebel Girl."[55] Soon after, Jane learned that Flynn would be in California the first two weeks of May, including Oakland on Friday evening, May 14.[56] Jane probably

Joe Hill's song "The Rebel Girl" instantly propelled Elizabeth
Gurley Flynn into labor lore.
*Courtesy of the New York Public Library*

did everything she could do to attend.[57] When Flynn finally arrived in Oakland to speak on "Small Families—A Working Class Necessity," the audience of mostly women showed deep interest. Birth control had become a popular, though unseemly, topic, and they asked numerous questions at the close of her speech.[58]

If Jane had not been able to attend the Oakland event, she definitely had the opportunity to read Flynn's words in the July 15, 1915, special ten-year edition of *Solidarity*, where Flynn drew heavily on what was now called the Ludlow Massacre. In a full-page article, "The IWW Call to Women," Elizabeth Gurley Flynn points out the chasm between working women and the elite, the "good women" of Colorado. She quotes Colorado's socialites whose comments are as cold-blooded as the Ludlow murderers themselves. One woman, the wife of a minister, is quoted as saying, "The miners probably killed the women and children themselves, because they were a drain on the union!" Another, the wife of a lawyer, is to have said, "There has been a lot of maudlin sentiment about those women and children. There were only two women (who died) and they make such a fuss!" Still another, the wife of the railroad superintendent, is to have said, "They're nothing but cattle! They ought to have been shot." Flynn then adds, *"The 'queen in the parlor' has no interest in common with 'the maid in the kitchen.'"*[59] Jane Street likely absorbed every word.

Grace Tuttle's anticipated tour ended abruptly, and she was now out of work. Her mentor, Professor Botta, who became depressed with failure and was incapable of assisting her, would take his own life months later.[60] Too many women, drawn by the exposition, had poured into Sacramento wanting work. Instead of more job opportunities becoming available, the significant unemployed population resulted in fewer jobs. *Solidarity* reported that an employment bureau for the exposition had posted that no person should come to the area unless she already had a position waiting for her or had sufficient funds to carry her over a period of four or five months.[61] In fact, only one in ten women whose applications were already on file would be hired, and because of the large number of unemployed women, a general cut in wages was reported.[62] Undaunted, Grace began nurturing a seed of an idea that could earn money and allow her to use her artistic talents.

In late 1915, the sisters made plans to relocate to Denver, Colorado. Grace would open a music school. Did Grace persuade Jane to move to Denver? Possibly. The reasons for Jane's decision to move are not recorded, and she clearly did not intend to seek work as a stenographer. Like Grace, she had begun to formulate a plan, one that required her feet to hit the ground running upon arrival in Denver. She would organize women—servants—for the IWW. Was she sent by the Sacramento local to organize a few housemaids, when the IWW was strongly focused on its new Agricultural Workers Organization (AWO) No. 400, with its three thousand members?[63] Not likely. With all the work that Sacramento Local No. 71 was doing to help unemployed men and to grow California's agricultural branch membership, it is doubtful that IWW members influenced her decision at all. However, if one views the intensity of propaganda concerning Colorado—Ludlow, dead children, callous Colorado mistresses, their servants—coupled with female leaders, Elizabeth Gurley Flynn's own words, and the allure and recognition that being a "rebel girl" brought, Jane Street may have sensed a calling. Even if this theory is flawed, one fact was true. Herbert Bumpass had just moved to Denver.

## Chapter Three
# QUEEN OF THE HILL

Deep would have been the blot upon his escutcheon if his
chocolate had been ignobly waited on by only three men;
he must have died of two.

Charles Dickens, *A Tale of Two Cities*

On a late September day, 1916, a span of spirited bays pulling
a handsome Victoria in clanking brass-trimmed harnesses
emerged on to Sherman Street on Denver's Capitol Hill. Behind them
stood an imposing three-story, white-pillared French Renaissance
Revival mansion, seven thousand square feet in all, the most recent
addition of space necessary for houseguest William Howard Taft's visit
five years earlier.[1] On the manicured lawn, a classical sculpture of a
nude woman holding lilies, in full view of passersby on their way to and
from the Colorado state capitol, was waiting to be draped to signal the
close of Capitol Hill's social season.[2] Denverites paid especially close
attention to the form's array, or lack thereof.

Sitting imperially on the carriage's black upholstered bench was
Louise Sneed Hill, also dressed in black, one of her two preferred colors. Although her mother-in-law had considered her a shameless social
climber, Louise's disdain for traditional social conventions and appetite for risqué amusements had made her the reigning queen of Denver's society, at least for the fast set.[3] In front, Carlson was just weeks
from exchanging his coachman title and the pair of thoroughbreds
for a chauffeur's hat and a new dark-green limousine. After holding

Louise Sneed Hill leaving her Sherman Street mansion, 1916.
*Courtesy of the Denver Public Library, Western History
Collection [Call # Rh-635]*

the reins over the Hills' horses for more than twenty years, he had
recently suffered the indignity of taking driving lessons, since Louise herself refused to learn how to drive.[4] But Carlson was loyal, and
whatever his mistress demanded, he acquiesced. On this day, however,
their horse-drawn conveyance was one of few, suffering defeat among
new twenty-horse-powered automobiles on the Hill's broad streets.
Certainly, Louise Hill did not mind. Capitol Hill was her realm.

   True to a pattern of nineteenth-century urban development was
the belief that the higher one resided physically, the more elevated
his or her status socially. Capitol Hill's 160-acre development certainly
provided investment opportunities for the "thoughtful and well posted
man."[5] Promoters, including realtor Charles Kibler, had guaranteed
pure air, pure life, and health-giving ozone, a boon to those who could
afford an escape from Denver's brown cloud of air pollution, given the
unpaved roads, smelters, heavy industries, and coal-and-wood fur-
naces.[6] Every lot was guaranteed an unobstructed view of two hundred miles of the Rocky Mountains, "a more beautifully situated sweep

of land not in existence."[7] With a beautiful boulevard system with widths of 190 and 200 feet, Capitol Hill was to be occupied by "palatial homes, parks, and the wealth of the rapidly growing Denver."[8] Kibler even provided a photograph of the type of home to be constructed on the Hill, its caption reading, "There will soon be many of them."[9]

In just a few years, mansions began to appear on Capitol Hill when the privileged realized they would have a "grand view of the Rockies away from the rush, noise, gambling dens, and even seedier areas downtown."[10] Ironically, the mansions' heads-of-households had made their millions mostly from the Front Range's silver and gold camps, such as Central City–Black Hawk's mining district in Gilpin County, about forty miles to the west. There miners enjoyed tents and shabby boarding houses, prostitutes, and gambling, along animal- and human-waste-strewn gulches, while their mine and smelter employers saw their bank accounts grow in Denver.[11]

The physical gulf between what was called the Richest Square Mile on Earth (Central City–Black Hawk) and Denver's mile-high Capitol Hill insulated the two classes from each other, and mine, smelter, and railroad owners, merchants, and their money-lenders could display newfound wealth for all to see among their newly built homes. With construction of their "Millionaire's Row" mansions and an expanding neighborhood, Denver's Old Guard spread to Capitol Hill. Prominent families included the Baxter, Boettcher, Brown (Junius F.), Cheesman, Fullerton, Galloway, Hendrie, Holland, Hallack, Hughes, Moffat, Newton, Peabody, Kountze, Teller, Van Kleeck, Whitehead, and Wood families, many of whose mistresses championed social causes, including the Women's Law and Order League.[12] Indeed, Denver was booming, and thus did the Hill, despite setbacks incurred during the Panic of 1893 and later 1907.[13]

In 1890 former Black Hawk mayor and Colorado U.S. senator Nathaniel P. Hill and his wife, Alice, purchased Capitol Hill lots from William Berger and his brother-in-law Charles B. Kountze. Hill had made a large portion of his fortune after constructing Colorado's first smelter to use the Swansea method of processing ore in the Central City–Black Hawk mining district in 1868.[14] Besides gold mines and oil companies, Hill also owned the *Denver Republican* to help further his interests. However, it was Hill's son Crawford and his pretentious wife Louise Sneed Hill who put the Hill fortune to use when they built the immense mansion at 969 Sherman Street. Though Alice Hill had been the grand dame of Denver society for years, a "force in every charitable and social uplift," her daughter-in-law quickly usurped her accomplishments in Denver's society pages.[15]

Miss Louise Bethel Sneed, born in 1862 to a prominent North Carolina family on the Forest Home Plantation, was raised with all the privileges that her southern social standing could afford. Since her mother died several months after Louise's birth, the baby girl was likely first thrust into the arms of an African American nanny, one of forty-nine slaves her father, dandy William Morgan Sneed, owned, possibly affecting Louise's future familial relationships with servants.[16] Four years later, Sneed was the primary suspect for the murder of a man whose wife Sneed had coveted and then promptly married. Though never indicted, the rich and powerful Sneed family appears to be not well liked and the second marriage "coolly received," casting a pall over Louise's social credentials.[17]

Still, a pampered upbringing in a sphere of house servants, a New York education at St. Mary's, and various social events contributed to crafting a confident, self-aware, and formidable, if not calculating, southern belle. Since the post–Civil War South afforded few wealthy and prominent men to match Louise's own social status and ambitions, and with the stigma of her father's dubious past, she accepted an invitation to live with her Denver cousins after her father's death in 1892, hoping to find an eligible suitor. Upon her arrival in 1893, a "roaring gala" held in her honor catapulted the scheming, elder debutante squarely in the path of a just slightly younger Crawford Hill, considered Denver's most eligible bachelor at the time. Louise, desiring wealth and prominence, captured Hill, and the "most brilliant" wedding "that ever occurred" was held in Memphis in 1895.[18] Afterward, Crawford Hill quietly, if not submissively, stepped into the shadows while his new wife absorbed most of Denver's gilded limelight from society newspaper pages. As one astute journalist put it, Louise "snagged Crawford while he was still gullible and naive, a condition from which he never fully recovered."[19]

Following her mother-in-law's footsteps, Louise could have participated in Denver's philanthropic activities. Most prominent Denver women supported public causes through leagues, assemblies, and clubs, some designed to help the rich ease their social consciences during leisurely hours. Certainly not all of Denver's club women participated in activities for selfish reasons, though many did. In fact, western women were known for pioneering women's suffrage after Susan B. Anthony's barnstorm across the West. In 1869 Wyoming legislatively gave its women the right to vote, followed by Utah in 1870. But it was Colorado that overwhelmingly gave women equal suffrage through popular referendum in 1893 after Colorado suffragists built a diverse political coalition in order to win votes for themselves.[20] Women's civic groups, faith-based organizations, and wives of bankers, politicians, and mine owners had all worked together. In 1894 the first woman to be elected to a state or territorial legislature or parliament *in the world* was a Colorado woman.[21] Almost twenty-five years later, Denver's suffragists continued to use their voting power to advocate and improve education and social standing for the underprivileged. "We don't ask for permission" to push for equality, a former Colorado female politician noted in 2015, "we, as women of the West, just move forward."[22] Still, Louise Hill demurred when asked how she would use her vote during her attendance as a Republican county assembly delegate in summer 1916. She coyly stated, "I suppose if I had not been a Republican when I married Mr. Hill, I would have become one. Women always are influenced by such things by their husbands. I vote as Mr. Hill does."[23]

Louise *had* agreed to experiment with a Women's Security League physical fitness plan in early 1916 when certain "women of suffrage" asked how they could support the war effort along with working-class women. But the *Denver Post*'s society page journalist Frances Wayne could not help but quip that though "Majoress" Louise Hill's "shadow had never fallen across" the path of an Irish participant named Maggie McGinnis before, Maggie would be "converted to the aristocracy by the charm of Mrs. Hill's democracy" during the exercise.[24] In fact, the only fight Louise Hill ever enlisted was to keep her public crown when an ambitious newcomer, Mrs. Verner Z. Reed, challenged Louise's leadership of Capitol Hill society three years earlier.[25] Louise Hill would not be a typical Denver club woman—robustly active in the Young Women's Christian Association (YWCA), Daughters of the American

Revolution (DAR), Monday Literary Club, Society of the Colonial Dames, Women's Press Club, Congress of Mothers, Citizens' Protective League, Pioneer Ladies' Aid Society, Denver Women's Club, or sundry other organizations. She would not become an educator devoted to the youth nor be inclined to minister to the poor. In short, Louise was not interested in any philanthropic or progressive political movement unless the activities benefited her comfort and entertainment. She had not even joined the Denver Women's Law and Order League, though her best friend Carrie Berger had.[26]

Instead Louise Hill enjoyed indulging in bridge lessons before hosting bridge parties on Fridays; lunching daily with select friends at her mansion, the Denver Country Club, or Brown Palace Hotel; joining couples at evening theater-box dinners or country club galas in either Denver or Colorado Springs; or hosting intimate repasts in the Hill mansion, the guest list always advanced for the public's pleasure in the *Denver Post*.[27] If a blank space somehow appeared on her busy, scribbled calendar, in between her shorthand notes about dates, maid information, and phone numbers, Louise took the time to enjoy trash novels or paste "cunning" invitations and newspaper clippings (naturally about herself) into her many scrapbooks.[28] Summer and winter trips to Europe, where she shopped and entertained in her French chateau; other annual trips to the Hill's Newport summer home; and occasional excursions to a New York apartment completed her life.

Her servants answered all phone calls ("Too many calls" and "too annoying,"), took all Louise's dictations ("I dictate all my letters, principally for the reason that my friends may find some pleasure in reading them, rather than suffer a terrible struggle in deciphering my handwriting"), and carried notes to her outer orbit of acquaintances, reminding them that even if Louise could not fit their requests or invitations into her busy schedule, she promised "to think of you often with admiration," and that would suffice.[29] Surprisingly, Louise Hill claimed to be lonely at times and was possibly bored.[30]

Louise Sneed Hill became prominent in Capitol Hill society for one reason only: her snobbery and rule over the "smart set" with an iron hand that would last more than thirty years. The Crawford Hill mansion would eclipse all homes as a site for the socially elite's legendary get-togethers, including champagne bridge club luncheons, nude

Louise Sneed Hill, dressed in her favorite colors of black and white, poses next to her sweeping staircase in 1910.
*Courtesy of the Denver Public Library, Western History Collection [Call # Rh-5816]*

bathing, lovers' trysts, and glamorous balls, with music emanating until dawn from an orchestra pit, specially built into the home's sweeping stairway.[31] Because the mansion's seventy-two-foot drawing room comfortably held nine card tables, each seating four bridge players, a newspaper columnist soon coined the "Sacred Thirty-Six" to describe Louise's exclusive guest list, a group of individuals intended to be a counterpart to New York City's famous "400."[32] Louise even created a new social register that included the Thirty-Six and other social and political leaders in 1906.[33] Journalist Caroline Bancroft described Louise's early circle as originally "less important" than Denver's Old Guard, but "fast" and subject to wagging tongues.[34] Later, Thirty-Six members matured into substantial members of society, though still socializing within Louise's inner circle. Bancroft wrote that like many early social leaders, these same individuals laid the foundation for present-day organizations in Denver.[35]

To become a member of the Thirty-Six, individuals had to have specific qualities that Louise deemed important—the most significant of these was possessing old wealth. She could make or break anyone with social aspirations, "sinking unfortunates" like Molly Brown of unsinkable fame, before they could get a toehold on the social ladder.[36] Brown had been both Irish and Roman Catholic, attributes often linked to lower working-class miners and domestics. The *Denver Times* commented that "Perhaps no woman in society has ever spent more time or money becoming 'civilized.'"[37] Margaret (Molly) Brown later labeled Louise Hill "the snobbiest woman in Denver" after several attempts to get invited to the group.[38] A half century later, surviving Thirty-Sixer Carrie Berger explained Brown's rejection more tactfully—that all of Capitol Hill's newcomers were embraced with caution.[39]

Thus, Louise Hill choreographed her own presence in Denver, crafting meticulous if not titillating details about her dress, parties, and other social activities to be released to an adoring public, ad nauseam, by the city's newspapers, whose reporters' favor Louise courted with gifts. In return, society page editors whispered secrets in their stories about the Thirty-Six, meant to cause intrigue and envy.[40] Caroline Bancroft was such a reporter and also the last person alive to have known members of the Thirty-Six.[41] She afterward identified them on the front of an old photograph and gifted it to the Denver Public Library. But there was another group who intimately knew the activities of their masters and mistresses, including within the homes of the Sacred Thirty-Six and the Old Guard. Denver's elite depended on housemaids, butlers, cooks, nannies, gardeners, laundresses, and chauffeurs to staff its mansions and liberate its mistresses for crusading and socializing.

An informal census of the number of dwellers taken between 1890 and 1910 is revealing, estimating that each household allowed an average of four "living-in" domestics, in addition to parents and children.[42] During the same period, the Crawford and Louise Hill mansion also employed four live-in maids besides chauffeur Carlson, who lived in his own home.[43] By 1916, a survey found that Capitol Hill's demand for houseworkers was greater than the supply, and that the supply was untrained and unhappy.[44] With the ability of a dissatisfied servant to leave one job for another in quick succession, an interconnected servant community—with mutual backgrounds, experiences, and grievances—developed. Without a doubt, a layer of servitude floated beneath the shimmering surface of Capitol Hill's glamorous society, supporting its foundation of leisure and virtuous activism. And, it collected all the dirt. Into this milieu, Jane Street would interject herself, intent on organizing those dissatisfied housemaids. And with her doing so, Louise Sneed Hill, whose servants *were* contently employed, now saw an opportunity to humor herself with a new diversion, superiorly interjecting herself into Denver's 1916 housemaid rebellion, stunning club women and mutineers alike.

## Chapter Four
# FIERY LITTLE JANE STREET

Speak gently to your cook, or you'll get on the blacklist,
and no girl will remain with you and wash your dirty
dishes.

Frances Wayne, *Denver Post*, March 20, 1916

The two eggs lay side by side in a kitchen icebox of a prominent merchant's residence on Capitol Hill in Denver, Colorado, one early spring morning. One was virgin-fresh while the other exhaled age, cheapness, and cold storage. Inspecting the icebox for her mistress's morning breakfast was Mary, the cook. She pondered its contents. She knew that the freshly laid egg was specially ordered, but a momentary inspiration niggled at her brain. As Mary reached inside to grasp the egg, memories of a long list of grievances against "Mrs. T," her mistress, suddenly erupted. The cook hesitated. As uncertainty turned into deliberate decision, Mary selected the newer egg and tossed it into a pot of water heating on the stove. Minutes later, she ate it. Mary next boiled the older egg and served it to her mistress. How the esteemed madam could determine her breakfast consisted of an old egg is up to speculation, but the cook soon found herself out on the street. Only after calling a policeman, could Mary retrieve her clothes and money from the great home.[1]

That same night, March 26, 1916, Mary, in her best clothes and carrying a worn purse, arrived at her first "experience meeting," joining other disgruntled servants who had ridden a creaky elevator to the third floor of the ancient Charles Building on the corner of 15th and Curtis Streets, a low-rent property engaged for the new Domestic Workers Industrial Union (DWIU), Local No. 113.[2] Housemaid after housemaid, cook after cook, rose to describe her experiences working in the homes of Capitol Hill's rich. The *Denver Post* later reported that the women did not "murder the King's English" when they got up to speak, and though their clothing was not as "smart" as that seen behind the department store counters, "their faces were the faces of intelligent, determined American women."[3]

After Mary shared her story, one cook empathized with her. "I worked for 'Mrs. X.' She always bought the best for the family to eat and the cheapest cold storage eggs she could buy for the servants to eat."[4] When one "neat, efficient-looking" cook asked if anyone had ever worked for "Mrs. Blank," laughter rippled through the room, many indignantly answering, "I should say I did!"[5] The cook went on to describe how she was dismissed for serving "too heavy," or too much food, despite the wishes of Mrs. Blank's husband and daughter who liked the servant's cooking.[6] Another "pretty, refined-looking" girl also commiserated, testifying that her mistress was so penurious that the cook had to spend her own wages every week to purchase meat for herself.[7] Mary probably felt exhilarated to hear others tell similar stories. This was a sisterhood, for certain, since everyone shared her pain and indignation.

More women spoke out boldly though politely giving the floor to timid girls inexperienced with speaking out. Mary heard shared tales of tyrannical, bad-tempered mistresses who demanded fifteen, eighteen, and twenty-hour workdays that culminated in poor beds in drafty attic rooms. One poor girl admitted that working a month on any one job was so taxing, that, before going to her next assignment, she had to have rest.[8]

The meeting was secret, and a "sharp lookout" was engaged to keep an eye out for reporters and spies from Denver's mistresses. Yet, next day, the *Post*'s light commentary sympathetically confirmed the housemaids' testimonies, stating that insurance companies considered the servants "the worst risks of any class of women on their books."[9] The fact that the meeting was reported in two Denver newspapers afterward, though humorously concealing the names of outed mistresses, suggests immense failure regarding the meeting's intended secrecy or perhaps a certain calculation on the part of the organizer.

Leading the discussion of this second official DWIU Local No. 113 meeting was "fiery little Jane Street," as described by the disguised *Post* reporter in attendance, who gave her own experiences working in the kitchen of one Denver mistress. Mary and the other women viewed Jane with curiosity. The diminutive woman standing in front of them was energetic, feisty, and fearless, not tired, downtrodden, and submissive. How could she talk rebellion? It was unnatural for servants to question their masters and mistresses. In fact, the entire meeting seemed surreal, even illegal, though no laws had been broken. This young woman was awakening them to the realization that they could voice complaints about work, share commiserations, and unite with purpose. They could not peel their eyes away from Jane Street.

Jane's appearance had changed from her smart business dress, reflecting her new roles as domestic worker and union organizer. Instead of a stylish feather hat or a tam hat with matching plaid gown, a 1916 photograph shows how she may have first appeared to her audience—a small, mousey face below a likewise small black pilgrim hat, her abundant black hair tucked above her simple dark coat. A sentiment on the photograph, however, written in Jane's scratchy handwriting, profoundly reveals her complete transformation. "Yours for the D.W.I.U. Jane Street." Despite her domestic appearance, the *Post* described the petite brunette as "pretty."[10]

Jane's physical transformation was not the only change she had undergone since 1915. She had reinvented herself to become a union organizer, using her capable business skills and stenographical experiences to create a business model for creating a domestic workers' union. Sacramento's IWW local surely contributed to her newborn knowledge of organizing—how to gather at least twenty signatures of wage workers to form a temporary local, apply for a charter, and hold an initial union meeting to elect a temporary secretary and chairman— but no ephemera or, more importantly, IWW documentation, exists concerning her initial schooling.[11] Since organizing domestic servants was quite different from organizing factory or agricultural workers, Jane had to become a domestic herself to lend any kind of credibility to her purpose.

"Yours for the D.W.I.U., Jane Street," 1916.
*Courtesy of Guy Leslie, Jane Street Family Papers*

Scarred and cautious from her earlier marriage to Herbert Bumpass, Jane did not resume an intimate relationship with him, though she probably recognized the sensibility of his sharing the boy's custody while she directed her passions elsewhere. Under the name Jack Street, Bumpass rented a room for both himself and seven-year-old

Dawn Street in a "shabby boarding house," formerly a pretentious dwelling, at 1205 Acoma Street in Denver sometime during late 1915.[12] No other family members—mother Mary Ann Tuttle, who had passed in early 1915 in Hot Springs, and sister Grace, now occupied as a Denver music teacher—could afford Jane childcare as she began working on Capitol Hill.[13] In the beginning, Jane likely moved into her mistresses' homes, while Grace rented a room in a two-story red-brick building also on Acoma Street.[14]

For the next three months, Jane worked at housework and collected names of other domestic servants whom she planned to approach about unionizing, describing her method as "tedious."[15]

> When I was off of a job, I rented a room and put an ad in the paper for a housemaid. Sometimes I used a box number and sometimes I used my address. The ad was worded something like this, "Wanted, Housemaid for private family, $30, eight hours daily." I would write them [domestics] letters afterwards and have them call and see me. If they came direct, I would usually have another ad in the same paper, advertising for a situation and using my telephone number. I would have enough answers to supply the applicants. Sometimes I would engage myself to as many as 25 jobs in one day, promising to call the next day to everyone that phones. I would collect the information, secured in this way. If any girl wanted any of the jobs, she could go out and say that they called her up the day before.[16]

By March, Jane had collected 300 names of housemaids and cooks. Of this number, she selected "the most promising" women and sent them invitations to attend a first meeting. Jane never mentioned the IWW to any of the women because she feared they would be "prejudiced," but later wrote that this "did not prove the case."[17] On Sunday evening, March 12, 1916, Jane held her first meeting with housemaids and cooks behind closed doors, introducing unionization for "self-protection."[18] Of the one hundred women invited, only thirty-five attended.[19] The following Sunday, March 19, Jane held a second "secret" meeting, though the *Post*, armed with the meeting's contents, next day reported in detail that Jane made a "short-right-from-the-shoulder speech" before officially establishing DWIU Local No. 113:

You do the menial work of the town, the dirtiest work in the world. You cook for rich women. You scrape the food from their plates into the garbage can. You wash their dirty clothes, you wash their dirty dishes in their greasy dishwater. You take care of their babies and scrub their floors. You make your hands rough and red and ugly doing these things. You have no time to yourself. If you do have an hour or two, it is to rest so you can do more work. You have your room. Your mistress tells you that you are free to read or sew there. You can't have company there, and you must stay right there. Even the employment agency that gets you your job is for the mistress, and not for you. You have the privilege of taking her job. But you have one great advantage over your mistress. She must have you in her home. She won't wash her own dishes![20]

Jane's use of the words "dirty" and "dirtiest" is provocative, as she points out that Denver mistresses' cleanliness is made possible by the housemaids' dirtiness. Women's studies historian Phyllis Palmer describes the evolution of this belief, pointing out that that the "division between whose body was clean and tended to accordingly, and whose body became relatively unclean in the process" became stronger by the nineteenth century.[21] A sweet-smelling, clean woman reflected superior mental and moral capacities.[22] Images of "good (clean) and bad (dirty) women were easily projected" onto mistresses and housemaids.[23] Thus, work distribution among women reflected the moral superiority of higher-class women and the moral degradation of working-class women. Jane, on the other hand, uses the comparison between classes to point out Denver's mistresses' primary weakness—aversion to menial labor and dirt.

Of the women attending the March 19 meeting, only thirteen signed the application for a new charter, each paying a dollar initiation fee and pledging fifty cents a month afterward. Jane was ecstatic, nonetheless.[24] Months later, when she described her methods of union organization, she emphasized that money was very difficult to get, especially from those who were out of work, so she invited all women to future meetings, including those who could not afford to join.[25] Jane described her vision, claiming that the new union would not hold strikes but "wear down the nerves of the individual (mistress) until she came to their terms."[26] In other words, new union members would train the women of Capitol Hill by sabotaging their homes.

"A long series of maids who leave once a week, serve meals late, take no back talk, and demand the privileges for which they have been asking in vain, is going to do the training," Jane promised.[27]

To soften the sacrifices of giving up their jobs on a weekly basis, Jane pledged to rent a "temporary barracks" where union members could live between jobs. The use of the word "barracks," typically a place to house soldiers, further supports Jane's vision of domestics doing battle on Capitol Hill. Instead of paying someone to cart their trunks between jobs, women could travel light, leaving their trunks at the union house. Mothers with children would be provided childcare as well.[28] Then Jane's maids and cooks would demand their terms of peace in the households: twelve dollars weekly wages, no work on Sundays, and better treatment.[29]

An odd letter from a sympathizer helped bolster the women's will. The author congratulated the women and girls on their organization, pointing out, "Can you tell me why, when the eight-hour law was passed for women, the housemaids were not included?"[30] Remarkably, the author of the letter was a Capitol Hill mistress, who claimed, "I do not call my girls maids: they are my companions. I see that they get rest in the afternoon, as I take mine. When they have finished, their time is their own. If I gave a luncheon, I would hire extra help. If I couldn't afford to do this, I wouldn't entertain."[31] The mistress had dared to diverge from the pack of Capitol Hill socialites and club leaders' views—that housemaids needed to be obedient, on hand at all times, and respectful.

Even more frightening for Denver mistresses who read the *Post*'s front-page article on March 20, 1916, perhaps was Jane's plan for blacklisting all "cross" and undesirable mistresses. A long list, kept like a "secret archive" of every employer of house servants in Denver, would list its owner's character ("without mincing words"), house size, and number and disposition of children.[32] Jane threatened, "Don't think the housemaids' union is a joke. It's deadly earnest."[33]

The *Post* headlined the March 19 meeting as a "war" and the housemaids' tactics as a "guerrilla campaign" juxtaposed to international headlines about Pancho Villa escaping across the Chihuahuan desert and Allied bombings in Belgium.[34] The attention to the new union in this context promised a public battle, with Jane Street and her union taking the fight to mistresses and employment agencies. But who could have attended the supposedly "secret" meeting and provided the information to the *Post*? And who was the sympathizer mistress?

Likely sitting in the room at 303 Charles Building was a grand-motherly looking woman with large, kind blue eyes on an otherwise small-featured face.[35] Atypical of Denver's transient domestic population, fifty-year-old Cora Cowan had already worked twelve years as a housemaid for one well-known employer, Louise Hill.[36] She was also earning well and had already begun stashing jewelry, stocks, bonds, and money in a black suitcase hidden in her closet.[37]

Characteristic of many other servants, however, she had had a trou-bled family past that eventually led her west. Cora had been orphaned at seven years old after her young father and Dutch-immigrant mother died of tuberculosis. Six children, split up among relatives, traveled different destinies, some dying of tuberculosis also, and one finding a life in politics.[38] In 1887 twenty-one-year-old Cora and her younger sister Ida left to work as maids in "old" Dayton, Ohio, much like their step-grandmother had done after their grandfather, Cornelius Kor-tina, died of the disease.[39] By 1900 Cora began working as a nurse for three children in a grain merchant's Chicago household, and three years later appears to be working in Boulder, Colorado, near Denver.[40] Cora, surely armed with impeccable references, found final employ-ment as a nanny in the Crawford Hill household in 1904, immediately traveling with the family to England.[41] The ensuing years were filled with other European trips twice a year—Paris, Cherbourg, Le Havre, London, Liverpool, Southampton—as well as traveling on a private railcar north where she could visit her niece Ethel Bertling O'Hair in Ohio, waiting on eminent personalities such as President William Taft and author Samuel Clemens, and engaging in Louise Hill's personal daily routine.[42]

Cora was more than a maid—she was a companion. Just three years earlier, both Cora and Louise had been placed under temporary arrest upon arrival in New York City from England, after being accused of smuggling French designer clothes. The two women had conspired to remove foreign labels in two silk dresses and one coat valued at $751, substituting them with names of American makers in order to avoid paying duty tax.[43] Only because of Louise's connections were no arrests made, the complaint dropped, and a $300 fine assessed.[44] Cora was the perfect servant—obedient, educated, unmarried, borne of a respectable family that produced an Ohio state legislator (her brother John Cowan), and absolutely devoted to the Hill family. She acted as a foster mother for the Hills' sons and secretary for all of Louise's personal communications. It was she, the first greeter, who opened the front door to world notables and the Hills' friends and acquaintances, including the owner of the *Denver Post*, Frederick G. Bonfils.[45]

Promoter Fred Bonfils moved to Denver in 1895, and along with bartender Harry Tammen, purchased the *Post*, quickly establishing it as a formidable competitor to the *Rocky Mountain News*.[46] Both newspapers dished contemptible journalism at various times and provided the best show in town according to some, while waging battle with each other all the way through the 1990s.[47] While the *Rocky Mountain News* had been Denver's indispensable standard for several generations since before Colorado even was a state, the *Post* used outrageous stunts to lure the *News*'s readers away. As an example, Bonfils and Tammen once hired a comedian to jump off its twelve-story building. A crowd of twenty-five thousand gathered to watch what turned out to be a dummy thrown off the roof. Unabashedly, Tammen claimed that "The public not only likes to be fooled—it insists upon it."[48] In short, while the *Rocky Mountain News*, called "my Rocky" by its loyal subscribers, exposed crime and corruption wherever it found them, the *Post* reflected the Wild West—trigger-happy, lawless, and shamelessly colorful in its ultraconservative and often biased reporting.[49]

Though Bonfils was criticized for the yellow journalism he brought to the *Post*, Louise Hill courted his paper to gain complimentary feature stories about her activities. In return, Bonfils was invited to socialize with the Sacred Thirty-Six, and the two became good friends. When the 1913 story broke about Louise Hill and Cora Cowan smuggling gowns into the country, the *Post* softened the facts, even providing arguments against Louise's deliberate criminal actions while the *Rocky Mountain News* printed a more objective yet devastating account of the event.[50] Time after time, Louise crafted her public face, using the *Post* and its reporters. After Bonfils accommodated her on one occasion years later, Louise wrote him, "You are always so wonderful to me in the *Post*, I really cannot tell you how much I appreciate it. . . . I think I am the grandest lady in the land."[51]

Indeed, Louise Hill held a high opinion of herself, and she had no intention of reading about a "Mrs. H" in Denver's newspapers. If Capitol Hill's housemaids and cooks were giving names publicly, Louise would make certain that her household was advertised above the fray—her superiority in employer-employee relationships would glare in the face of Denver's servant problem, the Old Guard, and certain prudish mistresses. Thus, sending Cora Cowan to gather information and possibly deliver sympathetic correspondence is not beyond the

From Charles Devlin, "Who Will Feed Us?" *One Big Union Monthly*, November 1920.
*Courtesy of the Industrial Workers of the World*

*Visions*

realm of disbelief. One fact is certain—only the *Post* had the scoop on March 20, one day later.

The March 26 "experience meeting" was about to conclude. Mary and forty-nine other women had just joined DWIU Local No. 113 and added their mistresses' information to the union's blacklist.[52] When Jane announced a need for financial help in securing new headquarters upstairs at 404 Charles Building, the cook who had lost her job under the stingy mistress led off with a contribution of twenty-five dollars. Though she could not afford to give, Mary contributed, joining others who pulled liberal contributions from worn purses and out-of-date handbags, placing monies into the hat.[53] Afterward, a "goodly" collection of bills, gold pieces, and silver "rattled into its crown."[54]

The next morning, as mistresses opened their newspapers, reading about the abuse meted out in their homes, a significant number of servants gave notice that unless wages increased, working hours decreased, and living quarters were made more attractive, mistress and house would be boycotted, likely reddening some faces over soured breakfasts. Many servants left their jobs without even the formality of a notice.[55] Denver's so-called servant problem was about to become exposed in an unconventional manner, emboldening the train of cooks, housemaids, and parlor maids who were being led by fiery little Jane Street.

*Chapter Five*

# THE SERVANT GIRL QUESTION

Present-day domestic service is only a transient and
defective state of slaves, bearing the most sumptuous
slavery. True servants always have been slaves.
Mme. Valentine de Point, *Denver Post*, April 2, 1916

Harriet Parker Campbell warmly greeted her guests the moment
each club woman walked through a great oaken door, its
flanks opposed by symmetrical oval windows that peered outside to
the stream of women climbing broad steps to the mansion's porticoed
entrance. She had invited certain Housewives' Assembly members to
meet in her grand home on Thursday afternoon, March 23, 1916, several
days after the *Post*'s initial story on the new domestics' union. Harriet
intended to direct a conversation regarding the servant problem that
would give representative voices from other Denver women's organizations. Her husband John, retired to general law practice, had been a
Colorado supreme court justice, and the couple resided alone in their
6,200-square-foot mansion on Capitol Hill's 1401 N. Gilpin Street.[1] The
fact that she had no children and no residing house servants did not
disqualify her from facilitating a discussion with the ladies of the Hill.

Harriet's civic contributions, included in *Representative Women
of Colorado*, present a college-educated woman whose pioneering
fortitude helped mark the Santa Fe Trail. An American blue-blood,
she was active in DAR and Colonial Dames and also had dedicated
her time to charitable endeavors, including organizing the Colorado

Springs Boys Club and other targeted activities identified through her membership in Denver's Fortnightly Club, an organization for volunteerism, literary pursuits, and comradery. When she died in 1937, her obituary stated that "one of the finest qualities of her character was her ability to mix, without any shade of condescension, with all sorts and conditions of people."[2] Most significantly, she had served on the YWCA's state board.[3] Lately, the YWCA had been taking a hard look at the relationship between American mistresses and their domestics.

The women settled in chairs and on sofas, the laces, taffetas, and other satins of their skirts and dresses softly rustling in front of an elegantly carved, oaken fireplace in the mansion's front parlor. A few sat stiffly, corseted in somber-colored suits, while the younger women likely wore more fashionable attire, short-waisted, perhaps loose and hemmed almost midcalf. All wore hats, some small, most wide-brimmed. The room was airy, with large, easterly windows on either side of the fireplace and a similar window on the north wall casting early afternoon light.

The ladies certainly knew each other, though they were diverse in age and experience. The youngest of the group, at forty-one years old, was Mabel Costigan, a former schoolteacher and suffragist with no children or full-time servants. She and her politically connected lawyer-husband Edward, a future U.S. senator, did not even own a home. She represented the Denver Women's Club, an organization that primarily supported women's endeavors in journalism and literary fields. The oldest lady, at sixty-four years old, was Ellen Van Kleeck, a charter member of the Colonial Dames.[4] Ellen was an ardent American patriot, as her Colonial Dames activities show, donating to war refugees and knitting surgical masks for the European front. She was also a bona fide member of Denver's Law and Order League.[5] Her large, childless household on Grant Street had consisted of Scandinavian maids for years.

Van Kleeck was joined by Olivia Kassler, another member of the Law and Order League representing West Side Neighborhood Association, and society woman Gail Writer, a Monday (Literary) Club representative, whose husband was an officer of the Colorado Fuel and Iron Company, the Rockefeller Corporation subsidiary responsible for hiring Ludlow's gun-thugs.[6] Members of the Monday Club had finished studying industrial and labor difficulties several years earlier, at first lauding the Rockefeller Plan for employee-employer relationships. After Ludlow's attack, the ladies determined the plan as one founded on patronage and not on equality of opportunity.[7] With the European War in full progress and refugees entering America, the organization was now busy studying "from Alien to Citizen."[8] Gail employed no full-time servants, while Olivia was owner of a new 6,649-square-foot mansion at 727 Washington Street, staffed with the most servants of any individual in the group.[9]

Fanny Galloway, also representing Denver's Women's Club, had been a true suffragist, now involved in philanthropic and progressive political movements.[10] Unlike the other women, she responded to her first name Fanny, and not to the more formal Mrs. William K. Galloway. She had employed a live-in Norwegian servant when she had small children, but not in her home at 107 Sherman Street in 1916.[11] Ray Sarah David, the only naturalized American in the group, represented the Jewish Relief Society. The wealthy widow took in boarders, almost

Club women required domestic help at home in order to pursue women's suffrage, improved morality, and education of the underprivileged. 1909 Dunston-Weiler Postcard. *Courtesy of the Palczewski Suffrage Postcard Archive, University of Northern Iowa, Cedar Falls, IA.*

all first-generation Eastern Europeans and wartime Polish refugees. Ray was the only woman who claimed her occupation to be a social worker in charity endeavors.[12] She certainly hired day-workers but had no resident servants. Other ladies sitting in Harriet's parlor representing various clubs included Mrs. Florence Dick, Mrs. Nettie Casper, Mrs. Lillian Winter, Miss Jennie Hendrie, Mrs. G. Holden, Mrs. Maude Downs, and a few others.[13]

Harriet Campbell had also invited *Denver Post*'s features reporter Frances Wayne, "the uncrowned queen of Denver reporters," to cover the meeting, the invitation a routine action when Denver's elite met to discuss noteworthy civic issues or wanted to instigate gossip in the *Post*.[14] A Frances Wayne byline guaranteed a large reading audience and a chance for the ladies to manufacture and control their publicity. Since Harriet, among others in the Housewives' Assembly, believed the organization to be on the right side of the servant problem, she probably expected Wayne would report their discussion as such to the public. But she was wrong.

Regarded as the *Post*'s last "sob sister," Frances Wayne was drawn to covering sensational social issues of the day, including abused women, immigration, and orphaned children.[15] Daughter of a Republican politician and progressive temperance activist, Wayne developed her progressive and empathetic views while growing up in Central City's mining camp.[16] It was no surprise that she had traveled to Ludlow and Trinidad to interview the massacre's survivors and report on the ensuing fallout. Nicknamed "Pinky" because of her flame-red hair, Wayne was also *Post*-owner-editor Fred Bonfils's favorite investigative reporter, and he placed her in an office directly next to his, the only features writer to have such an office.[17] No matter that Wayne exposed her personal feelings in her writings, her high-drama reporting thrilled *Post*'s readers.[18] If Harriet Campbell thought that the ladies would elicit empathy from the fiery-haired reporter, she misjudged. Pinky Wayne understood the backstory relating to the housemaids' rebellion.

Wayne had her eyes open and ears alert, well aware of the differences in what was expected of her in reporting the women's virtuous views, what made a good story for the *Post*'s readers, and what the actual facts revealed. Her March 26 article would meet all three expectations. She wrote that the Housewives' Assembly had organized earlier at the first whiff of servants conspiring to organize.[10] She also reported that the housewives all admitted from the outset that there was "something rotten in the 'back stair' realm," despite the women's varied opinions.[20] Wayne expertly let their direct quotes expose their snobbery and biases, though Wayne was careful to assign ownership of comments only if given permission.

The meeting had begun with several ladies sharing personal knowledge of abuse to servants in Capitol Hill homes. One club woman began, describing two sisters—motherless farm girls—whose father had freed them to take domestic work in Denver homes. One slept in the basement next to a coal bin, living on food scraps left from the family's plates, and toiled from daylight to sundown. Her sister slept in an attic and enjoyed "scenery" three times a week, looking down into a washtub so that the home's debutante daughter might be "spic and span."[21]

A voice responded immediately, "Now that is all wrong. It is our duty to abolish such abuses, jot down the number of the housewives who practice 'this sort of inhumanity.'"[22] The notion surely made certain mistresses squirm. Another woman, possibly Harriet Campbell, diplomatically proposed the YWCA's current view of standardizing domestic service and educating employers to lift the stigma of degradation from housework. Immediately, a few ladies offered small, conciliatory remedies. "Give them sitting rooms for the reception and entertainment of friends," one woman offered. "Call the maid by 'Miss Dawson,' instead of just plain 'Dawson' or 'Maggie,'" another said.[23]

The Housewives' Assembly membership had previously determined to follow the Golden Rule in view of recent developments.[24] The move was too little too late. Jane Street was already wise to the background of certain ladies who made up Capitol Hill's newest organization.[25] Of the three women associated peripherally with the Ludlow Massacre—Van Kleeck, Kassler, and Writer—only Gail Writer publicly expressed an open mind to the new housemaids' union, though she doubted that it would be able to solve the servant problem. "Mistresses and servants should each try to be just to the other," she suggested, "and perhaps the mistress should oftener consider the servants' side of the case."[26]

With that, discussion turned south when discussion of servants' deficiencies took over. A club woman, probably Ellen Van Kleeck (though

Frances Wayne does not identify her), sourly called the maids "hot-tentots," an old Dutch, derogatory epithet labeling African nomadic Khoikhoi tribal members. She complained, "Many of them can't cook; they know nothing about cleaning; waiting on tables is an unknown art to them; as laundresses, they are 'jokes,' and they demand big wages and become abusive when they are corrected or asked to do better than they are doing."[27] Wayne included these remarks "unof-ficially" except for president of the Mothers' Congress Lillian Winters's public opinion: "I think the union will have the effect of making many girls too independent."[28] This sole sentiment surely stirred up anxiety, and perhaps even alarm, in the brocaded and befrilled bosoms of some attending the Housewives' Assembly meeting.

One would have to go back to the early 1870s to find mention of a "servant problem" in Denver, and then the term would have a vastly different connotation from what it meant to the club women sitting in Harriet Parker Campbell's front room on March 23, 1916. It all had to do with supply and demand—and gold. In the late 1850s, after pros-pector John H. Gregory first discovered gold in a gulch that was to bear his name, eastern corporations capitalized on his and other discover-ies in the new Central City–Black Hawk mining district. Financiers, engineers, and metallurgists, along with their families, quickly moved to the district to develop gold mining interests further.[29] With the rise in corporate wealth, many of these families moved on to Denver, forty miles to the east, long before there was ever a Capitol Hill, avoiding the rough-and-tumble mining camp and its frigid winters.

As the mining district prospered, so did Front Range households that desperately desired domestic help and were willing to pay a pre-mium to get it. Because the WFM supported Western European work-ers over people of color, domestics from mining camp households, like the miners, were mostly white.[30] Many of the Irish and Cornish who worked the mining district were unmarried, and those who had wives and daughters content to work as servants were diminishing, growing an earlier domestic shortage. A tragedy and Denver's professed good-will changed things.

On October 8, 1871, a great fire broke out near or at Chicago's O'Leary home at 137 DeKoven Street on the city's southwest side, an Irish neighborhood crowded with wooden houses. With timber readily available in neighboring Wisconsin and Michigan, and waterways on which to transport lumber, Chicago had become a distinctive city of profuse wooden structures inhabited by an immigrant working class. Whether the cause of the conflagration was Mrs. O'Leary's fabled cow knocking over a lantern in her barn, carelessness at a late-night card game in the same barn, a comet, or some other incident is not important.

What is significant is that as the self-perpetuating inferno burst north and northeast into Chicago's primarily Irish, German, and Scandinavian neighborhoods, one-third of the population in a city of about three hundred thousand lost everything.[31] After the fire, more than seventeen thousand of the city's structures had been destroyed with damages estimated at $200 million, and Chicago's crisis became publicized nationally.[32] While the Swedes, many of whom were excellent carpenters, would be called upon to help rebuild the city, a mass of single women lost their jobs and homes.

Two days after the fire, the *Daily Rocky Mountain News* ventured a solution that would help solve Denver's servant problem and solve the homelessness of "hundreds of poor girls, dependent for their support upon the meagre salaries paid, in that overpopulated city."[33] The editor suggested that "colonies of this particular class could be reached with those facts (that) . . . servant girls from Chicago can find good homes in Denver, today, with wages averaging $20 per month, and all the necessaries of life supplied as cheaply as in the former city. One hundred good girls could find situations here at any moment of the present, and now that the matter of aiding the sufferers is before the public, and the railroads are making such liberal offers to transport supplies eastward, we think the same corporations would show their generosity and help the needy by placing them where they can help themselves."[34] It was a bold suggestion, requiring cooperation of mistresses willing to pay higher wages and corporations, after shipping goods east, agreeable to transporting the women back to Denver on their railroad cars at no cost. The idea appeared noble, at first.

On October 12, 1871, the *Daily Rocky Mountain News* editor again reinforced the magnanimous offer while revealing a far different reason for the gesture, aside from the scarcity of help. Importing a supply of young women from Chicago would punish Denver's haughty "would-be-kitchen-queens," who, despite their skill at housekeeping, were impudent and unreliable.[35] "We think that the arrival in this city of any number of good girls, competent, intelligent, and willing, would put an end to this kind of insidiousness, would make our girls more reliable, and more disposed to be of some service to those who pay them for their work," the paper's editor pronounced.[36]

By Friday, October 13, the mining camp's *Central City Register* was calling for a "concert of action" with the Denver paper in drafting petitions to be circulated for signatures.[37] Subscribers were asked to designate a number of servants they would require and the wages they would pay. The *Daily Rocky Mountain News* again reassured readers that the wages would surely be "reasonable" and probably run from twenty to twenty-five dollars per month.[38] In addition to the wages and room and board, some were already promising gifts of clothing. Once the lists were complete, the newspaper planned to forward them to Chicago's mayor, who would publish the offers to girls who could furnish "most satisfactory recommendations."[39] Meanwhile, railroad companies would make arrangements for the girls' transportation to Denver.

Almost immediately letters to the editor promised conflict among mistresses and servant girls. One author wrote, "Wanted—one hundred good servants, domestics, 'help' or whatever you choose to call them—in a word, one hundred packages of frame and muscle, with excellent background to comprehend the duties given them to perform."[40] The mistress, diminishing a former servant, derogatorily entitles the letter "Wailings from a 'Wictim,'" insisting that progressive American women are subject to "new world slavery" by tyrannical household help that is demanding, loud, and degenerate.[41] Claiming that western women do not make good servants, the mistress supports the effort to bring Chicago's Scandinavian immigrant girls to Colorado within her parameters. "There are hundreds of men and women servants out of employment; among the many Swedes from the Scandinavian colonies in Illinois. They are almost invariably good, faithful, industrious servants, frugal and cleanly in their habits, free from the wastefulness of the Irish and the indolence of the negroes, loving the mountains and the snow. . . . Let the fair-haired Swedish maidens be sent out," signing off as a victim (of having a terrible servant).[42]

In response, one servant girl defended her "much-abused" and "overworked" class demanding "one hundred good mistresses, domestic heads of families, or whatever you choose to call them—with unselfishness enough to comprehend that their servants are human—*not* made of iron and steel; with kindness of heart enough to comprehend that servants' endurance has a limit; with charity enough to make allowances."[43] She ends, "'A Wictim' should remember that while our mistresses and their class have time to cultivate the graces, we have toiled in the hot ill-ventilated kitchen for their comforts."[44]

The first letter to the editor clearly disparages Irish help, supporting a common notion that the Irish domestic was brash, disobedient, and unintelligent, though Irish American girls had been heavily engaged in housework for years. While the stereotypical "Bridget" had become a familiar fixture in hotels and homes because she was considered loyal, charged cheap wages, and maintained her good spirits, opinion changed swiftly as more Irish moved to mining districts bringing their militant views.[45] Kassler was the only mistress attending the March 23 Housewives' Assembly meeting who had a history of hiring Irish servants and may have offered up Maggie's name.

Maggie Dawson, a real person, was typical of many Irish immigrants or first-generation Irish working as domestics. She had been one of eleven children born in the United States to Irish immigrant parents. The family first moved to Chicago, departing for Denver sometime before 1900. By 1910, Maggie's mother depended solely on two daughters to support a rented household on West 29th, an Irish neighborhood in the Highland Park area. Twenty-one-year-old Maggie worked as a servant in a private home, and her widowed sister Mary worked as a waitress.[46]

If they employed servants, most of the club women attending the meeting had Norwegian or Swedish maids, confirming mistresses' preferences for Scandinavian habits. In truth, many of America's Scandinavian girls had been taught that good girls take jobs as domestics if they had to work outside their homes. By 1906 in the United States, the largest percentage of working domestics were Swedish, Norwegian, and Danish.[47] African American maids were rarer in Denver, though Harriet Parker Campbell employed a black housekeeper in 1900.[48] Instead, black women were overwhelmingly employed as cooks or laundresses and while in the South, many took "day-work" in homes or still worked as field-hands.[49] Lillian Winters had a black servant, a cook named Lizzice Legay, whom the family brought with them from Shreveport, Louisiana, before 1910.[50] Jennie Hendrie, an unmarried Housewives' Assembly member, employed a Japanese houseboy, a novelty.[51]

Clearly, the servant problem carried deep wounds from an earlier history than Denver's Capitol Hill ladies even considered. A house-maids' union had formed in 1901, organized by "lady-organizer" Mrs. John D. Pierce, an AFL member who approached Denver society respectfully, courting public opinion.[52] The union had been established when servants demanded a day off, instead of staffing and preparing Sunday dinners. Their demands drew light jests from some reporters who evidently described the new members as uneducated in appearance and speech. The union's new president, who rebutted their remarks, was not even a working-class woman, but wealthy philanthropist Etta Craig, who admitted she knew nothing about trade unions, and who defended the women as bright, intelligent, and "many educated."[53]

Unlike Elizabeth Gurley Flynn's and Jane Street's confrontational approach to union organization, Pierce's and Craig's efforts were pater-nalistic and even elitist. Pierce says: "The idea the mistresses have got-ten into their heads that the union is antagonistic to their interests is a serious mistake. We intend classifying girls into three divisions, first class, second class and third class, and in this way the mistresses will know what sort of a servant they are getting."[54] The union, not surpris-ingly, failed after one year.

Since 1901, the phrase *servant problem* had become part of pop culture, as ubiquitous as the products that were advertised to resolve the issue. As an example, a 1916 advertisement in the *Rocky Moun-tain News* reads: "The Servant Problem—who ever heard of it in the home where the housewife knows Shredded Wheat? In five minutes, you can prepare a wholesome satisfying meal with Shredded Wheat Biscuit without kitchen worry or work."[55] Popular plays incorporated servant girls as essential characters, though they were often portrayed as illiterate and as comic relief for audiences and readers. At a 1911 Denver's Women's Club performance, society woman and playwright Liska Stillman Churchill's play, "Two Phones and a Woman," portrays a prominent club woman dealing with a college-age daughter and an Irish maid in "delicious" humor. Mrs. Churchill herself played "Betsy, a negro maid," using southern dialect to bring down the house, "particularly the scene where the Ethiopian and Hibernian maids match wits."[56]

Contemporary novels likewise depended on kitchen and parlor humor. Alice Duer Miller's *Come Out of the Kitchen!* was advertised as "a story of the south and of a proud family who try to keep their old home by renting it furnished. How they cope with the servant problem, and the outcome of their bit of mystery, is sheer comedy."[57] Churches focused more seriously on the plight of servants. In 1902 the *Rocky Mountain News* reviewed Christian socialist Reverend Charles M. Sheldon's novel, *Born to Serve*, as the "Most Vexatious Problem to Women in America'—The Servant Girl Question."[58] Sheldon read every chapter to his congregation over the course of several weeks. Sunday school classes and women's clubs selected the servant problem for study groups, a 1916 group advertising, "Woman's Study club will meet tomorrow. They will discuss 'The Servant Problem.'"[59]

Newspaper editors incorporated fashion discussions on society pages. On a 1902 *Rocky Mountain News* page, mistresses were provided explanations and illustrations on how to dress parlor maids appropriately for fashionable afternoon teas, even as some maids were averse to wearing a cap and apron, a "so-called badge of servitude."[60] The article advised, "The parlor maid should always be dressed in black. Her dress should be neat and plain, and if any trimming is used at all it should be nothing more than white buttons or a white linen collar. Then there is the apron. A thrifty parlor maid will always take pride in keeping her apron as spic and span as possible. This apron is long and wide, covering the entire front and sides of the skirt."[61]

Across the Atlantic, as the European War unfurled, taking English men and women away from homes and thrusting them into wartime services and munitions' factories, the servant problem remained a catchphrase. As American papers reported, England's plan to allay its servant problem was to place Boy Scouts in households to work.[62]

In short, the aristocratic world could not exist without a servant problem.

A Denver housemaid, 1909.
*Courtesy of the Denver Public Library, Western History Collection (X-1839)*

The *Denver Post* had published Pinky Wayne's news story, recount-ing the Housewives' Assembly meeting, on March 26, 1916, the same day as DWIU's "experience" meeting. The ladies on the Hill could not have been too pleased. Wayne had written more than recounting the discussion in Harriet Campbell's elegant drawing room. She editorial-ized, providing an alternative view that "housewives follow an aged tradition of looking down on those who serve them and their fami-lies and refuse to practice patience or give counsel and regard to the women they hire as human beings with like impulses, like passions, like hopes and aims as herself."[63] She also had a complete copy of the Sympathizer's letter, probably given to her by Fred Bonfils, which she published fully, advising the Housewives' Assembly to read "with profit."[64]

Worse for the ladies of the Housewives' Assembly, since Louise Hill had not been included in the meeting, Wayne obtained Louise's opinion and used it at the conclusion of her story. Sounding much like the speaker in the Sympathizer letter, Louise said she held many of the same views as Jane Street, adding, "The only way to arrive at a practical understanding is for the girls to become more intelligent and for mistresses to become more humane, and for both to remember that any labor, however humble, may be dignified by the laborer."[65] Whether Jane welcomed the society queen's alliance is irrelevant. The IWW boys had just arrived in Denver to make certain that the new housemaid union toed the line, reminding its membership that "the working class and the employing class have nothing in common."[66]

## Chapter Six
# THE BOYS ARE BACK IN TOWN

She is a strange, little, unconventional social rebel.

Calenal Sellers

Claude Welday Sellers brooded next to a rented piano in the new DWIU meeting hall. It was early April on a Sunday evening, the weekly meeting time for the new Housemaids' Union, as it was now called. Despite his demeanor, his full attention was directed at Grace Tuttle, whose fingers glided nimbly over the familiar chords of "Home Sweet Home."[1] She was equipped with a portfolio of other old-time classics, and the soft bars were meant to instill a sense of sanctuary to the women who stepped from the old elevator onto the Charles Building's third floor. Though not a maid herself, Grace supported Jane, and now Sellers had begun calling Grace a "strange, little, unconventional social rebel."[2]

Smallish and slight of height at 5 feet, 7 inches, with dark hair, complexion, and eyes—one glass, Sellers exuded power and entitlement.[3] His moody stance publicly established his proprietary position among a small contingent of curious IWW men who had also arrived at the meeting, including his best friend, Albert Kohler. Kohler, too, was drawn to the former burlesque dancer. Of the two men, it was Sellers who was the fluent propagandist and aggressive IWW agitator, though his voice was feminine and speeches full of revolutionary platitudes.[4] And it was Sellers who boasted a robust revolutionary résumé, claiming to have participated in the Calumet, Michigan, strike three years

Unknown man, possibly Albert Kohler, standing next to Claude (Calenal) Sellers, sitting, ca. 1919. Note Sellers's crooked fingers, the result of an industrial accident. *Courtesy of Guy Leslie, Jane Street Family Papers*

earlier and every strike thereafter, though the Bureau of Investigation later reported he had joined the IWW just one year earlier.[5] Kohler, on the other hand, was a cook and a follower, but evidently more empathetic than his friend.[6] Grace would have no problem distinguishing the man best suited for her if she so chose.

Sellers unabashedly professed a number of intimate particulars. The grandson of a poor First Christian Church minister and even poorer dirt-farmer father, Sellers had enough education to work as a stenographer.[7] Yet at different times and places since he had completed two years of high school in 1894, he also claimed to have worked as a mechanic, miner, and waiter, though a Bureau of Investigation informant in Butte, Montana, maintained he never saw Sellers work at any trade.[8] Sellers readily admitted that he "had no great faith in the size of his 'intellect' and had been born in poverty and ignorance." Presently he was a great reader of radical literature, holding the pages close to his nearsighted, left eye when he read.[9] Sellers's most recent self-identification was that of an IWW speaker.

Both Jane and Grace had met Sellers as Calenal Sellers, not Claude, nor even any one of his other aliases—George William, Robert Thorpe, and cleverly, J. Gould.[10] In 1919 Sellers would use the alias J. W. Burns after his arrest for stealing a woman's overcoat at a Seattle carnival company where he worked as a mechanic.[11] A year later, when Sellers was arrested for organizing an IWW defense fund in Centralia, Washington, he was placed in a Tacoma jail cell with a common home burglar, Tilden C. Hardy. Within a week, the two men had dangerously burned their way out of the jail's ceiling and escaped.[12] Hardy was recaptured, but not Sellers. Sellers had already reinvented himself as he dodged local law enforcement and federal detectives for crimes that he had committed.

Not surprisingly, some Wobblies detested Sellers. The same informant noted that in 1917 when Sellers had to leave Denver, where he worked as a dishwasher, it was because he was about to be exposed as an "Agency" man.[13] Some even accused Sellers of being an undercover detective for the Thiel Detective Service, a Pinkerton competitor known for infiltrating labor union strikes. In Sellers, the informant said, "something is not quite right."[14] Sellers openly admitted to "pilloring" men with his fists in Butte, Montana, in 1919, where unions clashed with mining companies' hired thugs and each other. He bragged that some "thirsted" for his blood as a result. Sellers later wrote that he was "filled with seven devils sometimes. . . . I am a Dr. Jeykel [*sic*] and Mr. Hyde. Sometimes one and sometimes the other."[15] Although unstable, according to the Bureau of Investigation, Sellers was successful as a "leading agitator, advocating violence and destruction of property."[16] Many Butte miners applauded his speeches with approval, while others did not trust him.[17]

National IWW secretary-treasurer William D. Haywood did not trust him either, as future events would bear out. Sellers had just allied with Jane, who, in the face of opposition, was developing independent, decentralist views. Her ideas were likely influenced by the creation of mixed western locals where membership of several trades led to diverse self-serving philosophies and self-governance, and not to the One Big Union idea of universal organization. Historically, Denver's local IWW participation had mainly involved mixed trades, the last local—No. 26—most known for having fought in the 1913 Denver Free Speech Fight before it ceased its operations in 1915.[18] Now the same boys were back in town.

Sellers turned his attention to Grace's little sister, who was greeting each guest. Jane had contrived a brilliant idea—how to leverage Capitol Hill's mistresses. She began handing cards and pencils to women who entered the union hall. Each card was actually a blank form to be completed by prospective union members, providing essential information regarding former mistresses or those currently employing servants. How many people are in the home? How many are children? What kind of work do you do? What are your hours? How much are your weekly wages? What type of employer is your mistress? It was a novel strategy, capturing information about Capitol Hill mistresses and the working environments in their homes. Jane would later categorize the cards, creating a database of information to be used in matching housemaids and cooks to jobs through an application process that Jane had also designed. The Housemaids' Union could now serve the women as a free employment agency.

The piano music soon stopped, and all eyes turned to Jane. She proudly announced that the union already had three hundred employers on file—three hundred mistresses whose personal habits were known to all the maids and cooks who walked through the hall's doors searching for work.[19] Jane explained to the men and women that

> when a housewife advertises for a girl, we look over the cards
> you filled out to see what sort of a mistress she is. The card
> will show how much salary she pays and whether she is a slave
> driver. A mistress with a bad record will find that no girl will
> work for her. Sometimes we will send girls to her, but only
> to teach her a few things. The girls we send will treat her as
> she treats them, without consideration. And in time, they will
> train her.[20]

Jane also announced that she expected to have one thousand records by the end of the week.[21] She added that with mistresses already "on record," many of whom were good mistresses, servants looking for work already had recommendations for work situations.[22] On the flip side, several Denver housewives, cooperating with the union, had procured servants through the Housemaids' Union, according to Jane.

Sellers immediately decided he would share his organizational skills with the new Housemaids' Union instead of joining another men's mixed trades local. It is not known how the arrangement was made with Jane, and Sellers evidently was not a domestic. But one fact was clear—now both Tuttle sisters had captured his interest, and he was not about to let go. They needed him.

Denver's actual employment bureaus briefly appeared unfazed. A *Rocky Mountain News* story on April 17 shared the view of one employment agency owner, a lady "who numbers her acquaintances by the rich and fashionable."[23] She planned to try to negotiate between the parties with the "wisdom of Solomon," the paper reported, but "she doesn't think she can say anything about either side, except it is a 'three-to-one proposition,' as she held up four fingers."[24] The business-woman said, "Take a good mistress and a bad girl, you have trouble. Take a bad mistress and a good girl, you have trouble. Take a bad mistress and a bad girl, you have lots of trouble. There's only one way to have peace—a good mistress and a good girl."[25] Jane was not about to recommend negotiations with a third party. On April 16, 1916, *Denver Post*'s Sunday classified-ad section included an ad Jane had posted in order to grow the union's membership even more at the next union meeting:

> WANTED—500 housemaids, cooks, second girls, nursemaids
> and all domestic workers to attend meeting Sunday, April 16,
> at 8:30 P. M. 303 Charles bldg., 15th and Curtis Street. The
> Domestic Workers' Industrial Union.[26]

After spotting the ad, sixty women attended the April 16 meeting held just hours later, contributing more employer records to the House-maids' Union database. Jane emphatically now claimed the cards were not a blacklist, as initially reported, but a list of potential employers.[27]

Of more interest to a *Rocky Mountain News* reporter was that three black maids were among the women attending the April 16 meeting. The reporter noted that "no color lines" had been drawn.[28] The "colored" maids were welcomed as new members at the meeting per the IWW's vision. Also, seamstresses who sew by the day, the paper reported, now were to be included as domestic workers, along with cooks and laundresses employed in private homes.[29]

With the growing mutiny, Denver's employment agencies finally decided to fight back even as their initial remarks in local papers depicted otherwise. On Saturday, April 15, *Solidarity* reported that the agencies had posted ads recruiting "girl scabs" in eastern news-papers.[30] Also within the same *Solidarity* article, Jane asked for finan-cial assistance for the first time. She obviously recognized that to win an IWW fight against Capitol Hill, it would take money.

By April 23, Jane was ready to make her most significant announce-ment. Domestic Workers Industrial Union No. 113 was to have a club-house, just one floor upstairs at 404 Charles Building. There, at the clubhouse, all meetings and social events would be held. Girls also could find board and lodging should they find a mistress unbearable and need time to search for a more agreeable job. Should they desire, girls could improve their educations through coursework, Jane having procured several public-school teachers amenable to donating their evenings.[31] And that was not all. Jane had plans to engage an attorney and physician for the girls, free of charge. There would be childcare for working mothers.

Jane, upon observing a small measure of disbelief in the faces around her, further expounded her vision, "These are not idle dreams. We can do these things and we are going to do them. With a union attor-ney, you girls will be able to stand up for your rights. Only the other day I heard of a little girl in Denver having been discharged and accused of stealing a gown when she asked for her pay. The mistress had social standing and wealth and the girl could do nothing. She never got her salary, even though the mistress knew she had not taken the dress."[32] Jane reminded the domestic workers of the necessity of working in concert to achieve their goals. "All housemaids, second girls, ladies' maids, chambermaids, and nurse girls must all work for the same pur-pose and remember all are in the same union," she emphasized.[33]

An all-encompassing clubhouse was a remarkable idea for an IWW organizer, though not unique in some aspects. An instance where the IWW assisted women in order that they could participate in a strike had been in Lawrence's 1912 Bread and Roses Strike. Big Bill Haywood and Elizabeth Gurley Flynn urged striking-immigrant families to send their children to New York City out of harm's way. Flynn reports in her autobiography that it was Margaret Sanger who escorted the children to a New York City medical team, ready to examine them, before placing the children in temporary homes.[34] Other children were sent to Vermont, and one group attempted departure for Philadelphia, though the group's purpose was thwarted by troopers.[35] The IWW, advertising through their newspapers and union meetings, had also assisted financially, helped with soup kitchens, food distribution, and medical care.

The notion of comprehensive support had already been put into practice by social activist and suffragist Jane Addams in 1889 when Addams and Ellen Gates Starr founded Hull House, a Chicago settlement house for mostly poor immigrant women and their children. Hull House eventually expanded to other cities and would include employment bureaus, meeting places for trade unions, education centers to teach literacy, daycares for children of working mothers, child protection, access to legal aid and healthcare, and opportunity.[36] While the IWW advocated for a class war, Jane Addams's views were more nuanced. She encouraged women to move out of their "gender" spheres while working outside the home, striving to empower themselves within a male-dominated society.[37] As a lifelong pacifist, Addams later sympathized with the IWW, working to raise money for food and shelter for incarcerated Wobblies released on bail in Chicago after a mass trial in 1917. She identified with labor activists and other "wartime offenders" imprisoned under the Sedition Act during World War I.[38] For her work, in 1931 Jane Addams was awarded the Nobel Peace Prize.

In her autobiography, Jane Addams stressed the importance of working with civic organizations to sustain Hull House.[39] This included working with women's clubs. Jane Addams herself had grown up in a wealthy household and was familiar with the altruism associated with community groups. She, too, had memberships in organizations that supported women's suffrage, including an honorary DAR membership in 1900.[40] In emulating some of Addams's goals, Denver and Colorado Springs societies of the Colonial Dames of America strove to help certain immigrants. In a strange twist of hypocrisy, Law and Order League members Ellen B. Van Kleeck chaired the Dames' board in 1916, and Olivia Kassler led the organization's Philanthropic Committee working on "Americanization" of Denver's Italian Quarter.[41] Both women gave support for funding night schools for Italian immigrants and Austrian and Russian Jews. Van Kleeck even seconded a motion that would continue the unified work of the organization's Americanization Committee and Philanthropic Committee in 1916.[42] The Dames would study aliens in America at all board meetings and devote attention and money to education and training for citizenship of the "stranger in our midst."[43] Ellen Van Kleeck's zeal was especially documented.

A double standard certainly existed. Less than two years earlier, Law and Order League women had composed their side of the Ludlow Massacre in a letter to President Woodrow Wilson. It was plainly the immigrants' fault. "If the strikers had been American citizens, they would have gone back to work at the request of the militia," they argued. "The foreign element is uncontrollable," the epistle concluded.[44] Jane Addams, on the other hand, when told about the Ludlow Massacre, wept.[45] Several Ludlow women survivors and Denver judge Ben Lindsey had been en route to Washington, D.C., to meet with President Woodrow Wilson and request federal troops, when they stopped at Chicago's Hull House.[46]

National newspapers, reprinting the story of their meeting, mortified members of Denver's Women's Law and Order League. The League immediately set out to write letters to every magazine and newspaper in the country that had published statements about the strike, giving its version of the affair. A letter was specially sent to Jane Addams, informing her that the truth of Ludlow had not been presented honestly. Just before her letter was mailed, a speaker at a league meeting amazingly pronounced that the "battle of Ludlow was the most magnificent ever put up by citizen soldiery."[47] Clearly, club women's support for recently arrived refugees from war-torn countries in the face of their opposition to American immigrant workers and their fight for dignity was appalling. Thus, in planning her clubhouse, Jane endeavored to mimic Hull House's well-known attributes with one exception. Support from Denver's civic organizations was unwelcome.

At its final April meeting, Jane announced that the Housemaids' Union now had a total of one thousand records on Capitol Hill mistresses, causing a stir among its membership. One IWW woman observed, "Why look at some of the people who hire us? They're not fit for decent, respectable folks to associate with. Look at some of the society people who are so particular about the characters of their maids and cooks. There isn't a faster bunco of people in town, and if we told some of the goings-on on the Hill," she added, "it would make the public's hair stand on end."[48]

A speaker, probably Calenal Sellers, brought up a new concept. He told the Housemaids' Union membership that "It doesn't do any good to strike alone if there are other servants in the house." He counseled, "If you're a cook and go on a strike and the chauffeur and butler and yardman and the rest of the hired help walk out with you, you have the people of the house at your mercy."[49] As if preplanned, Jane quickly announced that now men—chauffeurs, butlers, and yardmen—were to be organized into an auxiliary of the union. Afterward, a naive, pretty young woman was heard squealing, "And let's have our beaux in it! Then they could sit in the meeting with us every Sunday night, instead of waiting for us in a cigar store or down on the corner."[50] Calenal Sellers had just devised his path into the Housemaids' Union. Even more foreboding, Jane Street's vision of the clubhouse was clearly being hijacked.

## Chapter Seven
# THE MAIDS' DEFIANCE

I can't help my loyalty bee
From buzzing around and busying me.

Jane Street, from "Why?"

W hen Jane Street skimmed the *Denver Rocky Mountain News* on the morning of May 1, 1916, she was probably disappointed that not one report on the Housemaids' Union graced the front page. Instead, headlining was an article about the Republicans' surefire campaign to help Teddy Roosevelt, "the only logical candidate," win the upcoming presidential election. Also featured was a story about a recent German agreement to abandon certain submarine warfare, brokered by the United States as a neutral observer. True to the fickle nature of politics and war, the United States would enter the European war less than a year later, despite reelected Democrat president Woodrow Wilson's pledge to keep the Homeland out of the conflict.

Outside, the day had begun gray and gloomy, trapping inside seven-year-old Dawn Street, who had recently returned to live with his mother on the fourth floor in Denver's downtown Charles Building. A slow-moving late-spring storm had delivered rain and snow over the last two days, leaving trees laden with fat, sparkling, half-frozen water droplets. Jane would have to caution Dawn to play quietly since Calenal Sellers now spent much of his time in the Housemaids' Union hall. Sellers does not seem to have liked or felt comfortable among children because, to him, they interfered with the One Big Union's goals.[1] Even pleasantly socializing with adults appeared to be an alien behavior for him. Still, Dawn had discovered books, possibly to escape the unusual circumstances of his home life, and could read quietly if necessary.[2] The *News*'s page five did cheerfully promise Denverites that sunny days were ahead with streams and irrigation ditches full.[3] Yet everyone who lived on the Front Range knew that the weather, just like political attitudes and military stratagems, could change in a frosty twinkling.

But Jane was not interested in politics. On the paper's society page, Jane next looked for bylines belonging to the *News*'s Mildred Morris, while in the *Denver Post*, Jane scanned for Frances "Pinky" Wayne's name. After Wayne's March 26 report on the Housewives' Assembly meeting at the Campbell home and the following day's revelations and testimonials from the Housemaids' Union meeting, there had been no more reporting on the topic in the *Post*. Someone must have complained to Fred Bonfils about Wayne's editorializing in favor of the rebel maids. The *News* had stubbornly carried stories until a week ago, but not so this past weekend. Evidently, Denver club women had peered closely at their tarnished reflections and believed their mirrors to be distorted. All Denver's newspapers had ceased penning articles and criticisms regarding the Housemaids' Union and the Housewives' Assembly.

Instead, Jane read Pinky Wayne's front-page May Day story highlighting the Denver Women's Club's dedication to impeding the reelection of Mayor Robert Speer, a "corrupt politician and grafter," at the ballot box.[4] Wayne now rendered certain Housewives' Assembly ladies as modern-day suffragists. Club president and Assembly member Mabel Costigan provided quotes supporting the club's efforts to save the city from "Boss Speer," certainly a more constructive view of the women's heroic activism.[5] Louise Hill, who aloofly but adeptly journeyed through society pages after she awoke each morning, was probably unconcerned. She was too busy making plans for her upcoming travels to New York and Newport. The European War had inconveniently put a halt to her international travel.

Even without local news coverage, Jane knew that her efforts had been productive. The clubhouse and its amenities had come to fruition. Jane had a bed in the same office where she worked and maintained her file system. Dawn likely slept with her. The hall had a kitchenette of

*Left to right:* Jane Street, her son Dawn (Phil) Street, and Grace Tuttle in 1916.
*Courtesy of Guy Leslie, Jane Street Family Papers*

some kind, and a lavatory was one floor up. With summer approaching, Jane did not have to worry about school, and Dawn could join other servants' children during the day, or Grace could watch after the child at her boarding house. Jane understood that Elizabeth Gurley Flynn was also responsible for a son about Dawn's age, and Flynn was still able to traverse the country lecturing and organizing. What Jane did not know was that Flynn's parents and sister did much of the child's rearing. Though Flynn's son Fred later boasted that he had been jailed twice for free speech before he was ever born, he had flourished with a family of surrogate parents after Flynn separated from his father.[6]

Instead Jane's new situation mirrored the circumstances of the other maid-members, and not Elizabeth Gurley Flynn's life path. Like many servants nationwide, DWIU servant girls generally had no families nearby for support, some were singles trapped in surroundings lacking opportunities for socialization, or if any woman did have children who stayed at the union hall, a father was generally missing from the equation. The new union changed their circumstances, providing a place to meet and opportunities to mingle.

The previous evening at the housemaids' meeting, the women composed their own rebel girl lyrics in Joe Hill–fashion amid much laughter. Few IWW songs had been written for or by women between 1909 and 1916, but Jane had urged the housemaids to have their own anthem. Even the IWW's *Big Red Songbook*'s editors noted much later that as "egalitarian as the IWW was in most respects, the (*Little Red*) songbook's editors appear to have been afflicted with at least a tinge of masculine prejudice."[7] As the housemaids and cooks called out their grievances, Jane helped put their words to rhyme. Grace likely sat at the piano, ready to put the words to the Irish tune of "Tipperary."[8] Jane later submitted that one housemaid wrote the five-stanza song, but "The Maids' Defiance" is regarded as a collaborative effort and a remarkable early IWW women's creation.[9] Union members immediately referred to the song (reprinted in full on p. vii of this book) as "Housemaid Mary."[10] Calenal Sellers, managing to make himself indispensable to Jane and the union, had wired the song's lyrics to *Solidarity*, so the rest of the industrial labor world would know that Jane Street had her own Rebel Girl song.[11]

There were other successes as well. Jane had installed a telephone at $4 a month for sixty calls (sometimes $14 to include excess calls) and subscribed to all the daily papers for $7 to $10 a month, where at least one DWIU ad ran daily, usually to help laundresses.[12] Owning a telephone, even collectively, was a luxury for a number of the housemaids. The clubhouse's telephone was weaponized immediately. Jane wrote, "Call up the woman and tell her you will accept the position at $20, that you will be sure to be out. Then she will not run her ad the next day. Don't go. Call up the next day and ask for $25, and promise to go and do the same thing over again. On the third day she will say, 'Come on out and we will talk the matter over.' You can get not only the wages, but shortened hours and lightened labor as well."[13]

Even though newspapers tried to discriminate against the union, charging "employment rate" expenses to advertise, Jane proudly boasted to another organizer that "with our handful of girls and our big expenses, we have got results. We actually have POWER to do things. We have raised wages, shortened hours, bettered conditions in hundreds of places. This is not merely a statement. It is a fact that is registered not only in black and white on the cards in our files in the office but in the flesh and blood of the girls on the job."[14]

At nine years Jane's senior, Calenal Sellers exuded worldliness and experience, just as Herbert Bumpass had done a decade ago. In fact, Jane found Sellers so knowledgeable in IWW matters, that she permitted an unusual management arrangement. She was the union's financial secretary, and strangely enough, Sellers was now assistant secretary in the all-female local, notwithstanding the domestic-male auxiliary.[15] DWIU Local No. 113 had officially received its charter on March 27, 1916, so election for an official local secretary-treasurer was overdue.[16] The IWW had no higher position in its organization—no bosses—promoting all its members as equal participants or comrades.

Sellers took over manning the telephone, writing news reports, and lecturing anyone who would listen. There were also membership books, dues stamps, constitutions, application blanks, report blanks, and literature to order and utilize appropriately. Jane, for her part, recruited new members whenever she could find them, making out their cards, putting in stamps for dues paid, and furnishing a report to the IWW headquarters for all monies collected. Not all the women coming to 404 Charles Building were dues-paying members, but Jane was not about to turn away any girl with an empty pocketbook and desperate circumstances. All were welcome. Still, accurate financial accounting was imperative.

Organizing member information and mistresses' personality and household management flaws on cardstock was not Jane's only analytic system. At some point in her life, she had begun making notes on herself, waking up each morning and jotting down her nocturnal dreams and ideas on a note pad so she could analyze them later.[17] Years afterward, Jane's teenaged grandson questioned the piles of rubber-banded notes that she had never thrown away. Jane found it easiest to rationalize the exercise as a form of "mental calisthenics."[18]

She obsessed about small details in others' lives as well. Once a loved one challenged her with, "Why do you always tell everyone what they should do?" Jane had responded, "Because I don't have time to be nice!"[19] She was also pragmatic, not liking anything that was not useful.[20] Jane managed the union hall, influenced by these same idiosyncrasies. Perhaps if the parameters of Jane's daily introspection were broader, she would have sensed the threat that Sellers posed in the union hall—and to her.

For several days, Jane and Sellers had been laboring on a news update for *Solidarity*. If they could keep the Housemaids' Union in industrial news, despite its recent suppression in Denver's newspapers, they had a chance of bringing in funds necessary for supporting the new clubhouse, the "big expenses," as Jane had called them. The finished article, published on May 13, 1916, reveals much about Sellers and the IWW men's view of Capitol Hill women.

Brought up in a home with a preacher-grandfather, Sellers was quite familiar with the ponderous rhetoric used to evangelize at church meetings. Absalom Sellers prepared God's word likely three times a week in the Sellerses' family home, and Calenal was not as uneducated as he would have Jane believe. Thus, the *Solidarity* article is structured much like an Old Testament Sunday-sermon. Referring to Colorado as the "hotbed of industrial revolt," Sellers sounds out an ancient "clarion cry" for battle.[21] Poor girls are rebelling against immoral, "painted dolls of Denver's exclusive homes," he writes.[22] The maids are "domestic slaves, toiling from dawn to long past dark" under conditions of "labor unspeakably hard," his words conjuring images of submissive Israelites laboring for the great Ramses II before Moses could lead them in revolt.[23]

Sellers further explains that the "powdered parasites" of the Housewives' Assembly are the faces of powerful female politicians, YWCA women, and members of Colorado's Law and Order League.[24] He reminds the reader that the sinful mistresses are the same gang of "society parasites" that "applauded the Colorado National Guard and lionized its officers" after they had "massacred" Ludlow's women and children.[25] The use of the words "parasite" and "slave" several times was red meat for IWW readers. America's industrial barons' wealth had been gained on the backs of poor working men and women, who truly enjoyed no profit. Workers, Sellers makes abundantly clear, are thus *slaves* to the elite. Finally, Sellers juxtaposes Jane Street, the "little rebel housemaid," against the rich and powerful, similar to the small boy, David, who smites a goliath.[26] Jane Street battled hard, opening up a new field, claims Sellers, presenting tremendous possibilities.

After lauding Jane's successes from Sunday evening House-maids' Union meetings where the "gospel of industrial unionism is expounded," Sellers gets down to the salient purpose of the article.[27] DWIU Local No. 113 needed financial assistance to support the club-house. He writes, "A little assistance now when the organization is young and meeting with much powerful opposition, the union can soon be built up to large proportions, and be in a position to render much material assistance to the men and women on the firing line in other industries."[28] One can almost envision a Sunday evening collection plate passed from row to row, while preacher Calenal Sellers stands up front on a dais. "They are slowly but surely aligning their forces to land smashing blows at the seat of the mighty!" he concludes in a stentorian voice, and thus commands, "Agitate, boost, contribute!"[29] And just like the *News*'s Mildred Morris and *Post*'s Frances Wayne, this reporter left his byline—C. W. Sellers.

Calenal Sellers sat next to Local No. 113's precious telephone in the Housemaids' Union hall making his calls. He had had a busy evening doing union business. Nearby, Dawn Street was entertaining himself, darting in and out of the office, where his mother was attending to her paperwork. Other women were in the union hall, some waiting out their mistresses and others in between jobs. Wobbly men, too, were free to come and go in the hall.

Sellers's mood darkened as the freckle-faced seven-year-old scrambled around the room, making childish racket that interfered with his conversations. It did not matter how unnatural it was for an energetic little boy to have to spend his playtime quietly inside the clubhouse's walls, instead of exploring and inventing games outside in fresh air like other children. Sellers went back to the call on hand, speaking into the black receiver.

Just as a dog is attracted to a person who least likes animals, Dawn went up to the ill-humored man, catching him unawares. In an instant, Sellers flung the child away from him, across the room, just as if he had instinctively swatted a bothersome insect. Immediately, Dawn fled to Jane, sobbing. A mother's rage embroiled Jane just as quickly as Sellers's own impulse to rid himself of the nuisance. Seeing her stormy face, Sellers immediately claimed that he "was forgetful of his [Dawn's] youth," and that the child had been interfering with his work.[30]

In response, Jane "bawled out" Sellers publicly, mincing no words—*her son* had been wronged, not Sellers. Furthermore, Jane warned ominously, "Dawn comes first over all things."[31] Some members of the Housemaids' Union witnessed Sellers's immediate humiliation as his sallow skin probably flushed. Jane had just placed a child over Sellers, and even worse, a child over his union work. At Jane's invective, he could only spit out what he felt deeply in his heart—Jane was placing "maternity before the revolution." That moment, he believed Jane's loyalty to Dawn made her a traitor to the IWW's movement.[32] Though Sellers's fulminations fell on deaf ears, a breach had begun between the two. For the others who had the misfortune to witness the outbursts, this point in time may have been the beginning of a sordid effort to keep Jane Street in her woman's place.

## Chapter Eight
# DARING DEVLIN

There are many pitfalls, and one can drop from sight and into oblivion quicker than scat unless they forever keep their eye on the ball and keep plodding.

Charles Devlin to his son Patrick, 1944

In early July 1916, as Jane contemplated just what to do with Calenal Sellers, IWW organizer Charles Devlin stepped into the Housemaids' Union office on the fourth floor of the Charles Building to offer his services. Upon seeing Jane, Devlin was smitten, writing later that "she was the most wonderful little lady I have ever seen," whose "large, brown eyes" had him "shaking."[1] The aforementioned eyes observed a slender man of average height who had a shock of unruly, brunette hair above a wide brow. He had kind gray eyes, set between ears that tended to stick out, and a confident, wide, full-lipped smile. Jane would not have noticed that Devlin had an odd gait, nor that he was unsettled upon meeting her. She gave Devlin a small smile of welcome and immediately switched to business.[2] Discounting Calenal Sellers's maniacal tirades, no, she told Devlin, she had never had a speaker for the Housemaids' Union, but she was willing.[3] Whatever plans Devlin may have had for his speaking itinerary, they were postponed. Instead, it was agreed that he would speak to the maids. "To say that I thought she was grand," he later wrote, "was putting it mildly."[4] Charles Devlin was staying in Denver.

Jane and Devlin immediately planned a strategy to draw the public's attention to the Housemaids' Union. Jane had already tried fliers, but they were evidently too costly for results:

> Fellow Workers: Do you belong in somebody's kitchen, attic or basement, doing their dirty work, attending to their most intimate personal needs, hiring yourselves out for all the time you are awake into the service of others who treat you as an inferior being? . . . Have you served others so long you have forgotten you have interests of your own? Join the Domestic Workers Industrial Union. THAT IS WHERE YOU BELONG.[5]

Denver's newspapers had continued to censor the Housemaids' Union as well. Instead, DWIU No. 113 would take the fight to the streets where Devlin had experience in soapboxing. He had previously street-preached in Des Moines, Iowa, and Lincoln, Nebraska, the latter location evolving into a more publicized free speech fight.[6] That Devlin was willing to alter his lifepath in hopes of gaining Jane's attention is not surprising. Challenges unfazed him, and he had changed course before. Central to his fearless approach is an incident that occurred when Devlin was fourteen years old.

Young Charley had read about a one-legged bicyclist named Dare Devil Kilpatrick who had ridden down Washington, D.C.'s Capitol steps.[7] An Adam Forepaugh and Sells Brothers colorful circus poster even featured Kilpatrick, on an ordinary "road" bicycle, "dashing" down a giant, lit stairway from Madison Square Garden's roof to the ground below, a sheer descent of over one hundred feet. The stunt had a name too—*Kilpatrick's Famous Ride*.[8] Soon after, Charley, staring down a lofty, wooden platform, had hoped to replicate a similar M. L. Clarke and Sons' Circus side act. Charles Devlin had only one foot, too.[9]

Years later Devlin recalled that he had become suddenly uninspired to try the feat—riding a bicycle down a ladder that was only one foot wide and sixty feet long at a 45-degree angle. To the boy, it had looked like it was an entire city block to the end of the ladder.[10] Still, he had studied the actual M. L. Clarke and Sons trick-bicyclist performing the *Ride for Life*, watching his every move in prior morning and evening exhibitions, before making the foolhardy decision. Devlin later wrote that he had been no longer satisfied with being a beggar after hoboing for over a year. He was convinced that trick-riding could provide a future where he could make a living without working a real job.[11]

On the ground below had been a throng of curious onlookers in front of an enormous white tent, its pennants fluttering softly in the breeze. They had arrived to see a bona fide stuntman give a free exhibition before the circus's ticketed performances. The stunt had been advertised as an electrifying feat, a "thriller," and the audience was primed.[12] Tingling with anticipation to see the afternoon's much-ballyhooed circus performers, parents tightly held the sticky-fingered hands of their children, their mouths in perfect O's and all pointing upward. The smooth-faced, fourteen-year-old boy in ragged street clothes, positioned high up on the platform, had been a complete surprise.[13]

Devlin recounted that after getting his balance, he took "one last, good look" downward and shoved off with his good leg. Not glancing to see if the bicycle was speeding between the ladder's side rails, he instead had focused his eyes at the feet of the ladder where a net was supposed to catch him. He knew that if he plummeted off the side on the descent, the flop would be his "hard luck."[14] Miraculously, the two-wheeler had flown true, hitting flat ground in an instant. The only drawback was that the circus roustabouts had forgotten to set the net. When Devlin landed, the bicycle's downward velocity powered both rider and machine for a distance before he could safely stop. He later admitted, "Here I was. I knew I was in for it if I did not do it." But he *had* succeeded—to the roars of astonished bystanders.[15] At this moment, the show business bug had bitten Charles Devlin, and the resulting contagion would consume him and certain members of his family for much of their lives. More importantly, the boy had confirmed that he could turn a handicap into success, his optimistic conviction and style of self-promotion profoundly shaping his actions toward Jane Street fifteen years later.

Devlin's early story is far more complicated than the classic tale of the boy who runs away to join a circus. Born Charles Carroll Devlin on August 11, 1885, to Scots-Irish American parents, Devlin initially lived on his grandfather John Devlin's six-hundred-acre homestead near Guttenberg, Iowa, on the banks of the Mississippi River. There his father, Louis Francis Devlin, farmed until becoming widowed in 1893, devastating the man.[16] Seven-year-old Charles's lot was to live with his grandparents in Guttenberg, where they had moved, for the next four years.[17] Shortly after Devlin finished his eighth-grade school year, his grandfather John, too, died.[18] In 1897 Devlin and his siblings moved again, this time along with their grandmother to Little Grant, Wisconsin, to live with his aunt and uncle. Immediately, Devlin began working on the Henry farm to help bring income into a home that now supported thirteen people.[19] Not surprisingly, the long, hard hours of labor induced Devlin to reconsider his circumstances.[20] Sometime after June 1900, thirteen-year-old Charles Devlin ran away to Chicago, where his older brother James worked.[21] He traveled by boxcar, where he immediately became introduced to another world—one of comradery and free spirit.

On board were hobos—also called "bindlestiffs," or just "stiffs," because of the blanket rolls slung by cords upon their shoulders—most, searching for seasonal jobs. American economic conditions between 1893 and 1914 compelled even skilled tradesman, their homes and families often lost, to jump empty boxcars and work job to job, while traveling freight cars to other promising work sites. Other men preferred drifting with no responsibilities and required little to satisfy their needs, including Charley's newest friends.

But freeloading train travel had inherent dangers. America's hobo culture generated hundreds of stories where someone lost a limb or even his life on train tracks. Because railroad workers were unionized, a paid-up union membership card usually protected men and provided them with a free passage. Brakemen otherwise booted off freeloaders without union affiliations, which Charley surely noticed.[22] Still, jumping on and off slow-moving trains was dangerous in itself. Some men—and boys—died or lost limbs. By 1909, IWW newspapers were regularly printing death notices and pleas for financial assistance for men who missed a step jumping into a boxcar or who unsuccessfully tried to ride the rods, the braking system underneath railcars. Devlin became an early statistic in October 1900, shortly after arriving in Chicago. Five railroad cars, including a car laden with coal, passed over his right leg and mangled his right arm. The accident almost cost him his life.[23]

Six months later, after multiple surgeries and extensive rehabilitation, Charles Devlin, minus his right foot, awkwardly shuffled out of Chicago's St. Luke's Hospital on crutches. His shoulder hurt, he could not walk fast, and he was wallowing in self-pity.[24] During his hospital confinement, he had lain in bed, trying to distinguish trains' arrivals and departures by their whistles, since the Illinois Central was just a few blocks from the hospital. He pondered how many "bums" were on each train, where they were from, where they were going. He believed he had no home afterward, at least no place where he could stay by earning his keep.[25] Without hesitation, the boy went back to hoboing, instead of taking what he called the "Dutch" route—suicide.[26] This short chapter in his life would help mold his social beliefs.

Charles Devlin loved listening to the "Bo's sitting round telling their stories."[27] There was Frisco Blackie, Chi (Chicago) Shorty, Boston Slim, invariably a "Punk," or some member of the "Johnson family," riding the rails, representing "the most interesting types of humanity," Devlin recalled in his memoirs.[28] In the hobo jungles along the tracks, the men counseled him about his future, forecasting success because Devlin was a young cripple. He would not get turned down when he asked for food or money, the hobos arguing that the boy "was made!"[29]

Indeed, the racket worked. Devlin approached homes and businesses, handing out "duckets" or cards that asked for help or donations, a practice he would use again to promote himself.[30] Even train conductors who caught him in the luxurious smoking cars of passenger trains allowed him to remain after Devlin gave them his card.[31] The boy got along nearly a year in this manner until he met veteran circus-man, M. L. (Mack Loren) Clarke, in Louisiana. Despite Charles Devlin's success at his initial *Ride for Life* stunt, Clarke could not offer him a contract until the next circus season. Devlin was, however, welcome to stay with the circus and practice.

Instead, in about 1902, Devlin made another bold decision on his own. He approached Artificial Leg Company in New Orleans, requesting help, a donation. It did not matter that the prosthetic he received was too long to use—Devlin had his wooden leg, and it would fit—after another amputation. Undeterred, he threw the artificial limb into a gunny sack, slung it over his shoulder, and "bummed" his way to

Dare Devil Devlin, One-Legged Globe Cyclist. Promotional card.
*Courtesy of Jack and Kathy Devlin, Devlin Family Papers*

Shreveport, Louisiana.[32] There he induced a charity hospital to perform his surgery, after showing doctors the wooden leg. Using a piece
of wet chalk, Charles Devlin himself marked the spot for the cut. He
had already determined how much muscle he would need to perform
his stunts.[33] Afterward, Devlin would always wear the prosthetic leg
except when giving exhibitions at fairs, carnivals, and other novelty
shows. As his act became more "hair-raising," including a high-wire
trick on his bicycle, Devlin gained his celebrity name—Dare Devil
Devlin.[34]

According to Charles Devlin, in 1912 the *Waco (Texas) Morning
News* was so intrigued with his act that the paper offered a $10,000
purse if he could ride his bicycle around the world within two years.[35]
Thus began Devlin's final bicycle stunt, a sixteen-country world tour
that began in May 1912 in Waco and ended in San Francisco two years
later.[36] Promoting himself as the "One-legged Globe Cyclist Making My
Own Way Around the World on a Bicycle," Devlin sold red postcards
along the way for five cents each to pay for a trip that first took him
across the United States. He encouraged reporting on his journey by
stopping occasionally at local newspaper offices along the way.[37] Devlin had joined the IWW in Chicago in 1908, and thus paused his cycling

to soapbox on a few midwestern street corners, sometimes getting arrested.[38] IWW free speech fights had broken out across the country, with most occurring in the West between the years 1909 and 1914, as more working-class Americans protested working conditions.[39]

In New York City, Devlin delayed sailing to Europe long enough to sell more promotional cards and stop in at the offices of the *New York Call*, a socialist newspaper, to promote himself further.[40] Then, he stowed himself and his bicycle away in hobo-fashion on a ship to Southampton. Soon discovered, he smooth-talked the captain into letting him work for his passage, a practice he would repeat several times over the course of the tour. At Dover, Devlin paid for his ticket to Calais, France, the only passage he paid on the entire trip.[41] Printing his red postcards in various languages for distribution and making stops at American embassies, Devlin took time to enjoy European sights, perhaps too exuberantly. He was arrested for disorderly conduct and striking a French policeman, spending twenty days in jail for the latter crime.[42] By the time he returned to the United States via the South Pacific, Charles Devlin emerged a seasoned raconteur, marketer, and traveler.[43] He had an affable personality, engaging political discourse and, like most IWWs, absolutely no fear of a jail cell. Devlin now occupied his time as an IWW speaker-organizer, earning his keep lecturing to locals and on street corners across the country, particularly assisting hotel and restaurant workers' locals, while occasionally working in the same industry.[44]

On May 17, 1916, Devlin was in Chicago when Hotel and Restaurant Workers Industrial Union Local No. 608 officially formed.[45] He surely read Calenal Sellers's *Solidarity* story about the "little rebel housemaid."[46] A month later, he read Jane Street's invitation, "You old-time rebels, who feel a thrill of satisfaction at the reports of the work started here. . . . Help us water our little wobbly garden here."[47] Devlin later wrote, "I had heard that there was a certain young lady in Denver by the name of Jane Street who had succeeded in organizing the Housemaids' Union. Most of my life had been spent among hard-boiled men in the field of Organization work. I was more than interested in the fact that here was a young woman who was not only doing this work but one who had had marvelous success in organizing. So naturally I wanted to go through Denver and see this marvel."[48] Indeed, other DWIU locals had begun popping up across the Midwest, a testament to Jane's work.[49]

In his memoirs, Devlin glowingly reminisced how he and Jane were together continually in Denver, holding street meetings every night among wonderful crowds while sharing their enjoyment of the "movement."[50] Devlin romantically attributes his optimism for the struggle "to make the world a better place for humanity" to his Irish ancestry.[51] Whatever the case with that, he was probably unaware of the difficulty Calenal Sellers was causing in Jane's life. As for Sellers, he was nonplussed to have another man step into the union hall with the same familiarity that he enjoyed himself. To make matters worse, while Sellers stayed aloof among the other male IWWs, Devlin made friends easily and immediately took over the job of organizing the men into an official mixed trades local.

Sellers's odd views about women and sex were disturbing, and lately he had begun obsessing about Jane. Sellers had found Jane like Grace in many ways, and he had imagined he had loved Grace. After Grace chose Albert Kohler as her beau, Sellers determined that his friend Kohler had taken Grace away from him. Later he wrote, "I was fiercely jealous for awhile—went back to the primitive in my hatred of him."[52] When the couple began living together in a boarding house on Lincoln Street, Sellers became even more bizarre, claiming that Kohler "worshipped on the shrine of sex."[53] That, according to Sellers, was all it was with Grace—sexual gratification—Sellers's usual fixation.[54] To him, both Grace and Kohler were "strange little" people, and he disliked and pitied both.[55] Now he pitied Charles Devlin, too, as a "poor lamed Irish boy," perhaps in an attempt to elevate himself over the intruder in his own mind.[56]

Nevertheless, on Friday evening, July 21, 1916, Calenal Sellers joined Charles Devlin and other men and maids on the corner of 18th and Champa Streets in Denver's Central Business District.[57] Little Jane Street stood just yards away from a looming, seven-story neoclassical-revival building, its identification printed in bold letters between floors four and six—*Denver Chamber of Commerce*.[58] The site selection was a deliberate statement, presenting a new angle of attack. Many of Capitol Hill's mistresses had spouses who owned or worked in businesses that were members of the civic giant. Employment agencies, in

Charles Devlin, Denver 1916.
*Courtesy of Guy Leslie, Jane Street Family Papers*

competition with DWIU's agenda, were also believed to be in league with Denver's Chamber of Commerce. Standing on a box, Jane opened up the street meeting to take up a collection for the Mesabi Range miners.[59]

In Minnesota, twenty thousand miners were on strike after one of their own had been murdered during a peaceful protest and others jailed. In retaliation, mining company gun thugs, along with local law enforcement, attempted to arrest Montenegrin strike leaders, killing several men in the process.[60] The Montenegrin miners were blamed for the deaths though they fired no weapons. Bill Haywood had wired IWW organizers Elizabeth Gurley Flynn and Joseph Ettor, and General Executive Board (GEB) chairman Frank Little to go to the Iron Range on July 7, 1916, to assist. Shortly after his arrival, Little was arrested, too. Jane had no way of knowing, but on the same day that she took to her soapbox in Denver, Little, the only GEB member sympathetic to Jane's organization, was to appear before a St. Louis County judge.[61]

On the Mesabi Range, Elizabeth Gurley Flynn estimated that of eight hundred families dependent on others for support, four hundred families depended on the IWW to help feed their hungry families.[62] Flynn also had a personal interest. Following separation from her husband Jack Jones, Flynn was especially distressed that, like Frank Little, her lover, Carlos Tresca, had also been arrested for "constructive presence," a legal twist where there is an alleged commission of crimes but the person charged is not actually present.[63] Authorities claimed Tresca's speeches incited the deaths at the Montenegrin's home. Later, Frank Little was released, but Tresca was held over for a grand jury. Flynn began working furiously for the prisoners' releases and called for contributions to strike funds. Jane had read Flynn's pleas through IWW newspapers and planned to ask for monies to support Mesabi's women and children.

In Denver, meanwhile, before Jane could utter any words, Denver police sergeant Cronin asked her to "move on" or be arrested.[64] After politely informing him that she was there for the purpose of holding a street meeting, one that she was determined to carry out, the cop left to find a telephone for calling in reinforcements.[65] Champa Street was thick with vehicles and pedestrians, and upon seeing a fracas about to ensue, a little crowd began to grow. Before more policemen could arrive, Charles Devlin took to the soapbox, orating to an "enthusiastic audience who were expressing themselves in no light terms."[66] Male IWW soapboxers typically used picturesque, if not salty, language that generated good humor but also delivered import. With his captivating storytelling, Devlin was soon speaking to about two hundred bystanders.[67] Officers Giles and Bear, along with Sergeant Cronin, soon yanked Devlin down from the box, "rushing" him two blocks away, in effect, dispersing the crowd.[68]

The next day, July 22, 1916, the *Rocky Mountain News* reported that "Miss Jane Street, chairman of the committee of the relief fund and an official of the Domestic Workers' union, a branch of the IWW; Charles Devlin, elevator pilot; Calenal Sellers, secretary of the Housemaids' Union; Max Cone, woodworker; and John Murphy, laborer," were arrested for disturbing the peace.[69] Devlin, who later reported the event to *Solidarity*, quipped that the group was escorted to the "City hotel," where they were registered and charged with refusing to move on.[70] Jane Street, like Elizabeth Gurley Flynn, had achieved her first arrest, and a city newspaper finally had broken its silence regarding the union.

The *News*'s use of the acronym IWW in connection with Jane Street's name for the first time is noteworthy. American public opinion had vehemently turned on the IWW. During earlier western free speech fights and strikes, the press had joked that the acronym "IWW" stood for "I Won't Work" and "I Want Whiskey" and later influenced public opinion with more serious tales of IWW-induced "death and woe, widowed wives, and orphaned children."[71] Now a willing media and corporations hoping to furnish supplies for the European war, including Mesabi Range iron and midwestern wheat, soon convinced the American public that the IWW was a German army of saboteurs. In August 1917, in front of the United States Congress, Arizona senator Henry F. Ashurst would add "Imperial Wilhelm's Warriors" to the list of epithets, further defining the IWW as a treasonous body.[72] Jane's small Housemaids' Union was now marked—a minnow swimming among larger radical fish, rushing upstream into the maw of a new Red Scare.

Jane never shared her thoughts about her arrest and first overnight incarceration. But if one were to contrast the personalities of the two men sharing her experience while competing for her favor—a moody pessimist and a cheerful romantic—Charles Devlin clearly had the edge. Jane needed someone who would tell her what was right instead of someone who constantly harped what was wrong, assigning her slipups to her sex. Now a war was coming—against America, against the IWW, and within the Housemaids' Union.

*Part Two*
# SHATTERED DREAMS

*Chapter Nine*

# SABOTAGE

Look out for soft "sabotagers!" They'll "queer" your social
affairs if you're not "good!"
              *Denver Rocky Mountain News*, July 13, 1916

Laden with IWW songbooks and picnic lunches expropriated
from their employers' kitchens, Jane jubilantly led members of
the Housemaids' Union and other Wobblies to a grassy area in Denver's 330-acre City Park on Sunday afternoon, July 23, not far from
the park's bandstand. She was celebrating her freedom. On last Friday evening, a municipal judge had refused initial attempts to bail out
Jane, who had never spent a night in jail. But on Saturday morning,
three "prominent" lawyers successfully won bail for all members of her
little soapboxing group.[1] Individual cases were now set to be examined
Wednesday next.[2]

Jane saw that the other maids were enjoying their freedom too,
by wearing fashionable, bobbed haircuts and discarding their drab
domestic servants' uniforms for dresses trimmed in lace and pearl
buttons. Most of the men wore white shirts, decorated with skinny
silk ties or bow ties. A few attired more casually, sporting popular
open-collared madras shirts. The men's modern, pale jackets donned
boutonnieres on their lapels. Almost all the fellows wore boaters,
popular flat-brimmed straw hats with wide colorful bands. This picnic
was not just a union activity but resembled more a social for working-
class girls who rarely had spare time or opportunity to mix with the

opposite sex. This was exactly what Jane had envisioned—comradery with purpose.

Besides Jane, the picnickers included her new beau, Charles Devlin, and her sister Grace, along with Grace's boyfriend, Alfred Kohler. Other attendees, associating together over the course of the 1916 summer and fall, included domestic workers Harriet Nillson, Violet Keib, Bertha O'Neill, Mary Shieber, Fanny Twohig, Olive Weaver, and "the Smith" girls. Wobbly men were likely Andy Barber, Max Cone, Dan Dailey, Meyer Friedkin, Charles Jacobs, "McClinton," George Meuret, John Murphy, "Skay," and "Pete." Pete was Jane's close friend, and his likeness appears in several of her photos dating through 1918. Whether Calenal Sellers attended the picnic is unknown, and his face is not recorded in an existing photo of a union get-together.

When the picnickers finished their "dandy" lunches, a female solo voice arose, singing the first verse of "Housemaid Mary," the union's common name for their new anthem.[3] Jane's and others' voices soon joined in the chorus, making "the air ring," and before long a large crowd collected around the songsters. Afterward, while an orchestra was warming up for an afternoon of classical music nearby, Jane took the opportunity to put up a short talk.[4] On cue, rebel maids quickly took up a collection before the audience could disperse.

Charles Devlin described the picnic for *Solidarity*'s readers in his usual upbeat manner, boasting how Denver's IWW spirit was booming once more.[5] He noted that the girls did not heed the Park Association's solicitation ban, as they were consumed with anticipation for the DWIU's newest diversion.[6] The Wobbly men and women had begun holding skits at their picnics, even using props to lampoon and caricature their employers, members of the Housewives' Assembly.

With their upcoming courtroom appearances in mind, the group held a mock trial. The accused was Mr. Block, a recurring comic strip character that appeared in IWW publications. Mr. Block (Blockhead) represented the average, uneducated worker who tends to "shoot himself in the foot" and thus "blocks" or sabotages his path to progress.[7] The housemaids' Mr. Block was charged with stabbing a donut to death. In Wobbly jargon, the quest for the elusive donut meant looking for work.[8] Charles Devlin described his own rousing performance as counsel for the defense, while hearing his arguments was presiding

Wobbly picnic, ca. 1916. *Sitting bottom row, left to right:*
Grace Tuttle and Jane Street. *Standing top row, left to*
*right:* Pete, 4th, next to, perhaps, a petite Phil Engle, 5th.
Note skit props—baby doll and lamp shade.
*Courtesy of Guy Leslie, Jane Street Family Papers*

judge Jane Street. Naturally the jury, represented by the hysterical audience, unanimously found Mr. Block guilty of the deed. Jane immediately pronounced his sentence: three weeks' kitchen labor while wearing a muzzle.[9] Interestingly, for the housemaids, the verdict may have been a liberating inversion of the sexual division of labor, that is, a housemaid sentencing a man to silence in the kitchen.[10] Just as clearly, the rebel soapboxers challenged their own sentencing for speaking publicly, contrary to Mr. Block, who would obediently and mutely work off his sentence of domestic work.

The summer day was lovely. In front of City Park's main pavilion, the bandstand extended out over the waters of Ferril Lake, a large, comma-shaped body of water. Beyond the floating bandstand, lovers and families boated in all sizes of watercrafts around the lake's center fountain. At the maids' Sunday picnic a week earlier, the municipal band discoursed classical music to what Charles Devlin described as a "bourgeoise crowd."[11] The IWW group had entertained themselves by singing "Housemaid Mary" in competition with "La Paloma" and a Wagnerian opera for entertainment.[12] Later the group had boated on a public launch, poking fun at three khaki-clad soldiers to others' applause, unsettling "their scissorine" girlfriends by singing "Stung Right," an IWW tune about the effects of war.[13]

> Some time ago when Uncle Sam he had a war with Spain,
> And many of the boys in blue were in the battle slain,
> Not all were killed by bullets, though; no, not by any means,
> The biggest part that were killed by Armour's Pork and Beans.[14]

Now the girls and their escorts took the same launch, singing IWW songs and listening to the orchestra. Charles Devlin reported their fun too, presenting his involvement in third person, writing that afterward the maids went home, "well satisfied and longing for the next picnic," namely, future melding with the IWW boys.[15] Devlin signed off his *Solidarity* story as "C. D."[16]

At the same time the Wobblies poked fun at Mr. Block's self-inflicted wounds, a small faction led by IWW Philip Engle declared war on Jane. Did Engle just not like Jane personally? Or, was his reaction more indicative of his social beliefs? Despite being an IWW, like many working-class men, he may not have easily accepted that working-class women belonged anywhere else except within traditional roles, including working at home, where men dominated. Generally, wealthy, white, high-class women had leisure time to build and lead organizations that combatted barriers limiting women's rights, but poor girls who could not afford to miss a paycheck did not.

At best, Engle was an insecure bully whose pint size, 5'4" and 133 pounds, may have influenced his behavior.[17] At worst, he was a misogynist with a following of members of the previous Denver mixed trades local who may have been uncomfortable with women taking a lead in their IWW affairs. Engle and his friends had dominated Denver's soapbox corners since their last free speech fight in 1910. He surely knew of Sellers's humiliation and even may have witnessed Jane's attack on Sellers. Perhaps he felt emasculated by Jane's organizational

*Shattered Dreams*

successes. One thing is certain—Engle's future actions would disrupt the positive achievements of DWIU Local No. 113, eventually reaching the ears of IWW national secretary-treasurer Bill Haywood in Chicago.[18] That IWW men would impede the efforts of IWW women was troubling and certainly counterproductive.

Born of Russian-Polish-Jewish immigrants in New York City on September 2, 1875, Philip Engle had been raised in poverty, living in a basement flat, along with five other families, on the city's lower east side.[19] When Phil was ten years old in 1885, his father, groceryman Benjamin Engel (Engle), died of pneumonia, leaving the small family even more impoverished. Engle's mother soon remarried in Detroit, Michigan, in 1887, and the family grew.[20] Leaving Detroit, an adult Phil Engle had lived since at least 1909 in Denver, where he worked "odd jobs" before landing employment at the Denver Distributing and Marketing Company, about the time that the Housemaids' Union formed.[21]

Although women usually figured in Wobbly imagery as idolized symbols of the class struggle, some men in the movement could also describe wives as the proverbial "ball and chain," and Engle certainly articulated this belief.[22] By several accounts, he bragged he had no wife and no car—in other words, no responsibilities, and his cynical personality and suspicious nature attracted no girlfriends.[23] Future history would show that Engle avoided most societal affiliations and personal commitments. A ghost in public records, he provided little census information, lived briefly in boarding house rooms, and formed few intimate relationships. The only persons connected to him were his mother and siblings in Detroit, Michigan.

Engle had boycotted the July 21 joint soapboxing event, though he was a spectator in the crowd. Not only had he refused to speak, but when the others were arrested, he avoided associating with them.[24] Engle pettily claimed that the intersection of Champa and 18th Streets had been the men's corner to speak, and he resented the women's presence. After Jane admonished him for his lack of action, Engle threatened her, and she later recounted "that he would see me on the outside of the IWW before he got through with me."[25] Indeed, Engle continued to work "with maniacal fervor toward that end ever since," Jane later wrote an organizer in November 1916.[26] Though IWW men had previously claimed the corners of Larimer and Market Streets on

17th Street, as well as a spot in front of the Majestic on Curtis Street, Engle and his followers would hold down the Champa and 18th Street corner for months to come.[27]

Engle's early actions reflect the IWW's distinctive ideas about gender. The organization had built its ideology on the idea that universal class conflict overrode all other differences including gender. Where earlier labor movements had excluded women, the IWW included them on the principle that women and men were united in the same class struggle. But unlike the paternalistic labor movements of earlier eras, the IWW still saw the universal working class as a different kind of masculine.

The working class was depicted as a single man robbed of his rightful chance to have a wife and family of his own. [28] This notion fit with the IWW focus on predominantly western industries where miners, timber workers, and other rough-and-tumble men lived in all-male barracks and camps far from any family. In Wobbly images and rhetoric, women often symbolized what the working class had been deprived of and hoped to win back. Their class struggle sometimes appeared to be a fight for each worker—implicitly male—to get a girl of his own.

As far as the women in the union, one slogan even reminded members that the rebel girl "of today is the helpful and encouraging wife of a union man tomorrow."[29] In the old Western Federation of Miners, a union that once had been the mining arm of the IWW, good union women were encouraged to support union men through their domesticity.[30] In effect, women should step aside and let men take the alpha roles in industrial unionizing.

Thus, while Jane Street saw herself as an equal partner, the IWW men around her could not help but observe her through a gendered lens. Prime examples are Jane's relationships with Calenal Sellers, who perceived her maternity as an inherently feminine weakness, and now Phil Engle, who, perhaps, believed she overstepped traditional divisions between sexes by overshadowing the men's organization. If Jane Street saw herself and her housemaids as the protagonists in their own struggle, the men saw her and the women around her as their dates for the revolution.

Dr. Francis Shor, in his study of this contradiction within IWW ideology, coined the term "virile syndicalism" to describe it.[31] Virile syndicalism is best defined as an organized, gendered form of protest in a workplace where working-class men are uncertain about their manly status. In response, IWW men often used direct action such as sabotage and striking to achieve power. But, in Denver, it was Jane Street who had achieved power, and not the men's mixed local.

Despite her success, the IWW marginalized her role in the movement's history. When prominent IWW historians such as Melvyn Dubofsky and Fred Thompson analyzed the IWW's past, rarely if ever do they mention Jane Street, in effect dismissing the organizer's right to history, even as the union touted inclusion, even propulsion, of women into industrial unionism. Journalist David D. Kirkpatrick, in his early discussion of Jane, remarks that to early union historians such as these, she was an "aberration in a masculine organization in its least adulterated and most radical region" (the West), and therefore, not considered worthy of note.[32]

In an unexpected surprise, all charges were dropped against the soapboxers the morning after the picnic, July 24. Charles Devlin noted that attorneys from the Free Speech Defense League convinced Denver's mayor, Robert Speer, that the housemaids had "all kinds of backing and threatened to call in 10,000 IWWs" if they were not given the right to speak.[33] It was agreed that the union could continue street speaking, unmolested. Local No. 113 wasted no time, and that night, another meeting was held. Though Devlin collected seven dollars for the miners on the Mesabi Range, he noted in his reporting that Jane, too, was also in need of funds in order to continue her "wonders." Every day the union office was packed by girls who were supplied with jobs as fast as they came in. According to Devlin, Denver employment agencies were nearly out of commission.[34] But he was wrong.

A strange event happened on Tuesday, the next day. A "sad-faced" gentleman who claimed to represent the Housemaids' Union made a tour of Denver's city office buildings asking for contributions of money to be used in wiping out debts incurred by its union organizers. The "Domestics Servants" union, he said, had "blown up."[35] The man despondently added that "the union had failed to catch on."[36] Now the *Denver Post*, which had not posted any stories about the Housemaids' Union since March 26, headlined that the attempted boycott of Denver was ending with a "sad, dull thud."[37] As for Jane, she had no clue who the collecting agent was and certainly did not send anyone out to solicit money from businesses.

The union office in the Charles Block probably exploded in recriminations, reproaches, and frustration. Who had sent the bogus collector? Who contacted the *Post*? Local employment "sharks" or Phil Engle? Jane's repudiation came on Sunday, July 30, 1916, in the *Post*. She argued:

> There is more money in the treasury than at any previous time.
>
> The number of members recruited daily is greater than ever before.
>
> The work in the employment office is heavier than at any time since the union was started last March.
>
> The social times enjoyed by the girls have been great successes.[38]

In fact, Jane announced, the union's books were always open for inspection of all members.[39]

Thus began a two-prong assault against the union. Phil Engle would perpetuate the idea that Local No. 113 was beset by financial difficulties caused by Jane's own mismanagement. And, the wound opened a weakness that employment agencies could penetrate. Even worse, in Chicago, Bill Haywood, hearing well-planted rumors, wrote Jane to "keep the objectionable characters away from their headquarters" referring to the misfits attracted to Local No. 113 and who had freedom of association.[40] Even as Jane's rebel maids enjoyed national attention disproportionate to their numbers in both national newspapers and IWW publications, and more women were organizing, a manufactured crisis, likely spawned by an employment agent and propagated by a disgruntled Wobbly, was about to derail the Housemaids' Union.[41] The glow of success, the fellowship with the Denver Wobblies, and all Jane's good, organizational work was beginning to dim in Denver.

A news story further damaged the Housemaids' Union. Mildred Morris of the *Rocky Mountain News* first reported on July 13, 1916, that Capitol Hill maids needed to be evaluated carefully—they could be members of the IWW! Once again, an unnamed source provided damaging information to the Denver press, this time that the Housemaids' Union had announced that maids, cooks, and laundresses would begin a campaign of sabotage. "'Sabotage' *is* the chief weapon of the IWW," Morris claimed, going on to explain that a common IWW method was dynamite, though, with tongue in cheek, she assuages readers' worries.[42] "Blacklisted mistresses will be permitted to live," she writes, "but some of them will be 'sabotaged' until they feel there are worse things than death."[43] The reporter elaborates further, claiming that there are trained union "experts" who will be sent into the homes of one thousand or more "listed" housewives.[44] A litany of illustrated scenarios—from using too much starch to breaking dishes to peppered soup, or even worse, sabotaging the next bridge party by pouring a whole pot of tea on an $150 exclusive-model frock—accompany the scare.[45]

At first read, the article is humorous in its silliness. But, *Solidarity*, also finding the situation amusing, weakened DWIU Local No. 113's strength by reprinting the absurdity, a tactical error. Suggesting violent methods of sabotage, particularly appealing to the "notoriously virile IWW," in the hands of "timid servant girls" inadvertently created a mockery of the female domestics, even as the images frightened Denver's elite.[46] In effect, the caricatures of saboteur-housemaids could be likened to a Mr. Block comic strip, degrading the rebel girls. Wobbly men found humor in the cartoons but certainly not the women who had been empowered to believe they had a momentous labor fight. Jane Street, for her part, makes no mention of sabotaging the domestics' duties in newspapers or her personal correspondence. To Jane, the fight was using certain systems to acquire a desirable job—or schemes to leave employment until better conditions prevailed.

Like Denver's propaganda, a concerted effort to discredit and neutralize the IWW was also underway in America. Newspapers, many owned by the very corporations that the IWW challenged, printed stories of IWW treachery, growing a Red Scare by 1917 that would not culminate until 1920. Even Mildred Morris's Denver sabotage story was quickly weaponized by other national newspapers hungry for salacious stories about America's newest enemy.[47] Well-known authors further incorporated anti-IWW and anti-labor themes, such as popular Western author Zane Grey. In his novel *Desert of Wheat* (1919), Wobblies sabotage farm implements and labor. To counter misinformation, progressive authors, such as Helen Keller, Jack London, and Upton Sinclair exposed corporate greed. Sinclair's *King Coal* (1917) exposes the truth about Colorado's coal wars and its maligned miners. Still, IWWs would be accused of fires, livestock poisonings, sabotaged harvesting equipment, and murder. With pop-culture literature and daily newspaper reports of IWW sabotage, fear began to pervade American homes by fall 1916.

Elizabeth Gurley Flynn did indeed publish a pamphlet titled "Sabotage," advertising it in the June 17, 1916, *Solidarity* issue. Within, Flynn generally defines sabotage as "the withdrawal of efficiency," while in industrial production, it means interfering with quality or quantity.[48] It is hitting "the boss" in his solar plexus, according to Flynn.[49] Yet, as much as the IWW, including Flynn, used sabotage in its rhetoric, sabotage was rarely practiced. The myth of IWW sabotage, cooperatively produced by both the IWW and its enemies, instead instigated vigilante action and anti-syndicalist legislation.[50] In 1918, when many IWWs were finally tried for sedition, all charges of sabotage were dismissed.[51]

Despite Phil Engle's conflict with Jane, Charles Devlin cheerfully lined up the IWW men to help make the Housemaids' Union a success. "Altogether, boys," he encouraged, "Do your best for the Denver rebel girls!"[52] On Wednesday, August 2, 1916, the IWWs held a street meeting at Charles (probably Curtis Street) and 18th Streets, chivalrously taking up a collection of five dollars for the Housemaids' Union.[53] Afterward, the group walked to the Mars Apartments, once an unemployment hall, where a larger crowd was assembled.[54] There, Charles Devlin formally began "reorganizing" Denver's Mixed Local No. 614.[55] While the rest sang songs, Engle and a Mr. McClinton signed up members, getting more than enough signatures for a charter. Devlin was then elected chairman and McClinton, secretary pro tem, leaving Engle still hungering for recognition. The group planned to meet again on August 9, with news of a new meeting hall.

A week later, Devlin left town, finally resuming his schedule.[56] His mission originally had been to help organize Hotel and Restaurant Workers Industrial Union locals, and in his mind, now that he had helped Jane, he could finish his obligations and then return. A pattern of short stays in Denver mixed with other union work would define his and Jane's working relationship. Personally, it must have been frustrating for Jane, who would have to deal with any more sabotage on her own while she awaited Devlin's return.

## Chapter Ten
# OCCUPATIONAL HAZARDS

"My dear young lady, I hope you pray God every night to keep you a good girl."

—"I don't have to. I get eight dollars a week."

*Industrial Worker*, July 3, 1913

J ane was still working in her office. The empty bed on one side of the room was a testament to her small orbit—she both worked and slept in the small area where privacy, at best, was minimal. Anyone entering her space would have sensed a personal intimacy with Jane even as she strove to mentor the girls and women in her office. Jane could hear sounds emanating from other parts of the Housemaids' Union Hall, where housemaids had been congregating with their Wobbly beaus this August evening. She was alone—until Calenal Sellers walked through the open door into the room.[1]

A truce apparently had been established between the two, but Sellers still held a grudge—her choice for motherhood—writing Jane later, "I resent it and always have and always will."[2] Yet since the encounter over Dawn, his desire to overcome her had actually increased. "There were times," Sellers admitted, that when around Jane, "I found myself trembling on the brink of the precipice."[3] So when he entered her room, his intent was not necessarily union business. Later, he declared that it was Jane's fault he had made an advance on her. She had *lured him*, Sellers claimed.[4] In his righteousness, he also wrote later that

Jane had apologized to him, in fact begging him to forgive her for what happened next.[5]

How the assault began is vague. Sellers must have pushed Jane's childlike body underneath his five foot, seven frame as he fumbled with her clothing. His hands were strong, workingman's hands, though later, the Bureau of Investigation would be able to identify Sellers by a newly mangled right hand, its fingers jutting at odd angles like a child's game of pick-up sticks. Jane apparently did not or could not resist or cry out for help before Sellers pulled away, likely flustered. He could not perform, another mortifying episode between him and Jane, threatening his manly reputation.[6] Even worse, though his bungled attempt had ended abruptly, a young machinist had walked past the open door just in time to see Jane in the "compromised" position.[7] Phil Engle would surely revel in the news, an imminent disaster.

Claiming he was not impotent, but sterile, Sellers privately defended his inability to have sex with Jane.[8] It was the usual excuse, later admonishing Jane in yet another tirade that "The difference between yourself and myself is that I [could] see the wrong I was doing the revolution and acknowledge that wrong. You glory in your actions [motherhood] and deny that you have been unfaithful to the revolution."[9] To further minimize his guilt, Sellers added, "You also seem to overlook the fact that you were a party to the wrong I tried to do you."[10] None of Jane's writings record her reaction to Sellers's assault if indeed it was an attack. During the 1910s, many intimate actions, including acts of domestic violence, were behind closed doors—private—and not to be discussed. These types of incidents, much like today's sex crimes, were often unreported, likely due to embarrassment, guilt, or fear. Jane's experience had been publicly exposed.

A letter to Jane, however, written by Calenal Sellers and confiscated by the Bureau of Investigation in 1919, is rich with detail concerning the event and must be evaluated considering its source.[11] A conflicted man with convoluted notions regarding his relationship with Jane, Sellers condemns her and praises her in the same breath, while rehashing moments and relationships in Denver during 1916 and 1917. His recollections expose a self-pitying fanatic who places Jane on a plane high above him, only to dash her to pieces because of her personal decisions. In this way, Sellers manipulates Jane's emotions in

*Shattered Dreams*

order to control her. Even one Bureau of Investigation agent, who after reading Sellers's letter to Jane, condemned Sellers for taking Jane "severely to task for subordinating the interests of the revolution to the desires of sex" and motherhood.[12] Special Agent in Charge F. W. Keely remarks in his report that Sellers "appears to be the most deserving" to be prosecuted first for crimes against the government.[13]

Despite Sellers's protestations in his letter, the description of Jane as willing partner is unproven and doubtful. Jane fully understood the danger of appearances, and even Sellers was concerned about what Phil Engle would do when he certainly heard what the machinist had seen.[14] Sellers immediately tried to convince the young man that his eyes had been fooled.[15] Nothing had happened, Sellers promised, at the same time advising Jane not to approach the machinist with any explanation. Jane was innocent of the event, Sellers now claimed.[16] But the damage had been done. However innocent, encouraged, or forced Jane's encounter with Sellers, sex or even the hint of it in a union hall dedicated to domestic workers was dangerous. Such indiscretions among domestic workers—often accused of prostitution or themselves the targets of sexual exploitation—had broader implications that could resonate badly. Clearly, permitting Wobbly men free rein in the union hall, if anything, was an occupational hazard.

Free love. Often attributed to the Baby Boomer generation, the hippie youth of the 1960s and 1970s, the concept has deeper roots in a broader context. In the mid-nineteenth century, the movement was called "voluntary motherhood," a push to liberate women from forming often loveless, political, or economic unions meant to procreate or provide security.[17] Victorian women wanted more—not only to have freedom to decide whether to become wives and mothers but also to choose because of love. Well known to Wobblies was anarchist Emma Goldman, who in writing a 1911 essay, "Marriage and Love," declared that "marriage and love have nothing in common; they are as far apart as the poles; are, in fact antagonistic to each other."[18] She claimed marriage was akin to capitalism, imprisoning women as dependents, or slaves.[19] In one 1913 *Industrial Worker* article, another writer affirmed that "Marriage today is a cold-blooded business-proposition!"[20] With activist Margaret Sanger's pioneering of birth control methods about the same time, voluntary motherhood thus gave way to women's choice to have a husband or a lover or both. Radical women during the 1910s, such as IWW general organizer Matilda Rabinowitz, called the view the "free love idea."[21] The concept did not mean having multiple sex partners but having sex outside marriage, just as IWW Elizabeth Gurley Flynn had openly carried on her affair with anarchist Carlo Tresca, though separated from Jack Jones.

Jane and her sister Grace evidently embraced free love, though the notion had been spawned from eastern radical intellectuals. Grace now openly lived with Albert Kohler, and Jane would continue to choose motherhood in her future—engaging in sex but not marriage. Her history with Herbert Bumpass had seen to that. Even still, Jane Street walked a tightrope if she chose to have sexual relationships with any one of the IWW men because of domestic servitude's historic proximity to prostitution. After working passionately to elevate the women of Local 113, she surely wanted to prevent them from making choices that would debase them further.

Joe Hill wrote in "The White Slave" (1912):

> One little girl, fair as a pearl,
> Worked every day in a laundry;
> All that she made, for food she paid,
> So she slept on a park bench so soundly;
> An old procuress spied her there,
> She came and whispered in her ear . . .
> Girls in this way, fall every day
> And have been falling for ages,
> Who is to blame? You know his name,
> It's the boss that pays starvation wages.
> A homeless girl can always hear
> Temptations calling everywhere.

Hill's popular lyrics, satirically sung to "Take Me Away to Dreamland," succinctly illustrate how a domestic worker could easily fall into prostitution and degradation. It was about economics and unscrupulous employers. In the 1900s and 1910s, women frequently began their labor experience when young, working continuously in their parents' home until they married, if indeed they even married. And then, marriage was late, and the percentage of women who never married was correspondingly high.[22] Girls who did leave home to work often gave their entire salaries to their families. In 1900, 38 percent of all single, urban working women over the age of sixteen lived with their employers and away from their families, such as Denver's Irish housemaid Maggie Dawson, who helped support a widowed mother.[23] Many of the western and midwestern farm girls, sent into cities to find employment, were mostly young, uneducated, and unskilled. They had few options. They could only seek work as servants, laundresses, and seamstresses, earning low wages. If they were bumped out of a job, they faced humiliating alternatives—begging or prostitution.[24]

The lack of a uniform job description for a domestic servant placed her in limbo between private and public spheres of life—identity and work. Even though the two spheres influence each other, the maid, "like the prostitute, operated in the space between the two worlds, symbolically ordered and imagined in different ways."[25] The IWW claimed that many employers sexually exploited the maids, just as the servants prostituted themselves for the chance to work.[26] Typically, there were no organized strikes to address undefined working conditions, including sexual exploitation, such as what women could do in eastern textile factory or western cannery protests.[27] That said, low wages prevented men from marrying and compelled them to seek female companionship in other forms, just as the women who would be their wives were driven "into the districts," including on Denver's Market Street.[28] Thus, unmarried women were out on the street because they did not earn enough, and men did not earn enough to put them in homes as wives.

Not surprisingly, the IWW saw prostitutes as "fallen" women, part of the working class and victims of the capitalist system, rather than morally deficient.[29] Because of this view, their plight was a favorite topic in the IWW press, and prostitution was the IWW's favorite metaphor for the exploitation of the working class.[30] But western Wobblies were a different breed than their eastern counterparts. They were more independent, often American-born and unmarried, such as Phil Engle and Calenal Sellers.[31] While they supported prostitutes in defying capitalism and welcomed their support at times of other labor conflicts, the women, in their eyes, were still prostitutes, whom the men themselves patronized.

At the 1916 IWW Convention, not all delegates and committee members appreciated the proximity of women's labor difficulties to prostitution. One female letter writer, begging for special women's literature to be included in IWW publications, described the ignorant woman who "works at lower wages, and longer hours than man, and robs him of his job, and at the same time robs herself of her honor, and is forced into prostitution which is a menace to our community." She added, "No doubt you all realize the power of the woman in fighting the unjust conditions in the industries as well as the social world."[32] Though a motion was introduced to educate women through literature, the attending male delegates buried the motion in committees, and ultimately, it was never passed.[33]

Still, the IWW talked a good game, and where women had strength in numbers through a thoroughly publicized direct-action campaign, the men supported them enthusiastically in union publications and even as vanguards on picket lines. An example is a Portland, Oregon, cannery strike in 1913, where women fought over increased wages, underlying safety issues, and unsanitary working conditions. The IWW contributed to the needs of these women and their families, physically fought against strikebreakers, and helped carry the strike. More significantly, Wobblies vigorously supported the women's fight to have control over their labor decisions and bodies, pushing against a Progressive move to manage the women's morality by defining proper womanhood relating to how and when a woman should work. The IWWs supported the notion that women should be able to make the best decisions for themselves.[34]

Ultimately, the Portland strike concluded, but not before protestors' voices had been censored and the IWW remarkably fought for a delinquent young woman on the periphery who had been arrested and incarcerated for perceived immoral behaviors.[35] Thus, the One Big Union, as a rule, viewed men and women equally, with women needing no special considerations because of sex. Prostitution was an economic concern, not a moral concern. Even so, Denver's Mixed Local No. 614 behaved paternalistically over the women in Local No. 113, where there was no traditional frontline.

Though no federal legislation protected domestic workers in 1916, including work hours, minimum pay, and workman's compensation, the Mann Act, passed in 1910, did prosecute human trafficking to protect young women who had immigrated or had come from farms to work in urban areas.[36] Passed to curtail "white slavery," the White-Slave Traffic Act, as it was commonly called, made it a felony to knowingly transport in interstate or foreign commerce "any woman or girl for the purpose of prostitution or debauchery, or for any other immoral purpose."[37] Quickly the act became a source of frustration for the court system when humiliated wives retaliated on their philandering husbands if the men traveled with girlfriends across state lines and money exchanged hands. Other wealthy men had to beware of liaisons with potential blackmailers.[38] Though Denver had a Bureau of Investigation office to handle such matters, its agents could not apply the law to sex trade within Market Street, Denver's red-light district, if the prospective prostitutes were not crossing state lines. Even more frustrating, city reformers had just recently forced the trade underground.[39] There the flesh market was still alive and well.

Between 1870 and 1913, approximately eight hundred women worked in Denver's tenderloin district at one time or another, while housing several hundred working girls at a time.[40] In Mattie Silks's brothel, a prostitute could earn between $100 to $200 a week, plus receive two meals a day, medical care, and plush accommodations.[41] Other working girls fared badly, working in nasty cribs that were sparsely furnished. Of these were women who worked prostitution part-time, moving in and out of other employment, including domestic service, as their economic fortunes rose and fell. As an example, soiled-dove Minnie Mundsack, alias Lillian Powers, first worked as a domestic servant earning two dollars a week. She later moved into prostitution, where she charged a dollar a date in her own crib.[42] Another prostitute, interviewed for a *Solidarity* article, "Prostitution and Wage Slavery," reported that she could earn more in one week than other girls in one month.[43] But, she was comparing herself to a factory worker. Domestic workers fared even worse.

There was reason to be concerned about the morality of domestic servants. On March 4, 1913, just hours before Woodrow Wilson took office, outgoing president William Howard Taft reluctantly signed a bill establishing the Department of Labor. The new labor department was an indirect product of the early 1900s Progressive Movement, which in part promoted improved morality. President Wilson appointed W. B. Wilson (no relation) as the first secretary of labor. Secretary Wilson had been a union man, secretary-treasurer of the UMWA, and later a congressman who had led the legislative drive that created the Department of Labor. And, he immediately ordered an investigation into the working conditions of women and children wage earners, including domestic servants.

The lengthy charge of this investigation was to obtain details about "the industrial, social, moral, educational, and physical condition of woman and child workers in the United States wherever employed, health, illiteracy, sanitary, and other conditions surrounding their occupation and the means employed for the protection of their health, person, and morals."[44] The final results appearing in a nineteen-volume report are astonishing in their discoveries, especially one volume that determined that of all occupations, the housemaid was the most vulnerable to danger, including prostitution, at the hands of white slavers and their employers.[45]

In fact, employment agencies, or "sharks" as the Wobblies called them, were prime players in the sex trade. Girls would go to employment agencies searching for jobs. There, unscrupulous agencies, after advertising qualified jobs they did not have, charged each woman a registration fee. Some firms were shams, taking the women's registration fees and then disappearing, while others demanded bribes to furnish employment of women who had already paid fees. Working conditions were often misrepresented, and sometimes, women were sent to questionable places for work, including prostitution, under the ruse of domestic service positions.[46] In 1913 the *Industrial Worker* angrily pointed out that even girls seeking honest work ran the risk of falling into vice through procurers posing as employment agencies.[47]

Jane's plan to impair Denver's employment agencies evidently had been too successful. With women applying at the Housemaids' Union Hall, instead of going to the city's "free" agencies that operated for the pleasure of Denver's Capitol Hill mistresses, the sharks' businesses had been crippled.[48] Previously, the agencies had cashed in on unhappy servants who job-hopped regularly, paying fees each time they applied for a different job. In fact, the "servant problem" had been lucrative.[49] Local 113 now cornered the domestic service market, and the employment agencies had a plan for retaliation.[50] So, when white slavers turned up at the six-floor, commercial Charles Building, on the corner of 15th and Curtis Streets, openly entering the union hall, another target appeared on Jane Street and her small local. If white slavers, sent by employment agencies, thought her girls could be persuaded or duped into prostitution easily, then what did the rest of the world imagine? Suddenly Calenal Sellers's latest transgression appeared minor to what was about to happen next.

White slavers began invading the Housemaids' Union Hall at Sunday union meetings to capture new recruits for what they surely claimed was a more worthwhile employment opportunity. The invaders, most likely men in the guise of union members, easily gained access into the public, women's union hall. Jane and the others later claimed that this "element" was from the "lower end of town" with connections to the underworld, though they had no idea of the men's associations at the time.[51] Jane soon realized that some sharks were attempting to establish a recruiting station for white slavery from within the ranks of her domestic workers.

When the uninvited guests refused to leave, disrupting her meetings, Jane had no choice but to call for assistance from the boys in the Mixed Trades Local No. 614. That included Phil Engle and his cohorts. With a membership now of forty men, the Wobblies were more than capable of manhandling the invaders out of the union hall.[52] At the next Sunday business meeting, they successfully drove out the white slavers who showed up, though threatened with bodily violence themselves. Calenal Sellers is never mentioned as having helped provide a barrier between the slavers and the girls, and Charles Devlin had not yet returned from his business.

Once again, Denver newspapers had not been keen on reporting any more news about the Housemaids' Union, and there would be no more reporting until the end of November 1916. Even if a reporter had gotten wind of the problems occurring at 404 Charles Building, no Chamber of Commerce member, employment agency, or mistress would have wanted possible connections revealed publicly. In effect, no one was talking. But, Local 614's Press Committee made certain that the heroes were glorified in industrial papers. Much later, on November 25, 1916, *Solidarity* posted its account of overcoming white slavers attempting to secure victims: "These fellow workers, though repeatedly threatened with bodily violence at the hands of the gang of white slavers, stood their ground and defended the girls. Credit should be given to Dan Dailey, Secretary of Local 614 and Fellow Workers Charles Jacobs, Meyer Friedkin, and Phil Engle. Our rebel girls must be protected!"[53]

Journalist David D. Kirkpatrick makes the observation that, in proving their manhood to the women and industrial papers, the Wobblies might have been acting out a role in the drama of the class struggle as portrayed in the IWW press. In a corollary to the depiction of the struggle as a fight to win wives and families, the IWW also often portrayed themselves battling to defend working-class women from the degrading prostitution imposed by capitalism.[54] Kirkpatrick adds, "In the process, the Wobblies also demonstrated the potential of the IWW's inclusive concept of class solidarity for women, helping Street resist the exploitation of both the housemaids' class—dependence on wage labor, and their gender—sexual commodification and entrapment as 'fallen women.'"[55]

It seems a rosy outcome, this brief story of heroism protecting the weaker sex. While it was true that Jane had had to depend on the solidarity of her fellow workers in the men's mixed local, she was now beholden to Phil Engle, surely a bitter pill to swallow. And, the affair was about to provide more bad press for Jane, when Chicago's IWW headquarters received reports from Denver, likely from Engle himself. Phil Engle and his friends had a new narrative they could exploit: Jane was a woman of loose morals, and the clubhouse and official headquarters was a place of "ill fame."[56]

Jane would later describe the harm that the men's mixed local actually caused. She ominously warned another organizer, "Sex can come rushing into your office like a great hurricane and blow all the papers of industrialism out the windows."[57] Jane would need to rethink her clubhouse and the Housemaids' Union's relationship with the men of Local 614.

*Shattered Dreams*

## Chapter Eleven
# DR. LOVE

Girls of 17 always crave for something romantic to happen
in their lives. What could be more romantic than to fall
in love with a soldier, a man of 40, who had served in five
wars, who had traveled all over the world, and who had
seen everything?

   Mildred Morris, *Denver Rocky Mountain News*,
             August 16, 1916

Even as Jane Street struggled with an increasingly volatile situation at the Housemaids' Union hall, another dilemma arose. Herbert Bumpass, identifying himself again as Jack Street after reappearing in Denver, now threatened her public narrative. His illicit actions in August 1916 just made himself the focus of a sensational story that would consume the city's investigative reporters, ultimately linking Jane to the con artist. This is not surprising since after Jane's divorce from Bumpass in 1909, his past had crescendoed with charges of immoral turpitude, felonious crimes, and related criminal investigations.

In late November 1912 Mrs. Cora Mickle Hoffer, the supreme high priestess at the headquarters for the Society of Natural Science on Chicago's Orleans Street, offered Herbert Ross Bumpass employment as an associate editor.[1] She had no idea of his past criminal activities, most recently his having dodged allegations in a forgery case in Little Rock, Arkansas.[2] Hoffer wanted Bumpass to help edit and print her

*The Thinkers' Magazine*, a new periodical for "Natural Scientists" of a new free-love cult.[3] He also was to write stories about his soldier-of-fortune days, about which he had evidently boasted, describing his experiences in the Boxer Rebellion, the Spanish-American War, and the Philippine insurrection.[4] The problem was, the high priestess had no money to pay Dr. Bumpass, as he now identified himself.[5]

Nonplussed, Bumpass asked for room and board in the Hoffer home as compensation, to which Hoffer agreed. But after moving into the abode and meeting Hoffer's daughter, the attractive Wilma Frances Minor, he informed Hoffer he would also require another payment. He had just "discovered that Mrs. Minor was [his] affinity," and he was due such "affinity as well as [his] room and board for work on the magazine."[6] It did not matter that the young woman in question was already married—after all, this was a society of free love and new thought. Hoffer, according to Bumpass, readily agreed, though later in court she vehemently denied this narrative.[7] Bumpass claimed that the husband of said-object-of-physical attraction acquiesced as well.[8] But after Bumpass took liberties with Mrs. Minor, the injured husband and vaudeville actor Mr. Minor forcefully disagreed and put on a riveting performance. Dr. Herbert R. Bumpass, newly engaged prophet of free love, found himself thrown out of the temple onto the street.[9] Then this weird story becomes even more bizarre.

In retaliation for a subsequent drunken riot at the Hoffer home, revelations of the love cult's secrets and general disruption of the peaceful sex temple's Zen, High Priestess Cora Mickle Hoffer and her daughter ratted on Herbert R. Bumpass and his brother Robert H. Bumpass. The brothers had set fire to the Continental-Chemical and Monarch Printing company, where Robert was part-owner.[10] They had plotted openly at the temple, and Bumpass had even brought back items he wanted to save in anticipation of the conflagration. On December 12, 1912, the Bumpasses and two others were indicted for arson.[11] Bond was set for $3,000, and the brothers released.[12] Later, at trial in March 1913, Herbert R. Bumpass remarkably was acquitted except for a $100 fine for lewd language and disorderly conduct during his testimony.[13] Not surprisingly, the story about the love cult affair was carried in national newspapers, including in the *Denver Post*. But Dr. Bumpass's story does not end here.

Four months later, on July 7, 1913, Bumpass convinced eighteen-year-old Lucy Cohan to marry him, though he was twenty years her senior.[14] The sticking point was Lucy's mother, Emma, an invalid after falling down a flight of stairs and who resided with the couple in St. Louis, Illinois. Bumpass demanded that Lucy sign a contract agreeing to leave her mother. It read: "This is to certify that Herbert Ross Bumpass, my husband, has this day given me the privilege of accompanying him where he will provide a home for me and give up my mother. He has in our marriage faithfully performed his part of the marriage contract. I sign this of my own free will, without persuasion or force of any kind."[15]

When young Lucy balked at signing the odious nonsense, Bumpass had a temper tantrum, making such a domestic disturbance that poor Lucy had to call the police to have him arrested. Later in court on July 31, 1913, as Bumpass quoted spiritual text about the necessity of his wife cleaving to him and giving up all her family ties, the presiding judge determined that the young lady was better off living with her mother.[16] This liaison, too, would end, and once again, Bumpass's extreme antics made headlines, from St. Louis north to Springfield. Still, it was another sensational scandal and tragedy that would bring newspaper headlines closer to home, much to the detriment of Jane, who was staving off the employment agency sharks at the same time.

Bumpass, still a social chameleon, had altered himself again after his move to Colorado in 1915. Denver's Colorado National Guard station offered him camouflage in a military milieu, along with assurances for action. Enlisting as Jack Street, and not Bumpass, he began building a new military career as a private in Company A. This military unit had been one of the same sullied National Guard companies that had attacked the striking miners' camp at Ludlow in 1914, although, in truth, many of its citizen guardsmen had been called back to Denver before the heinous attack.[17]

In March 1916, just three months before the sensational midsummer in Denver, revolutionist Pancho Villa and his compadres had brazenly raided the sleepy New Mexican town of Columbus, killing fifteen to twenty Americans, at least half of them U.S. Army soldiers. American response was almost instantaneous.[18] National Guardsmen from all across the country were called up for action, and Bumpass's group had been ordered to a mobilization camp at the Colorado state rifle range, also known as "Camp Golden" due to its proximity to Golden, Colorado.[19] Afterward, the soldiers were to journey to El Paso, Texas, where General John J. "Black Jack" Pershing was encamped. There, Bumpass's company and other guardsmen planned to help protect the United States' southern border, allowing Pershing to pursue Villa and his fragmented rebel army. Mexican general Álvaro Obregon was already balking at the invasion of his country.[20] But Pershing was not to be dissuaded.

Jack Street, as Bumpass was known, had been extremely popular with the younger men at the rifle range. With an attentive audience, one can only imagine the stories Bumpass fabricated about his soldiering days in Africa and China. By early summer, he had advanced to lieutenant as part of the First Cavalry squadron, still in Company A.[21] Apparently, Bumpass took Dawn Street's dog with him, too, and it became equally admired. A July 20, 1916, *Denver Post* photograph reveals a canine named "Third Lieutenant Jack Street" being initiated with a blanket toss, just like the unofficial initiation imposed on the soldiers themselves after taking the oath of allegiance to the United States.[22] The dog's owner is among a group of men, all with grins on their faces, gawking at the canine acrobat. For the human "Jack Street," the enlistment, along with its training, was a lark. He surely looked forward to Camp Golden's clubhouse where the men could host dances and "all 'lonesome' young women of Denver" were invited.[23] It did not take long for Bumpass's old habits to reappear in concert with his war stories, all as crooked as his dog's hind leg.

The sordid tale's background began when Mrs. Elizabeth Welborn of 1205 Acoma Street first greeted the charming man at the door of her "shabby boarding house" about eight months earlier, that is, in late fall 1915. She had no idea she was about to let a thief into her home.[24] Bumpass, as Jack Street, was looking for a room, and the divorced mother needed the income. He also had brought along seven-year-old Dawn, whom Welborn would be able to tend while Bumpass sought work, as Jane Street had begun employment as a housemaid in order to establish her credibility for founding Local 113.[25] The circumstances seemed nothing out of the ordinary.

Living within the household was Welborn's military-aged son, Lawrence, and her impressionable seventeen-year-old daughter, Gladys. It did not take long for Bumpass to woo the girl, filling her head with "pretty talk," and telling her he was only thirty-four years old when he was actually older—old enough to be her father.[26] With no idea of what was transpiring in her home, Elizabeth Welborn suddenly had to be hospitalized after becoming ill, leaving her older son in charge for two months.[27] While she was gone, Lawrence spent his days working as an elevator pilot in the Kaiserhof Hotel though he had enlisted in the Colorado National Guard.[28] Free from any oversight, Bumpass totally consumed Gladys Welborn, just as he had Jane, eleven years earlier. Much later, when Elizabeth Welborn found out that her daughter was in love with a divorced man, one who had been making love to the girl while she was absent, she was "horror-stricken."[29]

At Camp Golden in July 1916, Gladys Welborn had been unable to visit Bumpass. Yet, his new rank to second lieutenant and the "glamour of his uniform" had decidedly increased her desire to become a military bride.[30] When word came from Washington, D.C., that the National Guard was about to move to the southern border, Gladys immediately began pleading with Elizabeth to give permission for her marriage to Bumpass.[31] To Elizabeth, Bumpass's departure was a blessing, and she steadfastly denied Gladys's request. She had other plans for Gladys, saying that she wanted "clean young men who respect women" to court her daughter, clearly pegging Bumpass for what he was not.[32]

By early August 1916, about the same time Jane Street first discovered the white slavers, forty-one-year-old Herbert Bumpass found himself in another pickle. Elizabeth Welborn complained to the Colorado National Guard's headquarters that her underage daughter was the victim of an illicit relationship with one of its officers. Immediately Bumpass's superior officer had him removed back into Denver to work in the National Guard's office as a recruiting officer until the matter could be sorted out.[33]

Unbeknownst to Elizabeth Welborn, Gladys visited her lover on Monday afternoon, August 14, 1916, at the National Guard office in Denver's Commonwealth Building at Fifteenth and Stout Streets. There the two discussed plans to gain Elizabeth's consent to marriage.[34] Upon her exit from the building shortly afterward, Gladys stopped to talk with Sergeant C. E. Slater, who oversaw the station. He recalled later that she opened her handbag, smiling, and said, "See what I've bought?" half-jokingly. Slater peered deep within the purse, and there lay a glittering, blue-steeled .25 caliber automatic pistol. Without explanation, Gladys closed the bag and walked on.[35] She and Bumpass had made their plan. As for Slater, he put the incident out of mind.

Late Tuesday morning, August 15, 1916, an irate Elizabeth Welborn, accompanied by her daughter Gladys and son Lawrence, stormed inside the six-story, gray-stone Commonwealth Building. Triggering Elizabeth's ire was Gladys, who had just returned home after breakfasting with Bumpass earlier that morning. At issue was the fact that the lovers' date had begun at dinner the evening before.[36] Gladys eagerly and naively believed that this meeting with Bumpass would now convince her mother to permit her marriage to him.[37] Immediately, an argument broke out among Bumpass, Lawrence, and Elizabeth Welborn, with the latter exclaiming, "My daughter must *not* marry you, and I will *not* give her consent!"[38]

Gladys suddenly excused herself, turned, and walked out of the office, claiming she needed a drink of water. Sergeant Slater, suddenly remembering the pistol in her purse the day before, turned and hurriedly started after her. Midway down the hall, toward the rear of the building, Gladys pulled the pistol out of her handbag and calmly pointed it to her right temple.[39] Too late, Slater saw the flash of fire.[40] Inside the recruiting office, Elizabeth did not see the puff of smoke but certainly heard the pistol's report, as Gladys fell, "a staggering, crumpling heap which went to the floor," in the words of *Denver Post* reporter Ryley Cooper.[41] The bullet, entering her forehead and exiting behind her left ear, had shattered the brain.[42] Bumpass was the first to reach the lifeless body, cradling Gladys in his arms while the mother sobbed uncontrollably.

Afterward, Bumpass was held at the rifle range where he was on suicide watch.[43] After it was determined that he had not only gifted the girl the weapon, but that his love letters to her, found in the Welborn home, indicated a statutory crime had been committed, he was returned to Denver and jailed on orders of District Attorney John Rush.[44] Bumpass's commanding officer, Captain Dickinson, who accompanied him back to Denver, ordered Bumpass not to talk.[45] The boys back at Camp Golden, supporting his innocence, were rooting for him.

But Denver was talking. Enterprising *Rocky Mountain News* reporter Mildred Morris immediately dug into the salacious story, reporting it on August 17. She interviewed Elizabeth Welborn, who revealed all she knew about "Jack Street." He was a fraud. In fact, he was the divorced husband of Jane Street, who helped to organize the Housemaids' Union. He was also the father of their seven-year-old boy.[46] A printer by trade, Street had bragged about serving "as General Chaffee's personal orderly in the relief campaign of Peking and thru the Boxer uprising. In the Boer war, he was a member of the queen's imperial light horse brigade, the famous English organization," Morris reported. Clearly, Bumpass's military background had not impressed Elizabeth Welborn as it had Jane's parents, Frank and Mary Tuttle. Elizabeth ended her interview with Morris, claiming, "I tell you if that man is not driven out of the army, if the government protects him, I will hate it—Yes, I will hate it." She called Street, "That man—a dirty dog!"[47] For the first time, the name "Jack Street" was about to be revealed as the alias for Herbert R. Bumpass.

On August 26, 1916, Herbert R. Bumpass pleaded not guilty to statutory crime with a girl. His attorney, S. J. Sackett, offered that though Bumpass had the alias, it might be thought that he had a criminal record. In fact, Sackett assured the public, Bumpass was not hiding any unlawful activity. He offered a more reasonable explanation "that Bumpus, or Street, was adopted when a small child, taking the name of his adopted parents, but the adoption was not legal," thus defusing any need to seek out adoption documents for verification.[48] Once Sackett explained to the judge that Bumpass held a United States Army commission, a strong guarantee that he would appear at trial, the bond was reduced from $3,000 to $2,000.[49] Thus, Elizabeth Welborn had reason to be concerned about how the United States government might protect Bumpass. For his part, Bumpass confirmed his illusions of self-grandeur even as he mourned the girl's death. To him Gladys's death was heroic, and he declared to the newspapers that Gladys "showed all that was noble and womanly in her by the very act that ended her life."[50]

For the reading public, the Street-Bumpass case, that of a villain-ous military officer responsible for the violation and tragic death of a young maiden, was picked up by other Colorado papers.[51] In Denver, aside from European War stories and reports of Pancho Villa's travails, the sensationalism of the upcoming Street-Bumpass trial would be a reoccurring news story until almost October 1916, even as Jane Street worked to get positive press for the Housemaids' Union. Worse, Jane had been outed. Her lie about being a widow had been exposed. That she had entangled herself with someone as unscrupulous as Bumpass sul-lied her character as well. Compounding negative reports to the IWW headquarters in Chicago, the crimes of Herbert Bumpass now buried any advantageous reporting for the Denver's Housemaids' Union.

*Shattered Dreams*

*Chapter Twelve*

# RAID

Now that the "horse" is gone, the union has locked its
doors.
*Denver Rocky Mountain News*, November 1, 1916

Charles Devlin, when looking back, remarked that he had seen "disruptive forces" creeping in and that, "little by little," they were succeeding in breaking up "what Jane had built up."[1] His observation, twenty-two years later, obviously came too late.[2] But sometime in August 1916, an unconcerned Devlin had returned to Denver to work alongside Jane. There he moved into a boarding house, where he implemented an organizational structure, much like Jane's, to attract Denver's hotel and restaurant workers for a new IWW local. Jane appears to have moved into the same boarding house as well, away from the hazards of living alone in the Charles Block commercial building, as information later shows. Of the two—Devlin and Jane—she was the one anxious over recent events, even as she determined that the now three-hundred-member Housemaids' Union would succeed.[3] Though frustrated with Phil Engle's blatant dislike of her, combined with her vigilance in keeping Calenal Sellers in check, Jane showed no signs of yielding to duress—yet. Having Devlin back possibly buffered her reactions, insulating any future worries.

Evidently, his calming presence helped in other ways as well. As a result, Local 614's goodwill continued for a while longer, and remarkably, Phil Engle actually worked in tandem with Jane Street for the next month. On September 2, 1916, at a street meeting for the benefit of the Mesabi Range strikers, both took turns on a soapbox before a good crowd. After collecting $14.81 for the strikers' families, either Jane, Sellers, or a member of the men's Local 614's press committee optimistically notified *Solidarity* of the good work achieved by their renewed unity.[4] Other relationships improved too. Sellers admitted his guilt and actually made an effort to refrain from advancing on Jane again.[5] He remained engaged with the Housemaids' Union while keeping a close eye on Engle and his cohorts. Despite her indomitable efforts and Devlin's protection, what Jane could not control was her exposure to Bumpass, his trial, and the employment agencies who knew she was vulnerable.

Jane probably was not surprised to read in Denver papers that Herbert R. Bumpass had presented himself as a sympathetic victim as he played newspaper reporters, the courtroom audience, and his military peers. One paper reported that even when he first entered his jail cell, Bumpass dramatically removed his hat and uniform jacket, declaring that "it was Jack Street, not Lieutenant Street," who was about to enter the cell. Then he buried his face in his hands and wept, adding, "I never had a thought about that little girl that I wouldn't be glad for all to know."[6]

His histrionics did not go unnoticed. Some of his fellow guardsmen in Troop A, First Colorado Cavalry, who had been notified to testify, were conflicted. And now, one of the prosecutor's primary witnesses, First Sergeant Charles E. Slater, had gone AWOL. District Attorney Rush had detained the soldier in jail for several days in the hope of obtaining a statement but had to turn him loose after gaining nothing. Rather than be forced to lie on the stand and face a perjury charge, Slater declared he would rather desert and risk court-martial than injure Bumpass. U.S. Army officers and the sheriff had been out looking for him.[7]

Day one of the Street-Bumpass trial commenced Monday, September 25, 1916, around the same time that some of the housemaids began noticing "gimlet-eyed" men casing the Charles Building.[8] Whether they suspected the men to be employment agencies' hired thugs or criminal investigators working in concert with the Street-Bumpass case prosecution is unknown. Later, when the women's observations of the strange visitors continued beyond Bumpass's trial, Jane and others may have relaxed, dismissing the idea the men might try to connect the Housemaids' Union's leader to her former husband. They surely felt they could handle the employment sharks again if warranted.

Meanwhile in the West Side Courtroom belonging to Justice William D. Wright, Assistant District Attorney Foster Cline reflected on the Colorado National Guard's dismal record, tying the organization's past to the crime at hand in his opening remarks.[9] Bumpass's alleged crime should not come as a surprise, he implied, because the defendant was spawned from the same group of men whose spotty record illustrated blatant disregard for the rule of law. Cline may not have realized that he had stepped into a hornets' nest in trying to influence the twelve-member jury by linking the Street-Bumpass proceedings with Ludlow and other militia misdeeds. In the courtroom were also guardsmen, including Bumpass's commanding officer, Captain Julius G. Dickinson. A well-known Denver attorney recently featured in local newspapers, Dickinson had been assigned Troop A at the mobilization camp, and he was not pleased with Cline's defaming his men.[10]

Cline had not been wholly incorrect in his remarks, however. With little more than circumstantial evidence on hand, he gambled that using the Colorado National Guard's checkered reputation would win the case. The guard's public relations problem had begun with the 1903–4 Cripple Creek mining district strike. After that strike broke out, with mill workers and members of the Western Federation of Miners (WFM) union opposed to the mine and smelter owners, or Mine Owners' Association (MOA), Governor James H. Peabody called in the state militia. Peabody misused the guardsmen, however. The MOA bore the guardsmen's expenses and thus expected them to act on its behalf.[11] In fact, so flagrant was the abuse of the militia's power in concert with the MOA's directives that the editor of the *Army and Navy Journal* characterized this "curious condition of affairs" as a "rank perversion of the whole theory and purpose of the national guard," saying it was "far more likely to incite disorder than to prevent it."[12]

Brigadier General John Chase, of later Ludlow infamy, and Adjutant General Sherman Bell had arbitrarily used unconstitutional military force to repress the Cripple Creek and Victor strikers and their families, as well as their business associations. This included suspending habeas corpus, holding miners without charge, and denying their freedom of assembly, their freedom of press, and their right to bear arms.[13] Bell called it "military necessity," which, he said, "recognized no laws, either civil or social."[14] His subordinate, Major Thomas McClelland, after being reminded that his actions might be in violation of the state constitution, exclaimed, "To hell with the constitution," adding "we aren't going by the constitution."[15] He had attempted to suppress the press in Victor, Colorado, by arresting its linotype operators, including Emma Langdon's husband. Langdon then worked tirelessly to produce the *Victor Daily Record* despite McClelland, and she succeeded.[16]

At a subsequent trial on September 10, 1904, of four men arrested for making verbal threats against the MOA, militia cavalrymen surrounded the courthouse, picketing it with their bayonets bristling.[17] A Gatling gun was set up near the courthouse, and snipers assigned on roofs of buildings. After an entire company of infantry escorted the four prisoners into the courthouse with loaded guns and fixed bayonets, the judge could not refrain from commenting that the military display was "offensive to the court" and that it was "unwarranted and unnecessary."[18] The militia's overkill did not stop there.

In Trinidad ten years later, during the Colorado coal wars and under Governor Elias M. Ammons's watch, Adjutant General John Chase employed the same tactics using guardsmen as strikebreakers and ignoring constitutional freedoms, including holding Mary Harris Jones (Mother Jones) in jail without a hearing and filed charges.[19] His soldiers beat miners, and with their horses, rode down miners' wives who were parading in protest, and arrested many others. Ultimately, the militia's atrocities at the Ludlow Massacre finally drew national attention to the Colorado National Guard's soldierly reputation.

Just the previous year, in 1915, members of a college board for the Colorado State Agricultural College (now Colorado State University) balked at having a battery company of the National Guard formed on campus. One trustee stated, "We feel that it would be a disgrace to our students if they were connected with the guard. We feel that the guard, to put it mildly, is not all that it should be." She added, "We do not object to the government instituting a battery at the state agricultural college. But we do not want to have any connection, even by name, with the Colorado National Guard."[20] A *Rocky Mountain News* editorial also bemoaned that Colorado's National Guard was "unfit to take its place on equal terms with those of most of the other states as part of a national defense. It is disorganized and little more than a shell." The editorial writer added that a reorganization was "absolutely essential to save the militia from complete disruptions."[21]

Under Adjutant General Chase, the Colorado National Guard had obviously failed. Because of Pancho Villa's raid on Columbus, New Mexico, six months earlier, Colorado's militia had now been called out to join other guardsmen at America's southern border, but there had been no time to thoroughly vet its officers and rank and file. It was no wonder that the Street-Bumpass trial had been carried in Denver's newspapers. And, it is no surprise that Captain Julius G. Dickinson would not sit idly in court while the D. A. publicly insulted his military by painting another portrait of a guardsman-gone-astray for the jury.[22]

Bumpass's trial continued on Tuesday, September 26. The grieving mother, Mrs. Elizabeth Welborn, performed well as the injured party in front of the jury, telling how Jack Street had a hypnotic influence on her daughter.[23] Without benefit of knowing Bumpass's criminal past in similar circumstances, the court only had her opinion, her gut feelings about the accused, and some love letters between an adult and minor child. In fact, with the victim dead, all the prosecution had to share with the jurors was the National Guard's history, circumstantial evidence, emotional testimony, and the coroner's report.

The coroner had bizarrely claimed that he could tell from the deceased's examination that Gladys Welborn had spent the night out before the morning she killed herself.[24] Both the *Denver Post* and *Rocky Mountain News* sensationally claimed this would be the first criminal case in American history to be tried on just circumstantial evidence alone.[25] With the prosecution dependent on tying anecdotal besmirching of other U.S. soldiers' actions to Bumpass's behavior, the *Rocky Mountain News* declared that the military itself was now on trial, prosecuted by civil officers.[26]

On Wednesday, day three of the trial, Judge Wright sent the jury out to deliberate on the meager evidence on hand. Meanwhile, the Colorado National Guard ordered the arrest of Lawrence Welborn, the victim's brother, for desertion.[27] Apparently, Lawrence had joined the guard just before his mother became ill in August 1916, and it was

Bumpass who had given him leave to remain at home for the interim. After Elizabeth Welborn's recovery, young Lawrence never appeared at his mobilization unit, as required.[28] In addition, *Rocky Mountain News* reporter Mildred Morris had reported that Lawrence had met with municipal judge Ben B. Lindsey, the same day as his sister's death, in an effort to have Bumpass held responsible for her violation.[29] Evidently, this was payback.

The courtroom's gallery on Friday morning, September 29, 1916, was packed with guardsmen, including Sergeant George E. Smith, who informed the judge that he had orders to arrest Lawrence Welborn as soon as Welborn showed up to court for the afternoon's session.[30] Even worse, while Henry Bumpass sat quietly at the defense table, Captain Dickinson played his hand, informing Judge Wright that the Colorado National Guard would prefer charges against his assistant district attorney, Foster Cline, for his disparagement of the United States Army. If Bumpass were convicted, it would be because of Cline's comments about soldiery in general.[31]

By noon, to the consternation of Judge Wright, the jury foreman announced that the jury was at an impasse with two jurors holding out. Wright summoned each panel member to the bench in front of the large, intimidating military presence, and each responded if he or she believed it impossible to reach an agreement.[32] Displeased, Judge Wright sent the jurors back to the deliberation room with imperative instructions. After a last push two hours later, the reluctant jurors finally agreed to join their peers, and the group reached a unanimous verdict at 2 P.M.[33] Innocent. The cat had landed on his feet once again. As for the military, Captain Dickinson announced Bumpass would immediately be reinstated to Company A and, amazingly, awarded a promotion to first lieutenant for his service.[34] The guardsmen took their prize back to Camp Golden.

With the conclusion of the Street-Bumpass trial, the nidus fostering Jane's association with her ex-husband and his deplorable activities dissipated. How she felt about his exoneration is unknown, but she was probably relieved that he was out of Denver once more. Still, she observed that the curious wanderings of unidentifiable men about the Charles Building had not abated. In fact, some of the individuals had boldly stopped by the union hall to apply for work during office hours. Despite the notion that these were apparently annoying, "cheap 'detectives' of the gum-shoe variety," a warning niggled at her brain. Suspecting that something could happen to the Housemaids' Union Hall, Jane began sleeping in her office again. Shoving a "gatt," or pistol, under her pillow, she also placed a section of a gas pipe within easy reach.[35] When she used the upstairs washroom each morning, she locked the door after her, a new precaution.

On Halloween morning, October 31, 1916, while Jane was using the Charles Building's fifth-floor lavatory, the worst that could happen befell the Housemaids' Union. Upon her return, Jane discovered the door to her office had been forced ajar. Cautiously peering inside, Jane saw her world ransacked, leaving a few employer cards scattered over the floor. The thieves had apparently been in great haste exiting the union hall. Jane frantically searched for the rest of the important file kept on Capitol Hill's mistresses and became sickened in discovering its theft.[36] Indeed, someone had broken into union headquarters and stolen "the dope," that is, six thousand records on the Denver mistresses, records that the union had spent seven months preparing.[37] Picking up the telephone, Jane reported the theft at 404 Charles Building to authorities. The Denver police department's response was disturbing. No officer was interested in investigating a break-in for some missing paperwork for the IWW housemaids.[38]

Even without a proper investigation, Jane immediately realized that the raid had been carefully planned and that the thieves probably knew her schedule, expecting no one would be in the office between 7 P.M. and 9 A.M.[39] Furthermore, after discussing the crime with other union members, Jane believed the robbery had been planned by a "fly-by-night detective agency," probably aided by the same disgruntled element from the lower end of town that was blocked the past summer in efforts to establish a recruiting station for white slavery.[40] Characteristically, Jane's brain went into overdrive as she analyzed the crime and its effects on the women. She reflected as well on their sentiments concerning their security in the Charles Building. She knew she had been amiss in keeping the doors open to all visitors during the day, including men.[41] This was proof of her poor judgment and ultimately her fault.

This last blow should have been a coup de grâce for Denver's employment agency sharks and mistresses alike, but Jane was not about to become victimized or defeated. In a report to *Solidarity* on November 11, 1916, Calenal Sellers reported that the girls had met the situation bravely, resolving to fight all the harder against their "masters."[42] Jane had acted quickly. All members would be furnished with blank cards with which to gather raw data on jobs, and a new list would be constructed as rapidly as possible.[43]

There were other precautions as well. The new file would be kept in duplicate with one list in a safety vault while all records in the office would be guarded night and day.[44] Still, the loss of the card list was "inestimable" Sellers observed, adding that it contained data on practically every job in town where domestics were employed.[45] He likened the card file as "a fulcrum to the lever that the Housemaids' Union used on Capitol Mistresses" to force them to avoid employment sharks and "either openly advertise in the classified columns of the newspapers or come to the Union's office for their help."[46]

For the first time in three months, aside from the *Rocky Mountain News*'s reporting of Jane's connection to Herbert Bumpass, Local 113 was in Denver's news again. The same paper reported the break-in one day later, noting tongue-in-cheek that "now that the 'horse' is gone, the union locks its doors."[47] But Jane had not just begun locking the door to the union hall on 15th and Curtis Streets, she entirely severed the Housemaids' Union from the Charles Block building, moving its headquarters immediately.

The modest three-story house at 1614 North Franklin Street, in Denver's City Park neighborhood near Capitol Hill, had advertised cool, clean rooms with breakfast and dinner thrown in for five dollars a week, when Charles Devlin and probably Jane Street moved in sometime after Sellers's assault on Jane. There Devlin went to work to grow his new local, advertising management and blue-collar worker positions much like an employment agency. Publishing the earliest ad on August 22, 1916, in the *Denver Post*, his imaginary job seekers, offering repetitive information over the course of several months, were created to lure employers and workers alike into contacting the 1614 Franklin residence. In this manner, Devlin could build a file just as Jane had done with the housemaids the past year.

Phony positions included chauffeurs; hotel, apartment, and club managers; clerks and cashiers; and other "congenial" workers. The job seekers were advertised as healthy, white, unencumbered, and refined and educated.[48] One recurring, married couple sought positions together, managing properties, chauffeuring ("do own repairs"), and clerking. This ad is suspect. The male states his age as thirty-one years (Devlin was thirty-one), and the woman, a Mason's daughter, has ten years' experience in office work, which Jane had.[49] By all appearances, Devlin and Jane were also seeking legitimate work together while boarding on Franklin Street.[50] They were not married, however.[51]

During the week of the union hall break-in, a more attractive ad for the same Franklin Street boarding house read, "For Rent; Room & Board; 1614 Franklin; Steam-heated rooms, Glass enclosed sleeping porch; Serves best home-cooked meals, steak, milk, eggs daily; $30 & up monthly."[52] Not only was a luxurious board advertised, but rent had gone up substantially. The rooming house, it appears, was under new management. Five days later, on November 1, 1916, the house was completely under control of Jane Street for the use of DWIU Local No. 113's new headquarters.[53] Her snap decision and ability to move union headquarters to this particular boarding house in one day also supports the notion that Jane was already living there, and that she was now its manager.

Built in 1890, the new union headquarters was more homelike than any downtown boarding house room or commercial building office. The residence's facade was a traditional Victorian mixture of large stone bricks and fish-scale shingles, with an attractive bow window jutting out on the second story. Centered below the gabled roof on the third floor, a pair of windows looked out over a small front yard.[54] The broad front porch, accessed by six wide steps and running the width of the house, was large enough for groups to enjoy being outdoors. Though the house was narrow in front, it ran deep, and there were ten rooms inside its 3,067-square-foot interior, plus the sleeping porch. In the basement, a coal furnace heated water to warm the house, there being but one fireplace in the parlor. Still, Jane, for forty dollars a month, would be able to provide six furnished bedrooms for women who needed a place to stay.[55]

There were other benefits as well. The house's location near the Hill was in the very midst of the enemy.[56] The location, not far from City Park, was walkable to many Capitol Hill mansions or easily accessed

The Housemaids' Union Clubhouse
at 1614 North Franklin Street,
Denver, Colorado.
*Author's Photo*

by streetcar at Cheeseman, City Park, Colfax, and 17th Avenue stops.[57] With the Street-Bumpass trial over and the move out of the Charles Building concluded, Jane believed that the new start and location would facilitate growth and help the union's delegates line up other girls on jobs.[58] Surely, Jane also thought, the association of the girls with each other at the clubhouse would make them more rebellious, as they had more space and opportunity to converse and socialize among themselves.[59] At minimum, it was secure and provided a family-like atmosphere that the wounded union needed.

Thus, only one week after the Charles Building burglary, Denver's Capitol Hill mistresses discovered that despite their best efforts to use employment agency surrogates to destroy the rebel girl and her maids, Local 113 had been resuscitated right in their midst. The *Rocky Mountain News* reported the Housemaids' Union's new address, and Jane began running ads that included: "Nice Rooms, reasonable rent. Walking distance. Call Domestic Workers Union Employment Office and Rooming House, 1614 Franklin."[60]

Even more surprised were the Wobbly men who endeavored to attend the first Sunday Housemaids' Union meeting on November 5 at the new location. The front door was closed to non-DWIU members. With the exception of Calenal Sellers and Charles Devlin, no men, it seems, would be allowed.[61] Jane planned to make certain all vulnerabilities ceased. There would be no more early morning raids, unsolicited hanky-panky, or other surprises if she could help it.

## Chapter Thirteen
# JOB-ITES

They know nothing about living—
They do nothing remotely prejudicial to their jobs.
They don't love work—
They know nothing of the joy of creation.

Jane Street, "Job-ites"

Jane Street's successful Housemaids' Union forced board members of Denver's YWCA, commonly called the "YW," to join on Thursday, November 9, 1916, for a meeting in the YW's Rest and Recreation room on the sixth floor of the Wyoming Building at 14th and Champa Streets. Among the topics the women discussed was how to help housewives and housemaids coexist in a mutually efficient working atmosphere. Harriet Parker Campbell, new chairwoman of the new YW Employment Committee, laid the foundation for a broader discussion to be held on Saturday, November 18, featuring Henrietta Roelofs, visiting national secretary of the Commission of Household Employment of the YWCA. At the YW board meeting the past April, just after Jane had officially organized the Housemaids' Union, Mrs. Campbell had challenged board women to acknowledge the need for systemization of work for both employers and employees.[1] A few of the YW board members were also members of the Housewives' Assembly, and they likely had not been interested in modifying their personal behaviors.

Though Louise Hill's husband, Crawford, now sat on the YW Advisory Board and his mother maintained an honorary membership posthumously, Louise was not a member of the YW board, though she possibly could have been.[2] The Hill families had famously participated in the Denver YW's growth and success. Alice, Louise's mother-in-law, had been a charter member who led the organization with "clear-sighted judgement, her beautiful, sympathetic spirit and cordiality," and Alice's husband, Nathaniel P. Hill, had donated over twice the money ($5,000) than any other person or business for construction of the YW's first building on Sherman Street.[3]

Evidently Louise was not interested in an organization that histori-cally had "been with people, helping them to realize their full potenti-alities through increased skills, good health, effective citizenship, and the developing of inner resources through spiritual emphases"—the YW's first concern.[4] Or, perhaps, the organization, made up of Den-ver's more conservative Who's Who, was not interested in the socialite except for the Crawford Hills' philanthropic support. Louise surely did not mind—she relished poking the matronly movers and shakers on Capitol Hill too much.

A month earlier, Louise Hill had coquettishly peered out from under a plush black fur Cossack cap and produced a small smile on her lips for a Hopkins Studio photographer. Denver's own "grace of the South" forged with "the vigor of the West" had expertly posed at the foot of her oaken staircase.[5] Instead of her usual array in soft lay-ers of white satin, her throat and hands bedazzled with her favorite diamonds, Louise was smartly dressed for travel on Denver's streets. She had selected a trendy tweed jacket capped with a dark fox stole, its eared-head to white-tipped tail adding glamour above the jacket's belted waist. Her matching skirt revealed four or five inches of well-formed ankles that terminated in tall, white pumps. One kid-gloved hand was stylishly pocketed, and the other strategically rested on the crown of the heavy baluster. Mrs. Crawford Hill was ready for the world to see how she traveled for a front-page feature story in an upcoming *Denver Post* Sunday society-section.[6]

Louise had recently returned from the northeast at the end of the summer season, with her entourage of servants in tow. It did not take her long to catch up on the Housewives' Assembly's recently failed tactics and the YW's newest crusade. Not letting a good oppor-tunity to ensure her adoring public's awareness of her superiority in employee-employer relations slip by, while antagonizing the mistresses of the Hill simultaneously, Louise met with new *Denver Post* society editor Ella Miriam Sullivan.

The resulting full-page spread, published a week before the Housemaids' Union break-in, was guised to show off Carlson, Louise's chauffeur of twenty years. In the feature story, Sullivan avows that there are "few, if any, fashionable women in the city who can boast of having three maids in her home who have each been a member of the household for more than fifteen years."[7] Besides the ever-dependable Cora Cowan, even "Henry, the yard man," Sullivan writes, "has seen continuous service with the Hill family for fifteen years."[8] Though Sullivan claims these facts are merely incidental in her story on Louise, she does write that they are interesting in the "face of the eternal cry about the present day 'servant problem.'"[9] Sullivan goes on to gush that the "loving thought and consideration for those who have served [Hill] faithfully is one of many admirable characteristics of Mrs. Hill and one that has made her beloved by every member of her household."[10]

Though many in the Sacred Thirty-Six and Denver's up-and-coming fast set relished reading about Louise as they sipped their morning brews, the more grounded ladies of Capitol Hill certainly were not subscribing to the *Post*'s beneficent image. More astute *News* readers could imagine hearing the Housewives' Assembly's collective gag. In fact, they had reason to dismiss the Queen of the Hill's perfect domestic arrangement and ignore her passive-aggressive challenge to their household efficiencies. Since the YW now had plans to improve servants' morality and sophistication to match their mistresses' own attributes, Louise was just too naughty to be included in the newest affront on Jane and her maids.

While the Assembly discussed their next course of action regarding the Housemaids' Union, Louise Hill returned to her normal routine, holding "lively afternoon soirees" for her Sacred Thirty-Six friends with hired instructors to teach them the latest dance steps—including the "Turkey Trot" and "Grizzly Bear."[11] When her stodgy husband declined to participate, she had her lover, Bulkeley Wells, to accommodate her. Wells, too, was famously married—to heiress Grace Livermore, a Boston socialite. Wells was clearly an opportunist, and because of Grace's father's financial interests in Colorado gold mines,

*Shattered Dreams*

he had engineered a position managing the Smuggler-Union, Telluride's richest gold mine.[12] And, perhaps because of the ensuing labor unrest directly tied to her husband, Grace Livermore Wells rarely ventured to Colorado, leaving him to live a not-so-secret, "glamorous" life, as his lawyer E. B. Adams later described it.[13]

MaryJoy Martin, author and Telluride labor war historian, describes Buck Wells as "a peacock, all spangled, spurred and armed with a pistol."[14] In fact, the dashing, polo-playing military man seems to be Louise's male counterpart—egotistical, hedonistic, and wealthy, perhaps explaining the couple's mutual attraction.[15] That Calenal Sellers would tie Colorado National Guardsmen to the Capitol Hill ladies in the May 1916 *Solidarity* article is no surprise. His comments, labeling the women "'parasites' who 'lionized' the militia's officers after the Ludlow massacre," relates to Louise Hill and her Buck Wells as well.[16] Jane Street knew the history.

Under Wells's roughshod management, a decade before Ludlow, and which he likened to playing a polo match during an interview with "sob sister" reporter Polly Pry, mine and mill workers struck, demanding an eight-hour day and three-dollar daily wage, with the WFM leading the charge.[17] The Telluride labor war ensued with familiar Colorado actors—Governor Peabody, Brigadier General Sherman Bell, and the Colorado National Guard. Remarkably, by early February 1904, Wells was deemed captain of Troop A, First Squadron, a citizen militia, despite his direct involvement in the labor dispute. Soon he became the supreme military commander of San Miguel County, where he enforced martial law and his men terrorized brothels, saloons, and miners' homes, seeking out WFM members for deportation.[18]

In 1905 Buck Wells became Adjutant General Wells at the behest of retiring Sherman Bell even though Wells was, to union men and their families, one of the most despised officers in the Colorado National Guard. Most noteworthy, Wells was the third defendant named in the 1904 Colorado National Guard supreme court lawsuit—Charles H. Moyer vs. James H. Peabody, Sherman M. Bell, and Bulkeley Wells.[19] This particular case, some historians argue, prominently figured in the radicalization of the American labor movement, with one historical investigator remarking, "The IWW was hammered out in the fires of that conflict."[20] Indeed afterward, Moyer and the WFM helped found the IWW a year later for American workers who believed the courts were closed to them.

After Wells became a business associate of Crawford Hill's, he and Louise Hill entangled themselves in a remarkably open affair that would last for years.[21] Crawford apparently tolerated the relationship and appeared not to notice when Louise and Wells often left the Denver Country Club dance floor together, disappearing for extended periods, despite wagging tongues.[22] An immaculately attired Carlson even drove the lovers around town in Louise's elegant, open carriage, with Crawford sometimes joining them.[23] The three traveled and dined together, including within the Hills' immense mansion where, on the first stair-landing, Wells's full-length portrait prominently hung next to Crawford Hill's smaller caricature.[24] Perhaps reflecting Louise's views of her husband's inadequacies, Wells is dressed in tight polo trousers, displaying his physical superiority and overpowering masculine charm next to Crawford's weaker likeness.[25] Some maliciously whispered that the intimate group engaged in threesomes, though one journalist noted, it was highly "unlikely considering Crawford's personality."[26] Since the couple openly and remarkably flaunted their torrid love affair, some cynical observers noted that the couple made adultery "fashionable for the sophisticated woman."[27] The conservative ladies of the Housewives' Assembly, who surely paid attention to Louise's indiscretions, would have disagreed with this observation.

At the conclusion of another YW board meeting, Harriet Campbell invited all to come to a gathering at Mrs. Junius F. Brown's home on November 18, 1916, to meet labor reformer Henrietta Roelofs, and hear her talk on the Household Commission. Roelofs would be discussing the idea of "systemization" with Capitol Hill's housewives, sans Louise Hill. The mistresses should also bring their maids with them. Jane Street, housemaid organizer, was also expected to attend, Campbell announced.[28] Mrs. Gail Writer, who represented the Denver YWCA on Roelofs's national commission, would organize the details.

The housewives apparently were disenchanted with the *Denver Post* after Pinky Wayne's and Louise Hill's collaborative editorial following their March 1916 assembly meeting on Denver's servant problem at Harriet Parker Campbell's home. The *Post* feature on Louise Hill indicated that society writer Ella Miriam Sullivan planned to write similar puff-pieces about Louise under editor Fred Bonfils's management. Instead of the *Post*, Mildred Morris of the *Rocky Mountain News* was now given access to the YW board's plans and upcoming meetings that included Housewives' Assembly members. Morris, typically a features journalist, wrote the destructive story about the Housemaids' Union's inclination for sabotage the past July and broke the story about Jane's connection to Herbert Bumpass.[29] She was also a budding "militant suffragette," as she later referred to herself after being released from a Washington, D.C., jail in 1919, along with twenty other women protesting at the White House for women's voting rights.[30] While the Housewives' Assembly would not be able to snow Morris, she shared mutual ideas with some of the more progressive women and was a serious journalist.

Morris set the table for the public meeting at Mrs. Brown's home in a *Rocky Mountain News* article on November 16, 1916. She did her homework well, providing Denver's readers with quotes regarding Roelofs's views on making household administration "a business and economic manner."[31] In the article, the commission secretary claims that to solve the servant problem, a housewife "must put her house on a basis to compete with the factory in offering physical and social advantages to the worker," adding, "instead of talking about training her maids, she should make housework so attractive an occupation as to draw trained workers to it."[32]

Based on a 1915 YWCA Commission of Household Employment study, which Morris claims reads like a report on Jane's Housemaids' Union, women preferred to work in factories or shop jobs at much lower wages. There was, in fact, a revolution of domestics against long hours, servile treatment, and poor living conditions across America.[33] As a result, Roelofs's advice to housewives was "get ye to the factory and learn if ye would know why thy maid deserts thee for the factory."[34] For most Denver women, the factory analogy probably did not work. Roelofs's experience was based on eastern households that competed against eastern factories for workers.

Educated and powerful Front Range women were different from their Midwest and East Coast sisters, having little experience with factories. In fact, most women appear to be comfortably provincial in dealing with servants who had few other employment options.

When Morris quotes Roelofs's statement, "Let us begin by eliminating the words 'mistress' and 'master' and servant' from our vocabulary," these ladies were probably taken aback.[35] Educating their servants to behave and speak appropriately was acceptable; in fact, many of the mistresses, fearing sexual impropriety, supported attempts to reform poor servants. A few ladies were progressive reformers themselves, including Mabel Costigan, Ray David, Fanny Galloway, and Harriet Campbell.[36]

Still, placing Housewives' Assembly's employees on an elevated social plane, changing the household hierarchy, even as some house-maids simultaneously teetered on the precipice of prostitution, was an unusual, if not unacceptable, concept for many. For Louise, queen of Capitol Hill, who had been presented at the court of King Edward VII of England in 1908 wearing a famous train especially made for the occasion, and who hosted American dignitaries in her Sherman Street mansion, the notion would have been absurd.[37] Realistically, convincing members of the Housewives' Assembly that they were part of the problem would be the main challenge for Henrietta Roelofs.

That Jane could also be swayed with the new concept was also a pipe dream. Viewed through an IWW lens, the YWCA's plan was anti-thetical to the revolutionary organization's foundation as stated in the IWW preamble: "Between the working class and the employing class, there is nothing in common."[38] Not only did the elite women share little with their servants, the IWW believed, but they put their class loyalties above their gender. Jane and other rebel girls were reminded of Elizabeth Gurley Flynn's warning in Flynn's 1915 "Call to Women" that "the sisterhood of women, like the brotherhood of man, is a hollow sham to labor. Behind all its smug hypocrisy and sickly sentimentality lies the sinister outlines of the class war."[39] No amount of YWCA do-gooding would impress Housemaids' Union members to believe that progressive women, often the wealthiest of their gender, would actu-ally improve the domestics' circumstances.

A *Solidarity* editorial, published the same day as the Roelofs presentation, reiterates that these progressive reformers, "the more advanced in the woman's movement," were usually the "wealthiest women," who raise "their arms sky high in praise of woman's equaling herself with man by doing his work."[40] Calenal Sellers, in his May 13,

1916, article, reminded *Solidarity* readers that the YWCA progressives at the same time were "leaguing with the painted dolls of Denver's exclusive homes against the new union," adding, "to befool the workers by denouncing the I.W.W. and urging the slaves to join the association."[41]

After reading Mildred Morris's November 16 article, Jane Street, too, had her own take. The idea of infusing housework with scientific and efficiency principles did not make jobs more desirable for her.[42] Though she agreed that the current mistress-maid relationship was feudal, she, like others in the IWW and especially the miners, would have been opposed to forming modern business contracts with employers. Only a new state home economics curriculum, as part of an industrial endeavor to educate housewives and working women alike, might have interested Jane, who sought continuing education throughout her life.

Henrietta Roelofs pushed for such programs, believing that "non-wage-earning occupations in the household such as the wife and mother, should be considered under the subject of *vocational home-making education*."[43] Otherwise, "wage-earning occupations in the household should be considered under the subject of *vocational industrial education*."[44] Roelofs's clarification of differences between housewives and servants was judged by some to be "an act of historic importance in the solution of the domestic servant problem."[45] Her attitude signified a recognition of domestic service on an industrial basis with all that this involves in standardization of hours, division of labor, and so on.[46]

Jane was also averse to progressive ideas relating to Taylorization, or modern engineered assembly line employment, that were applied to factory work.[47] While the IWW's men and women did demand equal standardization of working hours and wages that the YW championed, they detested the consequences of "advances made in the simplicity and enlargement of mechanical devices for individual production."[48] New systems, requiring workers to use simple, repetitive actions in specially designed workstations, collectively increased factory output for the employer at great sacrifice for the craftsperson. Not surprisingly, individual artisans fell victim as workers became little more than wheel cogs in industrial operations.

Jane called such workers "job-ites," people who scurried to and from their repetitive, industrial jobs, including stenography pools, within which she would later work.[49] Jane's poem of the same name— "Job-ites"—appeared in the left-leaning *One Big Union Monthly* over twenty years later.[50] In the poem, she condemns people who only live to work, ignoring the beauty of individual creation. Now that Jane had pushed to organize nonindustrial, nonessential domestic servants who created no consumer products into a union, she could not stomach the consequences of organized, new progressive labor ideas and practices tied to domestics' vocational industrialization. She was all about resistance to capitalism's labor systemization.

At 3:30 P.M., on Saturday afternoon, the official "conference on the problem of household employment" commenced in the private art gallery of seventy-two-year-old Mary Louise Brown.[51] The collection of nineteenth-century French, American, and Dutch paintings in the 933 Pennsylvania Street mansion had been part of Mrs. Brown's late husband's estate.[52] Old-time Denver pioneer Junius Flagg Brown died in 1908 leaving his widow an estate valued at $1,005,712.14, an amount equal to $24,530,881.37 in today's dollars (2019).[53] The prominent art collection alone was estimated to be worth $100,000.[54] Mrs. Brown was currently in the process of negotiating a "loan" of the entire collection to the city to help found a new Denver Art Museum and Institute.[55] But for now, the prized paintings, including "Maternite" by Jean-Francois Millet, "Landscape" by Jean-Baptiste-Camille Corot, and "The Chaos" by Narcisse Virgilio Díaz, were displayed among the visiting ladies and their house servants in the opulent gallery.[56] This was to be a social occasion as well.

Gail Writer, a Denver representative on the YW's field committee for the West Central States Commission and wife of Jasper A. Writer of Colorado Fuel and Iron Company, presided. She appeared businesslike, wearing a black velvet hat that tilted jauntily atop her graying, pinned-up hair, a matching, somber suit with its white blouse open at her throat, and little jewelry. As Mrs. Writer's round, bespectacled face surveyed the attendees in the enormous room, her lips pursed, belying her attempted cheerfulness. Henrietta Roelofs had already arrived, but Mrs. Writer did not see the other prominent invitee, Jane Street. Absent also were Louise Hill and her maid Cora Cowan.[57] Otherwise, a

JOBITES:*

How lousy the world is with them!--
Mean-souled people who think
 They work to live
 While in reality
 They live to work!

They know nothing about living--
They do nothing remotely prejudicial to
    their jobs.
They don't love work--
They know nothing of the joy of creation.
Their minds are on their money,
And the money goes for food--
Unepicurean food
That makes for brawn
That makes for jobs.

How they hurry on their jobs!
Not with the thrill of getting somewhere
Or having something,
But like speeding electrons
In unchangeable orbits.

How they scurry, off their jobs,
Knifing blindly at each other,
For fear some other work pattern
Might be made by different vacancies.

All the deep purple of hidden murder
In the soul of man
For possession, for love, for power--
Leaks out in degenerate gray streaks
From the jealous eyes of jobites
Fearing for their jobs.

--Oh, life is nothing
Unless something is worth
More than life!            *Jane Street*

        *  "Job-ites", a term used in the I.W.W.
              meaning someone who cares for
By Jane Street        nothing but his job.
   141 No. Flower St
   Los Angeles, Cal.

*368 Museum Drive*

"Job-ites," by Jane Street.
*Courtesy of Guy Leslie, Jane Street Family Papers*

meadow of white-dandelion caps amid richly colored, elaborate hats—corduroys, satins, and velvets adorned with feathers, flowers, and con trasting ribbons—met her gaze as she noted that other uniformed housemaids were well represented in the audience along with their mistress-employers.[58]

After introducing the YW's featured speaker, Gail Writer took a seat, still straining to catalog the audience. She listened while Miss Roelofs, also fashionably dressed, with wisps of brunette hair escaping below her black velvet cloche, smiled broadly and greeted the women. Already a seasoned speaker, the college-educated, unmarried woman now lived with YWCA editorial secretary Rhoda Elizabeth McCulloch, also single, in both McCulloch's homes, in New York City and New Canaan, Connecticut.[59] Born to a Dutch father and American mother in 1878, Henrietta Gertrude Magdalene Roelofs had been raised a member of the Dutch Reformed Church. This explained the use of some archaic vernacular that reporter Mildred Morris, sitting somewhere in the gallery, would have to sort out.[60] Morris planned a feature for the next day's *Rocky Mountain News* Sunday edition.

Miss Roelofs announced that they were all gathered today to hear a discussion of the "servant problem." Morris noted that only the "fashionable part of the audience" applauded this statement.[61] Roelofs continued, "For the first time, women face a test of the sincerity of their stand for social justice."[62] The audience suddenly became quiet, expecting an explanation. A few may have reflected on their own motives for attending this meeting.

Before Roelofs's remarks could continue, Mrs. Writer's eye suddenly caught two unfamiliar men boldly seated at the rear of the gallery. Newspaper reports had clearly stated that all were invited to attend, but she quickly moved to inform the two that members of the opposite sex were not invited. Immediately, whispers that the trespassers were IWWs soughed among the rustling dresses throughout the room.[63] Gail Writer was probably puzzled. Where was Jane Street?

Unperturbed, Roelofs continued speaking.

"Before taking part in movements of community, national, and international interest, [women] should put their own houses in order. They cannot be trusted with big public problems when they stand convicted of selfishness, insincerity, and injustice of dealing with workers

*Shattered Dreams*

in their own households," Roelofs pointed out to the sinking faces in the audience.[64] Mildred Morris did not note how the housemaids reacted to the criticism against their mistresses. The maids were not attending this conference by choice, but at the behest of the housewives. The girls probably squirmed, avoiding eye contact that would show embarrassment or fear for their employers.

Roelofs elaborated. "What must you do? The first thing is to systematize your work. You must have a standard of hours for your workers just as business men have for theirs. If you employ a maid for eight or nine hours, you must not impose upon her at the end of those hours. In every field of industry except domestic service, a standard of limitation is observed. You must give your maid each day sufficient hours of leisure. And you must regard those hours as hers irrespective of what comes up."[65]

"What are you going to do if you have a late dinner hour?" asked Mrs. James D. Whitmore.

"Many women who have late dinner hours have their maids come late in the morning," Roelofs replied.

"But, if the maid comes that late in the morning," another housewife asked, apparently perplexed, "when does she do the housecleaning?"[66] And, so it went.

The next day Mildred Morris's story headline shouted, "Housewives Are Declared Failure; Unfair, Says Speaker at Meeting of Society Folk and Maids."[67] Morris's one-line declaration was no better than Pinky Wayne's editorial assessment of the ladies on Capitol Hill in her March 26, 1916, article. The Housewives' Assembly had made no progress in a bilateral attempt at conciliation with Jane Street and the maids on Capitol Hill. Louise Hill still reigned in household-domestic matters, and Jane, by her absence, had shown housemaids that she did not kowtow to the YW or Housewives' Assembly. Morris did note, tongue in cheek, that at least the "fashionables" were able to "fraternize" with their "help" at Mrs. J. F. Brown's home.[68]

The two IWW interlopers, most likely Charles Devlin and Calenal Sellers, reported back to Jane. Whether they were sent to spy, intimidate, or even participate is unknown. But clearly the ladies of Capitol Hill were split several ways in affirming a servant problem and dealing with its ramifications. In the face of the YWCA's attempt at domestic reformation, Louise Hill had boasted that a mistress could maintain a domestic staff with longevity while keeping all aspects of servile social divisions. Evidently other housewives, unlike Louise, lacked the secret ingredient necessary to retain servants and were unwilling to adjust despite progressive suggestions. A third group had no servants at all and nothing to lose, despite their fervent interests in changing the status quo. Mildred Morris's newspaper story next day, coupled with the men's early observations, assured Jane of one truth: she need not worry about the YWCA.

*Chapter Fourteen*

# BETRAYAL

No better way to restore the feeling of manhood to the
hearts of the workers than sabotage.

Big Bill Haywood

One of the maids answered a knock on the door of the House-maids' Union's Victorian clubhouse one early evening in late January 1917. When she opened the door, Phil Engle and some of the men from Local 614 made a sudden rush inside, muscling their way into the house amid women's terrified shrieks and Jane's furious shouts. Stunned, Jane tried to order the trespassers out and stand her ground, but she was helpless against their physical onslaught. Instead, Engle hatefully assaulted her, battering and shoving her small frame out of the way. Afterward, Jane could only watch defeatedly as men began ransacking rooms.[1] Where were Charles Devlin and Calenal Sellers? Their presence surely would have saved her. Evidently, Jane Street and the Housemaids' Union had overcome Capitol Hill mistresses and their tools—Denver employment agencies and the YWCA—but their gender alone could not combat the brute strength of the Wobbly bullies. The first act of the final betrayal had begun.

Before Engle and his thugs had even begun planning their offensive on the housemaids, forebodings of imminent disaster occupied Jane's thoughts. The clubhouse at 1614 Franklin Street was a financial wreck. Staring at the pile of bills and billings—the clubhouse's own debts and the DWIU's invoices that she had prepared for collection—Jane mused at her desk. Some mistresses had stubbornly denied payment for housemaids' services, which in turn, impeded contributions to the union. Worse, she was still having to advertise for female roomers in the clubhouse.[2] Without tenants, she could not pay the grocery and telephone bills. Now that it was late December and winter had arrived, coal expenses had also risen dramatically. "Even if we had the house filled all the time," Jane reflected later, "which was not the case, it [still] would not pay expenses" of keeping the coal bin full.[3] Still, organizing the paperwork by what she could pay and what she could collect, prioritizing each in the process, kept Jane's naturally analytical mind away from glitches that she could not control.

For collecting on the housewives, Jane began preparing "duns" bearing the IWW seal for a lawyer who volunteered his services to serve husbands of delinquent mistresses. Generally, she was able to settle most of these bills out of court using this tack. The trick was to include the name and business of mistresses' husbands on their file cards in case of nonpayment.[4] For the clubhouse's expenses and groceries, Jane had depended on donations and room rentals. But now Phil Engle was back to his old tricks again, this time blocking donations from outside locals while at the same time slandering Jane.[5] The Housemaids' Union was losing money quickly, and the realization had just hit her that, being "swamped with debts," the clubhouse was unsustainable.[6] Even worse, Bill Haywood had just sent his spy to Denver to investigate Phil Engle's rumors.

Big Bill Haywood, so named because legend claimed him to be a giant at well over six feet tall and weighing between 225 and 275 pounds, positioned his "slack bulk" in an office chair at his large rolltop desk in the IWW's headquarters on Chicago's "skid road," 1001 West Madison Street.[7] At the moment, he was distracted from his surroundings—the union hall, overflowing with Agricultural Workers Industrial Union (AWIU) men walking through its double doors and over an inlaid-tile greeting, "*Salve.*"[8] The floor tile then morphed into an aisle, dividing the large, narrow room, and coursed immediately behind Haywood's chair. His space was situated against one of two parallel walls, along with a string of other workstations filled with harried secretaries and busy clerks, also atop a cheerful, multicolored mosaic-tile floor.[9] A fog of smoke hazed upward, obscuring white-chalked harvesting jobs printed on blackboards and blurring windows that dimly permitted light into the union hall.[10] Haywood was a chain-smoker—a worrier—who liked to exert central control over all IWW activities.[11] At the moment, he was upset with the IWW debacle at the Mesabi Iron Ore Range. Its iron ore miners, after a failed strike, now questioned the IWW's sincerity and purpose. IWW general secretary-treasurer William D. Haywood was directly responsible.

Most of the rank and file saw Haywood as a "paragon of virility"—possessing great masculine power and militant purpose—a blue-blood radical who cut his teeth deep in the bowels of a gold mine in Ophir, Utah, when he was only nine years old.[12] Men wanted to emulate him and women nearly swooned in his presence.[13] Haywood himself carefully cultivated his western image of individuality by exaggerating his origins even as he styled himself an outlaw. Actually, he was more "bar-room-brawler," full of fierce rhetoric, infused with the sensitivity of a schoolgirl.[14] He dramatically impressed audiences in the East by declaring, "I'm a two-gun man from the West, you know." After a pregnant pause, he would pull a crimson IWW card from one pocket and a similarly red SPA (Socialist Party of America) card from the other pocket.[15]

Though IWW cartoonists helped create Haywood's enormous, myth-like image, symbolizing his manhood towering over his opponents, "the most feared man in America" made certain that photographic images captured only the left side of his face.[16] He rarely looked directly into a camera where others could see a physical weakness, his right eye, lost in a childhood accident.[17] But when he did pose directly for photographers, his face was in a perpetual scowl, and his good eye "a bit cocked."[18] He had reason to glower. His enemies attacked him from all sides. The Socialists had disavowed him for his violent language, warmongers feared him for his call to direct action, and the United States government was watching his every move.[19] Now Elizabeth Gurley Flynn, along with Joseph Ettor, had just betrayed the working class under his watch.

A December 1916 settlement between St. Louis County, Minnesota, prosecutors and IWW attorneys brokered a deal to reduce murder charges against the Montenegrin miners—who had never fired a shot at local law enforcement or Pickands-Mather gunman—in exchange for

*Left to right:* second, Carlo Tresca; next, Elizabeth Gurley Flynn, the original "rebel girl"; and last, William D. Haywood. *Courtesy of the Joseph A. Labadie Collection, University of Michigan*

the release of union organizers.[20] Not conversant in English, the miners were shocked to discover that instead of agreeing to manslaughter charges and one-year prison sentences, they had agreed to second-degree murder charges with sentences of five to twenty years.[21] Bill Haywood blasted IWW general organizers Flynn and Ettor, who had been in the region since July 1916, for helping broker the one-sided deal. He called their collusion in courtroom proceedings a farce.[22] Both weakly offered that "it was the best that could be done."[23]

Haywood believed otherwise, reminding them that the IWW "would not have permitted [any IWW] to plead guilty to anything, not even spitting on the sidewalk!"[24] As a result of Flynn and Ettor's duplicitous efforts, the freed organizers—Sam Scarlett, Joseph Schmidt, and Carlo Tresca—were released. It was a well-known fact that Tresca was Flynn's lover and not even an IWW man. Haywood might have contemplated that her actions resulted from being a member of the fairer sex. She had chosen Tresca over the unfortunate miners and their families.

*Shattered Dreams*

For this injustice, Haywood just decided that Elizabeth Gurley Flynn would have to leave the IWW.[25] And, one did not disagree with Big Bill Haywood.

Inarguably, Haywood was a pugilist, having earned his reputation in the Colorado labor wars beginning in 1903. In 1906 Colonel Bulkeley Wells, soon to be Louise Sneed Hill's lover, arrested him in Denver for the 1905 murder of Idaho governor Frank Steunenberg, the crime believed to be a retaliatory act.[26] During the arrest, Haywood allegedly struck Wells, and Wells's men pummeled Haywood with fists and rifles as retribution.[27] A badly beaten Haywood then joined George Pettibone and WFM president Charles Moyer, also accused of the murder, and the three were quickly and illegally deported out of Colorado to Utah. Later a sensational trial with Clarence Darrow as defense attorney successfully convinced a jury that a MOA stoolie named Harry Orchard was the sole murderer.[28] Orchard had fingered the defendants as part of the murder scheme at the behest of mine owners, who badly wanted to punish the WFM leaders. Orchard had a famous visitor on numerous occasions while serving his time in prison—Colonel Wells.[29] As for Haywood, he was vaulted to godlike adulation as a result of the labor wars and ensuing trial.

Though Haywood's history with men is well known, his views and actions toward women appear contradictory. Certainly, his early stances about women's place alongside men evolved along with his deeds in the WFM. The militant miners' union was known for its patriarchal view—women belonged in the home.[30] Still, Haywood himself had called the organizers together at the founding convention of the IWW in 1905. Of forty-three organizations responding to his call, five had been female representatives—women who could not be ignored—including Lucy E. Parsons, wife of slain Haymarket martyr Albert Parsons; Mary Harris (Mother Jones), widow and UMWA organizer; Emma Langdon, wife of the censored Cripple Creek linotype operator; Luella Twining, socialist activist and Denver educator; and a Mrs. E. C. Cogswell.[31] Within the more progressive and radical new IWW, two women were eventually elected general organizers—Matilda Rabinowitz (Robbins) and Elizabeth Gurley Flynn.

Nevertheless, the newly founded organization was predominantly male, and the WFM, known for its unapologetically rugged character, had the largest membership. Even though Haywood showed support for women mill workers in the Lawrence and Paterson strikes in the East, organizer Matilda Rabinowitz could not help but share her disappointment in the big man. He seemed to be about appearances, dancing with pretty girls, and surrounding himself with sycophants, unlike his predecessor, Vincent St. John, the first IWW general secretary-treasurer.[32] Instead, Haywood left the hard work to the rank and file. More recently, at the Tenth IWW Convention in November 1916, no women attended through most of the proceedings, although Flynn's credentials were approved for another year.[33] Journalist David Kirkpatrick sums up Haywood's dilemma: if power and masculinity were inextricably linked for the IWW, then women were inevitably relegated to a peripheral or symbolic role in the movement.[34]

Haywood's views on long-lasting relationships with women were also in line with other western Wobblies carved out from the WFM, whose peripatetic existences did not jibe with providing stable environments for wives and children. The men's romantic interests were often short-lived. Case in point, Haywood deserted his sickly wife Nevada Jane and his two daughters and reportedly found comfort in the arms of various prostitutes and other lovers before bigamously marrying again.[35] Though the IWW professed not to view prostitution with a moral lens, some men naturally placed women on a lower, disreputable rung. The Denver Wobblies used the false rumor of Jane running a whorehouse as an argument with Haywood to disenfranchise her. As a result, many women, including Jane, believed they had to fight hypocrisy to earn respect alongside western Wobblies, who publicly courted them as IWW warriors.

Now Haywood had another rebel girl concerning him besides Flynn—Jane Street would have to be dealt with, especially if she was running a house of ill repute, as Phil Engle would have him believe. Despite the glowing stories Jane and Sellers submitted to IWW papers about the Housemaids' Union, its rebel maids, and the spread of industrial unionism for the lowest group of workers, Bill Haywood could not ignore the rumors. DWIU No. 113's financial difficulties by themselves could substantiate malfeasance on Jane's part, rendering unnecessary distasteful accusations concerning using the union hall for the sex trade should Haywood decide to intervene. An investigation was in order. And so, the Colorado labor wars, Colorado National Guard, Capitol Hill women, the IWW, and Jane's Housemaids' Union became interconnected puzzle pieces in the broader landscape of western labor unrest.

Charles Lindsay Lambert had been Sacramento's secretary-treasurer when Jane first joined the IWW in 1915. A Scotsman, having arrived in the United States in 1906, he first had been employed as an electrical lineman in Kern County, California.[36] Eventually he worked his way to Sacramento and ultimately into the IWW's GEB. Another member of the masculine arm of the IWW, Lambert also appears not to have had any endearing relationships with women, at least long-lasting ones, remarking later, "I am never likely to have any wife."[37]

A jack-of-all-trades representative, Lambert now wore an auditor's cap as he investigated DWIU No. 113.[38] He was not about to disagree with Haywood's justification for an investigation. Famous Wobbly Frank H. Little had once pointed out, "When Bill makes up his mind about a thing, we are all supposed to toe the line, and we do, or try to—even to not drinking whiskey. Bill calls that 'teamwork.'"[39] Lambert would look for evidence, just as Haywood had directed. Jane knew Lambert well enough to loathe him. In a letter dated June 19, 1920, to Harriet Nillson, a DWIU No. 113 member, Jane reflects on all her "what-if's" and "I-wish-I-had's" regarding events that occurred in Denver late 1916 and early 1917. She tells Nillson, "You will remember how Lambert sneaked around Denver and did the bidding of the bunch there, and how he made a secret report to Haywood?"[40] Indeed, Lambert immediately fell in with Phil Engle and the mixed trades local.

To her credit, Jane had worked hard to provide the housemaids social activities in mixed company events. A week after the downtown union hall break-in, she believed it important to reschedule and relocate a Halloween party to 1747½ Arapahoe Street, a "neutral" location, on November 7, 1916, repurposing it as a masquerade ball.[41] The gathering had a dual purpose. Dressed in outrageous costumes, women could wait for national election results with their boyfriends, many of them Wobblies. The party was a success, "from a revolutionary standpoint," according to Jane, and their candidate, Democrat Woodrow Wilson, won reelection after campaigning that he had kept the country out of war.[42] The next evening, IWW speaker James Thompson addressed the women workers at their new clubhouse, further engaging the housemaids, who had been suddenly uprooted.[43] Since then, Sunday meetings had continued—but without men present, with the possible exception of Calenal Sellers.

The Housemaids' Union made their feelings known indirectly but publicly concerning the male Wobblies' treatment of their local. At Jane's direction, DWIU member Mary Shieber submitted an article, "The Education of Women," to *Solidarity* that was published on December 9, 1916. Initially addressing women readers, Shieber points out, "All you women who work for a wage, have you ever stopped to consider how you are being exploited at the point of production? How, because of your sex you are considered inferior to man?"[44] Though a good lead-in, most women knew this fact already, and the article is really about the education of men.

Knowing full well that most Wobblies would read *Solidarity*, Shieber reveals the trouble brewing in Denver without ever mentioning Local 614. She clearly has Phil Engle and his cohorts in her sights when she writes, "Women have continually been complimented upon their good looks; always been looked upon as a sort of toy," adding, "I don't mean this to be a moral lesson for anyone, but whomsoever the shoe may fit, let him wear it." She continues, "While sexuality may be a necessary factor in the worker's life, the economic question comes first, as it hits us first. That is the main issue." Instead, Shieber advises men, "We'd appreciate the cooperation of our boys. But don't continually feed her sweets. A little change would do her good. Industrial organization should be the main topic of conversation." Finally, a challenge to the mixed local. "What are you going to do about it, boys?"[45] They responded, but not the way the housemaids expected.

Charles Lambert concluded his investigation and sent a report to Bill Haywood. Jane called it a "secret" report, although its conclusions seemed to be well known to Engle's bunch. What is uncertain is whether Big Bill Haywood gave further directions to Lambert concerning the women's union, and if Lambert relayed them to Phil Engle or if Engle began acting on his own. Haywood prized the art of purposeful sabotage, even telling a crowd of socialists in Union Square that he knew "of no better way to restore the feeling of manhood to the hearts of the workers than sabotage," so it is likely that he either directed or deliberately turned a deaf ear to what Engle did next.[46]

By January 1917, Engle began interfering openly with the unity within the Housemaids' Union by going among the girls and in Jane's words, "stirring up trouble."[47] He gossiped and spread rumors "from one end of the country to the other," Jane later complained.[48] While she could defend her personal character among the older members of DWIU No. 113, new prospects likely were confused by conflicting IWW messages. Did Jane ask Charles Devlin or Calenal Sellers to insulate her from Denver's male Wobblies? Possibly, but not likely. Jane had fought hard to stand independently but equally along with other IWWs. To have to ask other men for help against what she surely considered rogue behavior would not have helped the Housemaids' Union's standing among other Wobblies.

How Charles Devlin reacted is not known because he was still traveling back and forth, organizing. Yet, Engle and the men from Mixed Trades Local No. 614 sabotaged the fruits of Devlin's labor as well, the new Hotel and Restaurant Workers Industrial Union local that Devlin and Wobbly Andy Barber were trying to organize.[49] Ironically, Sellers pointed out to Jane that it was her relationship with Devlin that was part of the problem. She was still putting sex before the One Big Union, perpetuating Engle's lies about her being a loose woman, according to Sellers. Jane's response to Sellers? "These are matters of which you know nothing."[50] Sellers shot back, "You know the psychology of the dupe of the type that Engle [uses] well enough to know that it is an easy mental step from this thing to a belief of all the others," simply meaning, Engle could convince others to side with him by saying all criticisms of Jane were likely true. Still, Jane chose to ignore what was happening around her, including the danger of Phil Engle, until Bill Haywood wielded Mixed Trades Local No. 614 to pound the Housemaids' Union.

Now an army of Wobbly men, whose charge was to work with IWW women as equal partners in a revolution for economic change, had burst in to wreck the housemaids' clubhouse. Furniture was thrown askew, drawers searched, files opened, and their pages tossed. Engle was searching for the most vital tool belonging to DWIU Local No. 113—its charter. Without the charter, Jane Street no longer had an IWW affiliation. And, without the affiliation, she would be finished in Denver. Inevitably, the paper was discovered. Holding it up and looking Jane directly in the eyes, Phil Engle maliciously tore the precious document into pieces.[51]

## Chapter Fifteen
# VIRUS OF PATRIOTISM

A plan to substitute women traffic cops, detectives, and patrol women in place of all Denver police, who may join the colors either through volunteering or conscription, has been evolved by Mrs. Jane Street, head of the Local Domestic Workers Union.

A Denver newspaper

Jane finally found time to write back to Mrs. Elmer Bruse, an Oklahoma organizer who had written her several times since the new year, the most recent letter dated February 28, 1917. In weeks past, Jane had been too full of anger to respond with cheerful optimism. When Charles Devlin returned, he found her still distraught, though furious, and the Housemaids' Union in shambles. He helped Jane put up a calm facade among the women and get back to business, even as she needed his comfort. Jane had immediately written Bill Haywood for a new charter, and while she waited for the replacement document, addressed other business. First, she reorganized the Housemaids' Union's new headquarters in the Quincy Building at the corner of 17th and Curtis Streets.[1] Satisfied with its two "nice" offices, she believed the location made the union look impressively prosperous and attractive for gaining new members.[2] They had, in fact, picked up twenty-eight new members since Phil Engle and his co-conspirators barged into the Franklin Street clubhouse.[3] Now meetings and organizational activities could go on as scheduled. Looking at her typewriter, Jane searched for the right words to use in her letter to Bruse, who wanted advice on setting up a new DWIU. This was difficult. Jane was still full of rage.

The March 1917 letter to Mrs. Bruse, discovered in the bowels of the National Archives in 1976, reveals a composed Jane—at least on the surface.[4] Jane matter-of-factly begins the letter by tediously detailing how to begin a domestic workers' union, collect dues, pay bills, and combat mistresses. Not until the third page of what was probably a four-page letter, does Jane turn to the difficulties she has had with the men. She writes, "I would advise you strongly against trying to have your headquarters in connection with the other IWW local there," explaining that the "Mixed Local here in Denver has done us more harm than any other enemy, the women of Capitol Hill, the employment sharks and the YWCA combined."[5]

Jane explains how the men had not been permitted to enter the clubhouse and, as a result, gave the Franklin Street house a bad name. She describes Phil Engle, who said he "'would see me on the outside of the IWW' before he got through with me," and the other Wobblies who broke into the house on Franklin Street.[6] She details how they "assaulted her physically," tore up her records, and ripped DWIU No. 113's precious charter to pieces.[7] She still had no dues stamps or membership books for new members, and no replacement charter because "they have probably told some big lie about us to headquarters."[8]

Buried beneath her words of caution is a harsher truth. Sexism abounded in the IWW. Jane condemns the male Wobblies, writing, "For a domestic workers' local to spring up anywhere and achieve success is a monument to their [men's] treachery and false prophecy against us, and they therefore discourage them [female locals] in an effort to protect themselves." She ends the letter with an apology:

> I am so sorry to tell you these things—you who are so full of
> hope and faith and spirit for the revolution. I have tried to keep
> out of this letter the bitterness that surges up in me. When one
> looks upon the slavery on all sides that enchain the workers—
> these women workers sentenced to hard labor and solitary
> confinement on their prison jobs in the homes of the rich—
> and these very men who forgot their IWW principles in their

opposition to us—when we look about us, we soon see that the Method of Emancipation that we advocate is greater than any or all of us and that the great principles and ideals that we stand for can completely overshadow the frailties of human nature. Stick to your domestic workers' union, fellow worker, stick to it with all the persistence and ardor that there is in you.[9]

Only later, after concluding the Bruse letter, did Jane allow a private moment of self-pity in verse:

> My friends seemed all to betray me,
> And my enemies, really to misunderstand.
> One blow after another,
> Without stop,
> Pounding on my soul,
> Like a storm upon the boy.
> Does it still go on?
> I do not know.
> I no longer feel it.
> The sun shines—
> Someone is smiling at me,
> Falsely or truly I do not ask—
> My delirium is gone,
> And I am well again.

Jane, undaunted, had decided to fight back. She just needed Lambert's report.

Haywood leaned back in his office chair, smoking, while he contemplated recent world events. With German submarines striking at American vessels and German spies infiltrating into Mexico, Haywood knew it was inevitable that America would soon join the European War, despite what President Wilson had promised. He, Bill Haywood, would soon have to navigate the IWW through a minefield of political and economic decisions. The United States' maneuvers toward allying with Russia and Great Britain in the war had the workers befuddled. The Irish typically sympathized with the Sinn-Féiners in Ireland, who detested British rule. The Finnish, most of whom were socialists, and their cousins, the Swedes, condemned Russia for its attempted "Russification" of Finland and other Baltic countries. Ancestral emotions made for rancorous divisions, and already men were taking sides, especially the immigrant workers who had brought their native prejudices and political histories with them. Certainly, IWW members wanted to know exactly how the union fit in. What would be the IWW's response to this war?

Haywood wanted to discuss options with the GEB and especially Frank H. Little, who was chairman of the group, but Little was too militant and brash. He would draw scrutiny that the IWW did not presently need. A national propaganda campaign had already spread through local newspapers claiming the Wobblies were in cahoots with the Germans and funded with German money. Haywood considered other GEB members. There was William Wiertola, a miner from Virginia, Minnesota; Richard Brazier, a British-Canadian miner and songwriter; Francis D. Miller, a weaver from Providence, Rhode Island; and of course, Charles L. Lambert, the Scottish immigrant and jack-of-all-trades from California who recently had reported on Jane Street. Aside from Haywood, each member represented a different section of the United States as well as a key industry.[10] Of the group, Dick Brazier was his closest confidante. So Brazier it would be.

Haywood bent his great head over his desk and painstakingly began a letter to Brazier. Haywood could not write, at least not very well, by some reports.[11] He was sensitive to criticisms about his writing, so he avoided sending out public statements in his own hand. Typically, he had a secretary take his correspondence, and when Brazier was in the Chicago office, he often acted as Haywood's secretary. There were too many spies about, and Haywood trusted Brazier implicitly. Dating the letter February 4, 1917, Haywood queried Brazier, "What effect will war on this country have?" Haywood paused, and then he added, "Do you think it advisable to mix a little anti-military dope?"[12] When the letter was completed, Haywood placed its carbon copy in his files. IWW offices across the country copied and filed all correspondence, unwittingly leaving a paper trail for federal agents in later investigations.

Brazier wasted no time in responding to Haywood. Small boned with a thick shock of dark hair and even thicker walrus mustache below a patrician nose, Dick Brazier was blind in his right eye like Haywood.[13] The two appeared to share the same sentiments as well. In his answer, Brazier suggested to Haywood that "a little anti-military dope with our organization talk" would "kill the virus of patriotism that will be sweeping the land."[14] But, Haywood was characteristically cautious. He ultimately decided that anti-war propaganda would be in-house—in IWW papers and correspondence—providing some direction to address readers' uncertainties, and not advertised on public soapboxes where the organization could possibly appear treasonous. This way, the IWW could keep its members out of jail.

In the weeks leading up to the United States' decision to enter a war that would be renamed the Great War and finally World War I, Haywood firmed up his stance more explicitly. The IWW would campaign on a policy midway between what Frank Little wanted—to initiate a nationwide strike if the country edged toward war—and that of using the conflict to organize more harvest hands, miners, and timber workers while avoiding anti-war soapboxing.[15] If Wobblies wanted to know the attitude of the organization toward supporting the war, all they had to do was read IWW literature, including within *Industrial Worker* and *Solidarity*, such as this verse:

> I love my flag, I do, I do
> Which floats upon the breeze,
> I also love my arms and legs,
> And neck, and nose and knees.
> One little shell might spoil them all
> Or give them such a twist,
> They would be of no use to me;
> I guess I won't enlist.[16]

The propaganda was obviously directed toward men who were in a quandary about their participation, but what about IWW women?

Elizabeth Gurley Flynn, before her IWW demise, offered her views on patriotism in a 1916 essay, "Do You Believe in Patriotism." Noting that the majority of IWW workers were foreigners, one or two generations removed, she wrote that internationalism is the "logical patriotism of heterogeneous populations."[17] In fact, she decried that America was *not* a melting pot, "that produces a jingoistic, mercenary, one-mold type," but instead "a giant loom weaving into a mighty whole the sons, the poetry, the traditions, and the customs of all races, until a beautiful human fabric, with each thread intact, comes forth."[18] Flynn retorts, "Count me for Labor first. . . . I despise the rule of Rockefeller and Morgan as much as that of King or Kaiser, and am as outraged by Ludlow and Calumet as by Belgium. Joe Hill was as cruelly martyred as Edith Cavell, and I cannot work myself into a frenzy of patriotism wherever a contraband ship is sunk and we lose a few prominent citizens."[19]

Flynn's attitude was certainly representative of many IWW men and women, especially the non-native-born. For others, the notion that this war would be a "rich man's war and a poor man's fight" began resonating in mines, factories, wheat fields, and logging camps. Still, with the IWW's deliberately ambiguous public stance on members' war involvement, some Wobblies operated on their inherited American beliefs, becoming caught up in the national fervor that was sweeping the country. Jane was not immune.

"WAR DECLARED" in large print shouted above the *Denver Post*'s masthead on Good Friday morning, April 6, 1917. Jane put down her paper. Like most Americans who read the expected announcement, she wondered what the conflict would mean for herself and the housemaids. Already news of hurried-up weddings, new women's first aid society organizations, and suspension of intercollegiate activities shared page space with stories of German bombs killing gray-haired grandmothers and citizen-organized roundups of German Americans. Aside from encouraging young men to join the military and disseminating powerful war-planning strategies with new allies in the fray, newspapers asked Denverites how they could help the war effort. Because men would be called up, leaving vacant, crucial jobs in Denver, Jane pondered how the Housemaids' Union could help, soon devising a way she and the housemaids could join the bandwagon fervor spreading across the country. Jane contacted Denver newspapers and proudly offered up the housemaids as substitute civil servants in the city. Besides, Haywood appeared to be ignoring her.

A plan to substitute women traffic cops, detectives, and patrol women in place of all Denver police, who may join the colors either through volunteering or conscription, has been evolved by Mrs. Jane Street, head of the Local Domestic Workers Union, who proposed to furnish the women to the city in the event of war vacancies in the local department. Not only will Mrs. Street furnish patrol women, but also will be prepared to supply firewomen, post offices, conductors, motor-women and female workers in all trades, she announced this morning. She declares that war will drain the west of men, and that women will be forced to fill up the depleted ranks of industry.[20]

Jane Street, born in Indiana into a Southern Baptist family headed by a civil-servant father, had naively decided that she, too, would help, while ignoring IWW sentiments. Service was in her DNA just as was helping an exploited class of women rise against their employers. Jane had become infected with the virus of patriotism, an anathema to Chicago's IWW headquarters.

Jane's newest transgression spread like fire over the wires and in the mail. In the IWWs' purview, she had suggested the unthinkable— supporting the capitalists in *their* war. A Miss Olive Weaver of Denver, a DWIU member who was concerned about Jane's offer, immediately wrote Frank Little in Arizona and enclosed the newspaper clippings.[21] After reading the articles, Little, amused, wrote Weaver back, saying:

Hope they are the usual rot printed by the capitalist press. Would hate to think they were true. Would hate to know that any member of the IWW would volunteer to aid the capitalists in their campaign of murder that they are preparing to carry on; the IWW is opposed to all wars, and we must use all of our power to prevent the workers from joining the army. If the regular wants to go to the firing line, we should not Worry. Why should we care whether there were police to protect the city of Denver or any other town or city. No member of the organization, whether man or woman, should act either as police or soldier. If the industrial pirates wants [*sic*] to have murder committed, let them do their own dirty work. I should hate to think that the domestic workers' union was aiding them in their work.[22]

On April 15, Little wrote Haywood, enclosing Weaver's letter, a copy of his response to her, and the newspaper clippings. Little noted wryly that Jane "had been doing some patriotic work."[23]

But Haywood had already received the same report four days earlier from Wobblies Joe Gordo and Elmer H. Groves, the latter a new IWW organizer. He wrote them back on April 13, enclosing another set of the same clippings for them to read. In the letter, Haywood compared Jane to his trade-unionist foe and AFL leader Samuel Gompers.[24] The AFL—ignoring unskilled workers, especially within immigrant groups and minorities—had competed with the IWW for union membership after the WFM split from the IWW in 1907 and rejoined the AFL in 1911. Haywood wrote, "Yours of the 11th received, note the clippings enclosed. It is interesting to know that the AFL men followed Gompers' lead and settled the strike on account of the war. Have clippings from Colorado which shows that Jane Street of the Domestic Workers Union had been badly bitten by the bug of patriotism. If the papers tell the truth, she is following the lead of Sammy, the toad, promising her members for all kinds of military service."[25]

Bill Haywood also wrote to Richard Brazier about Jane. He recalled that "a long time ago" he "wrote to Jane Street to keep the objectionable characters away from their headquarters," adding that, "since then things have gone from bad to worse. The latest antics, pledging the girls in the union to the war, makes her a laughingstock."[26] Bill Haywood, dismissing Jane as an embarrassment, had no intention of sending Jane a new charter now. He also had no intention of telling her why.

Six weeks after Jane wrote Mrs. Bruse, Jane was still fixated on acquiring a copy of Charles Lambert's report to Bill Haywood. In her mind, it was Lambert who had prevented DWIU No. 113 from receiving the replacement charter. He had listened to Phil Engle. None of her explanatory letters to Haywood and the "volumes" she wrote to the GEB had been acknowledged.[27] No one—including Calenal Sellers and Charles Devlin—could temper Jane's increased obsession with the secret report. Not waiting until the regularly scheduled meeting the next Sunday, Jane called a business meeting of the Housemaids' Union on Thursday evening, April 12, 1917. Candidly explaining the reasons behind not receiving their charter, Jane concluded that her personal character had been impugned. If the executive committee could simply vouch for her, perhaps Haywood would reconsider and send the new charter. Their response was immediate and read:

> 502 Quincy Bldg.,
> Denver, Colo.
> April 12, 1917

> To All Members of the IWW:
> This is to certify that Jane Street, as Financial Secretary of Local #113, has always been found faithful and zealous in her efforts to build up the IWW organization. The charges of graft and disloyalty directed against her by an element of disgruntled disrupters that have infested Denver and disgraced the IWW are absolutely without foundation in fact.

> (Sgd.) Fanny Twohig
> *Permanent Chairman*
> (Sgd.) C. W. Sellers
> *Asst. Secretary*
> (Sgd.) Violet Keib
> *Recording Secretary*

This letter was endorsed unanimously by Local 113 at a business meeting held April 12, 1917.[28]
(IWW Seal of Colorado)

But DWIU Local No. 113 never received a response to the endorsement, probably because Haywood had just received the Denver articles discussing Jane's patriotic offer. Jane next wrote Frank Little personally. He had been the GEB member who had requested a women's literature page in *Solidarity* five months earlier. Surely, he would help her. Jane waited.

Two weeks later, Jane was certain of one fact—she was pregnant with Charles Devlin's baby. Naturally, Devlin was not in Denver but traveling again, working his job as a Hotel and Restaurant Workers

Industrial Union organizer. Sellers did find out, and when he did, railed at Jane, even intimating that she should abort the baby in the name of the revolution.

"I have always fought for your good name," he wrote her later as he recalled events during the month of May 1917. "You know that once when we were walking around Denver and the matter of some of these lying, slimy stories came up, I told you I always have [had] every faith in you, no matter what happened."[29]

Now, Sellers declared, her pregnancy would prove the type of union she was running to Engle and provide Engle ammunition for everything of which he had accused her. "I do not condemn you as an immoral woman," Sellers told Jane, but he reminded her that Engle and others destroyed the clubhouse because they believed it a house of ill fame.[30] Sellers scolded, "When that critical time came for you to decide between sex gratification with Devlin or remaining true to the movement and avoiding all the disastrous results that would follow in the train of having a child by Devlin in Denver—disastrous results to the movement that we had tried so hard to build up, you decided in favor of sex."[31]

As in the past, Sellers's condemnations fell on deaf ears. Jane treasured motherhood even as she strove for equal treatment among sexes in the union. Irritated, Sellers considered leaving Denver. The fight was farther west—in the mining camps—and everyone was going. Because of the war declaration, Conscription Day had been set for June 5, 1917. Most Wobblies did not plan to be trapped in Denver. Sellers, like Phil Engle and other men, would try becoming ghosts to avoid registration. Sellers was already upset with Jane anyway because of her patriotic suggestion. He had made it clear that though he was born in the United States, he was prouder of being an IWW than being an American.[32]

No, Jane reasoned, the Housemaids' Union depended on her alone. She would regain the charter, even if she had to get it herself, at the same time fighting morning sickness. Frank Little had finally answered her—he had a copy of Lambert's report. She was to meet him in Bisbee, Arizona, where the IWW had just announced it was taking the revolution to America. She wired Devlin to meet her there. He was going to become a father.

*Chapter Sixteen*

# LAST HOPE AT BISBEE

They didn't think of themselves as radicals. Just union
men. We were all "German sympathizers." I bet you
there wasn't a German amongst the bunch. But a wobbly
had horns.

> Fred Watson, "Still on Strike!" 1977

To Jane Street, the high-desert town of Bisbee, Arizona, would
have seemed delightfully vibrant with its strong mix of ethnicities, yet a perceptible promise of conflict instead infused the air. Having never stepped foot into an actual western mining camp before,
Jane now encountered opposing elements of industrial grime and new-
wealth gleam upon her arrival in June 1917. The railroad depot, located
near the intersection of Naco Road and OK Street, was in plain sight
of Phelps Dodge's fabled Copper Queen mine to the south. There, an
armed presence stood, observing militant miners, whose task was to
pull dusty carts of copper ore out of its dingy maw. Working underground were many of the Queen's seasoned miners, some of whom
had migrated from Colorado, after being deported at the conclusion of
the labor wars thirteen years ago under Colorado governor Peabody's
administration. Of these former WFM miners, most were experienced
at fighting mine management, and a good number were still averse to
working with Eastern Europeans, Mexicans, and other darker-skinned
men. This history, Jane knew.

On a nearby El Paso and Southwestern Railroad spur, mostly immigrant, above-ground workers proceeded to load the ore into hoppers for processing at Douglas's sooty smelter, about twenty-five miles away, near the Mexican border. The IWW had begun organizing these workers too, indiscriminate of ethnicity or color, much to the dismay of the former "white man's camp" residents.[1] Though at least thirty languages could be heard in Bisbee, a move to keep the town traditionally "American" was underway.

When she glanced northward, Jane saw a burnt-red, scrubby mountain, locally called Chihuahua Hill because of its Mexican shanties coursing downward toward a noisy confusion of adobe-and-brick theaters, bars, hotels, sundry stores, and gambling houses. The jewel of Bisbee's delights, Brewery Avenue, paralleled OK Street at the base of the hill in a gulch of the same name, narrowing northward beyond the city's park to shabby, wooden-framed boarding houses and prostitutes' cribs. Between the rows of buildings, Jane could see other ascendant streets, with crude, concrete stairs laddered among them, inconspicuously herding residents—some well-heeled and others in poorer immigrant dress—along to their destinations within the steep canyon. Gripping Dawn's eight-year-old hand in hers, Jane began the climb upward to this seedier district in Brewery Gulch. She knew that the IWW met at Union Hall on OK Street at the base of Chihuahua Hill. It was there she planned to find Frank Little, chairman of the IWW's GEB.

Little had arrived in Bisbee shortly before Thursday evening, June 14, 1917, to attend the first meeting of the Metal Mine Workers Industrial Union (MMWIU) No. 800 convention after leaving Jerome, Arizona, one of many Arizona copper mining camps in turmoil. He should have been jubilant. There, the old WFM, now a branch of the AFL renamed the International Union of Mine, Mill, and Smelter Workers (IUMMSW), had vociferously opposed striking alongside the IWW, demanding full recognition as the only traditional American labor union. In recent months, the word "traditional" had acquired a more nuanced definition, helping characterize people and groups by their origins. With the United States joining the European War, a strong suspicion against non-native-born Americans had arisen, fomented by industrial bosses and the press.

Despite the IUMMSW's refusal to join forces, Little and MMWIU No. 800's secretary-treasurer, Grover Perry, had successfully engineered an IWW copper miners' strike and won, an especially sweet victory after Arizona governor Thomas E. Campbell's abrupt refusal to meet their demands—$6 a day underground and $5.50 a day above ground, and two men on every drill.[2] With the exception of Globe, Arizona copper miners were immediately inspired to strike elsewhere without IUMMSW assistance.[3]

But one week later, on June 8, 1917, the Granite shaft of the Speculator Mine in Butte, Montana, had caught fire, killing 168 copper miners—the worst underground hard-rock mining disaster ever recorded in the United States.[4] Many blamed the catastrophe on mine management's neglect. Butte miners had immediately gone on strike. Now all Arizona's copper miners were clamoring to strike in sympathy with their miner brothers and not because of the war. Frank Little had arrived in Bisbee to ask MMWIU No. 800's representative-members to restrain themselves until a united, organized statewide assault could be organized.[5] To him, Arizona was the frontline for the IWW's battle against the capitalists' European War. Wobblies from afar began traveling west to assist.

Working quietly behind this panorama of war preparations, disgruntled miners and smelter workers, and AFL and IWW organizers were the mine owners and managers. Their infiltrators were already reporting to Phelps Dodge's Walter Douglas, John C. Greenway of the Calumet & Arizona Mining Company, and M. W. Merrill, president of Bisbee's Loyalty League, about Frank Little's presence and the IWW's activities.[6] It was only a matter of time before they would take action against the miners who were bellowing "strike!"

Little had all this on his mind when he arrived in Bisbee, plus recent, exasperating correspondences with Bill Haywood. He was irritated, in fact, angry. Haywood, sitting comfortably in his great swivel chair in Chicago, had flatly refused to clarify the IWW's stand on war, despite Little's and others' passionate telegrams from the IWW's battlefield: the mining and logging camps, wheat fields, and factories feeding the war. Just as he had decided to ignore Jane's numerous requests for the charter replacement and an explanation for his inaction, Big Bill Haywood was still indecisive regarding IWW participation in World War I.[7]

When Jane finally encountered Frank Little face-to-face, she saw a lean, battle-worn figure in a drab, olive-green suit. Little carried only 135 pounds on his five foot, eleven frame, causing some in Jerome to nickname him "Wobbly Slim."[8] He still carried battle scars from being kidnapped in Michigan on August 12, 1916, during the Mesabi Range strike, where he had been beaten senseless, mock-hanged, and thrown out of an automobile.[9] Compounding these injuries, gunmen had jumped him in El Paso, Texas, viciously kicking him in the stomach, sometime during spring 1917. Now he suffered from multiple, exceedingly painful hernias.[10]

After several letters and wires to Chicago's IWW headquarters asking to replace him in Arizona, Haywood had finally acquiesced on June 4, notifying Little that he could have surgery at the IWW's expense after this brief trip to Bisbee.[11] Punctuating the turmoil in his life, a family telegram had just caught up with Little advising him of his mother's death in Oklahoma on June 9.[12] Still, Little had agreed to meet the Housemaids' Union's embattled organizer if she could come

Frank Little, IWW GEB Chairman who sympathized with Jane Street.
*Courtesy of the Joseph A. Labadie Collection, University of Michigan*

*Shattered Dreams*

to him. And Jane indeed had arrived. Frank Little was her last hope for the girls back in Denver. As for Little, perhaps he sensed that their similar experiences with Bill Haywood justified his decision to hand over Lambert's report.

Jane saw that Frank Little's weathered face, tan with worry lines, was amiable and strong, and his right eye—his seeing eye—blue with intense interest. She began to talk. Little listened patiently as Jane recounted DWIU No. 113's history with Phil Engle and the other men of Denver's mixed local. The history was tedious and certainly disappointing to process. Because she had arrived in Bisbee with the promise of seeing Lambert's secret report, he gave it to her and waited while she examined it, knowing full well what Jane would find. She would read Lambert's own derogatory assessment of her character, describing alleged improprieties she took regarding the Housemaids' Union. She would also read that Lambert found no fault with her financial management of the union. Afterward, Jane could only remark that the report "was a lie from start to finish—with the exception that he had to admit my books were straight," exactly what she had expected from Lambert.[13]

Evidently trusting Little, Jane did not hesitate to ask more of him. Could he do anything to help her with the other members of the GEB? Frank Little gave little hope with one exception. If "the girls" in the Housemaids' Union would write to him, including their accounts of Phil Engle's duplicity, then he might be able to convince Bill Haywood that DWIU No. 113 was worthwhile, and her character and union charter could be restored.[14] Jane had hope at last. With that, their meeting was over. The IWW had a much larger battle to wage, and Jane Street and her Housemaids' Union were minuscule in contrast. In fact, all focus was on working men in the West.

Jane remained at the union hall after her meeting with Little, likely the morning of June 15, 1917, where she quickly prepared a copy of the Lambert report and a cover letter to Harriet Nillson in Denver, delivering Frank Little's instructions, on the hall's typewriter.[15] Meanwhile, in the meeting room behind her, MMWIU No. 800 members had begun their first day of the convention. Unbeknownst to Jane and the men, while miners elected officers, outlined demands, and endorsed supporting the miners' strike in Butte, local enforcers were strategizing a method to mold Bisbee into a "community of American citizens."[16] Local leaders were further emboldened on June 15, 1917, the same day as this first convention meeting, when mining companies received the welcome news that Congress had passed the Espionage Act. The new law emphatically stated that if any person or organization interfered with military operations, supported America's enemies, promoted insubordination in the military, or interfered with military recruitment, they would be arrested. Now mine operators could justify circumventing legalities when engaging military assistance to prevent interruption of their copper output—it was wartime. The IWW now had a real battle on its hands, one that Bill Haywood could not dodge.

Southwest of the Phelps Dodge office building was Bisbee's post office on Main Street, its three stories framed by tall arches. Inside, postmaster L. R. Bailey was a valuable informant.[17] But Bailey did not know who Jane Street was when she mailed her letter with a copy of Lambert's report to Denver. Now all Jane had to do was wait for Charles Devlin to make his appearance in Bisbee. Then she had a decision to make—return to Denver to the struggling locals they had helped create or let Devlin guide her elsewhere for the duration of the pregnancy, much like she had done with Jack Street eight years ago. Jane never mentions any concern about leaving her sister, Grace, who was content running her music school and living with Alfred Kohler, who, according to Calenal Sellers, was now "entirely lost to the movement" and the IWW.[18] In the end, circumstances beyond Jane's control would direct her course of action.

When Charles Devlin arrived in Bisbee shortly after Frank Little and Jane Street's meeting, he was his generally confident self. He had been organizing in the East and visiting family when he received Jane's telegram to come to Arizona "post haste," stopping only briefly in Denver to collect his things.[19] He was going to become a father! That he would share a child with the woman he loved "more than anything in life" was the best news he had had in a while.[20] Devlin had a much better view of how the IWW stood in Denver and elsewhere, and he intended to convince Jane there would be no going back, at least for the present. The new wave of superpatriotism and xenophobia, now sweeping the nation, labeling IWWs dangerous threats to American industry, put their lives at risk, too.

*Shattered Dreams*

Devlin planned to leave his life as an IWW organizer, at least temporarily, to work a traditional job, one that would help him supply a home and good life for his new child. More than anything else, he wanted to find a job at a California movie studio, claiming to be most interested in "show life."[21] With naive optimism, Devlin wrote later that he had looked forward to a long life of happiness and contentment with Jane.[22] But none of Jane's writings—her letters, poetry, and essays—indicate that she came even close to reciprocating the same affection for Devlin. On the contrary, Sellers points out in a 1919 letter to Jane how she used Devlin, later causing him great suffering.[23] She had no intention of deserting the IWW and the Housemaids' Union if she went to California. Though not openly in step with Devlin and his new plans, Jane agreed to the move, one that ultimately saved them both.

Frank Little and Grover Perry may have known the mine owners' secret plans for Bisbee.[24] Shortly after Jane and Devlin's departure, Frank Little and Perry, along with Perry's small family, also left Bisbee, surreptitiously departing at night on an auto stage for Globe, Arizona, a distance of about 205 miles. Hoping to avoid law enforcement on Monday, June 18, they traveled an old wagon road, winding around mesas, through dark canyons and sandy washes.[25] Well into the night, their vehicle finally crawled into Bowie, about halfway to their destination. Leaving Bowie in the early hours of June 19, the car's occupants were probably asleep, a three-year-old lying between his parents. Under a clear, starry night, the chauffeur also drifted off.[26] Suddenly, the car left the road, somersaulted into the air, and landed on a steep incline. Both Frank and Mrs. Perry broke their left ankles; Grover Perry, his left arm; the driver, a rib. The Perry's toddler was bruised.[27]

Little was hospitalized in the Gila county hospital until June 20. He then hobbled out on crutches with his leg swathed in a cumbersome plaster cast and spoke briefly to Miami, Arizona, miners.[28] After that, he made his way to Chicago, where he met with Bill Haywood and the rest of the GEB to discuss posting an official IWW statement opposing the war.[29] Little afterward intended to travel to Butte, where miners had asked for IWW assistance. But, at this moment, while Frank Little was engaged in a contentious meeting with a yet-again-uncompromising Big Bill Haywood, all roads in and out of Bisbee were blocked and telegraph wires cut.

At precisely 6:30 A.M. on July 12, a siren at the Douglas smelter blared, alerting gunmen to commence what some called the Great Wobbly Drive and what would come to be known as the Bisbee Deportation.[30] Simultaneously, Bisbee's Sheriff Harry Wheeler, members of the local Citizen's Protective League, and other men with white armbands ambushed men arriving for morning picket duty outside Bisbee mines and businesses.[31] Vigilantes, armed with machine guns, rifles, and clubs, went door to door without warrants, waking up sleeping families. Husbands, fathers, and sons, prodded with gun butts, were ordered into the streets amid wails of protesting wives and mothers. While remembering their hats, many men dressed sockless.

Deemed a threat to Bisbee citizenry, a procession of men—including mostly Mexican, Eastern European, and American-born—began a three-mile march to the Warren baseball park at 9:00 A.M. where, atop the Calumet and Arizona Mining Company office roof, a machine gun pointed downward toward them.[32] At 11:00 A.M., a train with nineteen El Paso and Southwestern Railroad cattle-and-box cars arrived from tracks at the rear of the ball field on orders of its owner Walter Douglas.[33] Crammed into the cars, deep with manure, were 1,186 men, while armed guards stood on top.[34] As the temperature climbed above 110 degrees, the train departed. After fifty-two hours of travel with few stops, the train finally drew into a siding in Hermanas, New Mexico, where President Woodrow Wilson's *undesirables*—most not even members of the IWW—were abandoned in the hot desert sun.[35] Leaders of the infamous Bisbee Deportation justified their actions under the Law of Necessity.[36] Their illegal action was necessary, they claimed, to protect the greater good against the evil of the IWW.

Two weeks later, in the dark, early morning hours of August 1, 1917, another sinister plot was carried out, likely planned by managers of Anaconda Mining Company. Six men quietly slid out of a black Cadillac in front of a boardinghouse at 316 North Wyoming Street in Butte, Montana. There an exhausted Frank Little was asleep in his bed after thirteen days of giving speeches and advising striking miners.[37] After breaking down his door, the men yanked Little roughly out of bed as he futilely reached for his pocket watch and hat. Then they threw him into the car's backseat and began beating him. The black sedan drove back south down Wyoming Street, stopping abruptly just before it turned west into Butte's business district. Wrenching Little out of the Cadillac, his assailants tied him to the rear bumper and drove several more blocks, towing him in the car's wake over granite-paved streets.[38]

When the car was within sight of the Milwaukee Railroad trestle, about two miles south of town, it turned west onto a sandy road that led near the bridge. The car stopped directly underneath it, next to a dangling rope thrown over the ties. Someone quickly pinned a pasteboard placard on the right thigh of Little's dirtied underwear. Scribbled in blood-red crayon, its message read, "Others take notice! First and last warning! 3-7-77," the numbers referring to an old Montana vigilante code. After placing the noose around Little's neck, the men heaved him on top of the big black car. Then the car suddenly lurched forward, leaving Little's slender frame to swing about five feet above the ground.[39]

Jane Street's last hope had just been viciously murdered, and wartime hysteria had reached its apex in the West.

*Chapter Seventeen*

# VINDICATION

Those who are bold enough to advance before the age
they live in . . . must learn to brave censure.

Mary Wollstonecraft, 1797

Jane peered down at the newborn baby nursing at her breast. It
was December 13, 1917, and she had just delivered her second
son, this one fair-skinned with a promise of curly hair like his brother's.
Jane had agreed to name the infant Charles Patrick Devlin after his
father, and call him Pat, though she had not agreed to marriage.[1] Later
the boy, seemingly a bastard son, would take his mother's name, discarding his namesake for stage name David Street while in his teens.

In fact, all aspects of Jane and Devlin's relationship seemed transient. Though they appeared to live as husband and wife in Los Angeles
during the past months, uncertainty ruled their lives.[2] Jane was still
determined to fight in the IWW's rebel ranks, while Devlin optimis-
tically settled for domestic bliss. The couple's incongruencies would
inevitably lead to discord.

Charles Devlin had found his show business job immediately upon
their arrival in California. The job on a "Spieling" lot for a film production in Long Beach had lasted a mere three weeks.[3] Now he was
working as an elevator pilot in Los Angeles, bringing home a steady
paycheck. Normally Jane would have appreciated an ordered way of
life, but routine was not how she envisioned her immediate future.
Even as she nursed the baby, she calculated how to resuscitate her

Housemaids' Union. Still, a maternal respite permitted Jane's heart to fill with contentment as she looked at her baby's muddy-brown eyes. Jane had just given birth during a maelstrom, even as she and Devlin had managed to escape a wide net cast over other IWWs. Almost all the prominent Wobblies had been arrested in what the IWW now called the "Big Pinch."

After Frank Little's murder, with western industries virtually at a standstill, the Bureau of Investigation made preparations to end IWW anti-war propaganda and the union's efforts to cripple war production.[4] Besides, the public certainly demanded some sort of action after Red Scare propaganda falsely tied Wobblies to German sabotage. In cities across the nation, and especially in the West, federal agents planned simultaneous raids on IWW local halls and Chicago's IWW headquarters for September 5.[5] The greatest secrecy had been ordered.[6] At 2:00 P.M. Central Time, agents with legal warrants in hand barged into IWW halls making arrests of unsuspecting Wobblies, at the same time collecting supporting evidence of conspiracy as defined by the recent Espionage Act. In Denver, DWIU No. 113's hall had already closed, and the men's Mixed Local No. 614 had disbanded. However, in Chicago, Bill Haywood and other members of the GEB, who had been expecting some dire action, were promptly arrested.[7] Others soon turned themselves in, believing they had committed no crimes.[8]

In Chicago, agents gathered a trove of incriminating information—minute books, checks, correspondence, membership lists, typewriters, mimeograph machines, and even trash can contents—that would be used to bolster conspiracy charges against IWW leaders and associates.[9] Included in the gathered correspondence were the letters belonging to Bill Haywood, Richard Brazier, and Frank Little regarding Jane Street and her patriotism.[10] Haywood's damaging words regarding war and American patriotism would finally help define his views publicly at trial, while injuring Jane's reputation with other IWWs.

Jane had heard the news about Frank Little's tragic death while she and Devlin were in Long Beach. Only one letter had been mailed to Frank from the girls in Denver, which Bureau of Investigation agents also collected in Chicago.[11] In recent weeks, a few of the regulars from the Denver locals had shown up in California to join a Los Angeles IWW General Recruiting Union (GRU) that was still active, its skeleton crew also tasked with supporting a defense committee for newly incarcerated California Wobblies. Recruiting locals, aimed at eliminating mixed trades locals, were tasked with organizing workers into industries that lacked separate industrial trade locals.[12] Splintered groups of DWIU locals now joined hotel and restaurant workers merging as one industrial union, No. 1100. Friends Harriet Nillson and Pete Aguilar, who appears in several of Jane's private photos, had arrived, joining the Los Angeles GRU and bringing news from Denver. Calenal Sellers, however, remained in Denver, hiding in plain sight as a dishwasher at Gene's Lunch on 15th Street, while he cautiously tested the waters to see what IWW leadership would do.[13] He and Jane had begun exchanging letters. As for Devlin, he drifted back into IWW organization, this time helping with the new Hotel, Restaurant and Domestic Workers Industrial Union local while Jane remained at home.

As the days and months passed, Jane and Devlin's domestic interlude continued without interruption. Jack Street had been long gone from Dawn's life, and Devlin had been a good surrogate father to the boy, whom he believed to be genius, "very studious" and a "thinker."[14] With her Kodak Brownie, Jane took photos of Devlin clearly enjoying his own baby son. Devlin, in a rocking chair with baby Pat, the family dog sitting beside them; another, Devlin dressed in overalls, legs crossed, sitting in the grass, holding a toddler immersed in a small, wooden toy; and Devlin, joyfully lifting his child to the sky, as young Pat grabs his hat. What the photos do not illustrate is Jane's inner turmoil and the layer of insecurity that existed as both parents nervously awaited the Justice Department's future actions. Anyone affiliated with the IWW could still be arrested at any time.

On April Fools' Day 1918, Judge Kenesaw Mountain Landis opened the first wartime trial of Wobblies who were swept up during the September 5, 1917, raid. While Jane tended her two sons, she and Devlin, like other IWWs, anxiously read daily accounts of the four-month-long mass trial. A second trial for California IWWs would be held afterward, and their Los Angeles friends were making defense preparations.

Testimony and thousands of documents in Chicago supported indictments against 113 men with five counts of conspiracy—the first count, conspiring with Frank Little "and with other persons to prevent

*Left to right:* Charles Devlin, Dawn (Phil) Street, and Jane
Street with baby Pat (David) Devlin, 1918.
*Courtesy of Guy Leslie, Jane Street Family Papers*

Charles Devlin with son, Pat (David),
late 1918.
*Courtesy of Guy Leslie, Jane Street
Family Papers*

by force the execution of federal laws pertaining to the prosecution of war."[15] The second count charged the defendants with conspiring to oppress, threaten, and intimidate many persons engaged in furnishing, under contract, munitions, fuel, ships, equipment, and so on, to the United States—in other words, strike.

The prosecution expounded the belief that any man who struck in wartime was not loyal to his country, "by demanding stated wages and certain terms from the employers throughout the United States and unless the employers of labor will agree to pay the stated wages and agree to the certain terms demanded, the said defendants and the said persons, with whom said defendants conspired, would refuse to work for or give 'their services to said employers, and would engage in what is known in every day parlance as a strike.'"[16] Obviously, the right to strike and organize was on trial.

The third count charged conspiracy to aid, counsel, command, and induce thousands of persons to refuse to register, and other thousands to desert the service of the United States. The fourth count charged conspiracy to cause insubordination, disloyalty, and refusal of duty in the military and naval forces, as well as to obstruct recruiting and enlistment. The fifth count charged conspiracy to violate the postal laws of the country by depositing for mailing and delivery papers, circulars, and stickerettes advocating the commission of fraudulent acts against employers, such acts consisting of sabotage, secret interference with efficient service, willful slackening of production, and restriction of profits. The latter count was soon dropped with no legislation to support it. Lawmakers soon passed a controversial authorization.

A month after the trial commenced, on May 16, 1918, the United States made it much easier for federal agents to justify arrests of dissenters. The federal government extended the Espionage Act of 1917 with the new Sedition Act of 1918, overreaching the powers of the United States in direct opposition to the First Amendment. Now speech and expression of opinion that cast the government or the war effort in a negative light or interfered with the sale of government bonds would be a felony. Specifically, the act forbade the use of disloyal, profane, scurrilous, or abusive language about the United States, its flag, or its armed forces. It also allowed the United States postmaster general to refuse delivery of mail that met those same standards for punishable

*Shattered Dreams*

speech or opinion. In layman's terms, one could go to jail for his or her language against the United States of America.

In early August 1918, after less than an hour's deliberation by the jury, the Chicago defendants were all found guilty of a multitude of federal law violations. On August 31, Judge Landis, showing little mercy, handed the accused their sentences. Fifteen received the legal maximum of twenty years in jail, including Haywood, Brazier, and Lambert; thirty-three received ten years; thirty-one received five years; eighteen received lesser sentences; and together they incurred more than $2 million in fines.[17] All sentences were to be served in Leavenworth Prison. There would be four appeals.

Shortly after the final appeal of the courtroom's verdict, Charles Lambert penned a letter to President Warren Harding, which the Leavenworth prisoners all signed, expounding on the nature of Judge Landis's courtroom and its prejudiced proceedings. In a cover letter to a friend, to whom he gifted the original "Open Letter to President Harding" in 1953, Lambert describes what he originally wrote President Harding. "Manufactured mass hysteria by the press and from the platform made our conviction possible," Lambert wrote, "but the selection of the jury made our conviction sure. No juror was selected who was not 'a 100 per cent American.' (How often have you heard that expression?) We were convicted of one crime only, 'That of improper activities and the use of the spoken word.'"[18] Lambert continued:

> In other words we stood convicted of having thought for ourselves, spoken for ourselves, and in our own small way upheld the constitution of the United States which in the fourth amendment to that long forgotten document lays down that the right "That what one believes to be true, no one can be stopped from writing of it or speaking of it." (or words to that effect. I don't know if I have the exact wording.) How would you like to walk into a court and look up to the judge's bench and see a figure sitting there without a coat, collar undone, his shoes off and a wad of chewing tobacco in his face? That was how he looked every morning.[19]

The Justice Department had "indicted the organization," one historian later wrote, "on the basis of its philosophy and its publications."[20] The

Wobblies were guilty by written word and certainly not by criminal deed. With the successful Chicago verdict, the second IWW trial was scheduled, this time in Sacramento, California, in December 1918.

By the time the Sacramento trial commenced, Jane realized she was pregnant once again. But pregnancy was not Jane's concern—she found Devlin's presence unbearable. Whether past experiences with men affected her ability to trust and love men in general or differences of opinion about her continual quest for innocence affected her emotions, one can only surmise. On an early April 1919 morning, Jane apparently deliberately picked a fight with Devlin. He later minimalized the incident as a "small spat" that he could not even recall clearly.[21] Devlin certainly did not think their words were "serious enough for what followed."[22] When he returned home from work later that day, the home was empty. Jane, six months pregnant, and her children were gone, leaving a devastated father.

Jane and her boys fled to San Diego, the reason for the specific location also unclear. Though Sellers, not Devlin, still held the most radical influence affecting Jane and her decisions, she also broke off contact with him. She did not want to hear his recriminations about how she had treated Devlin. When Jane finally wrote Sellers several weeks later to tell him of her new residence at 1427 Market Street, a boarding house in San Diego, he responded exactly as she expected.[23] In the interim, Devlin, nearly frantic, had written Sellers asking for help to find Jane, further inflaming Sellers, who suddenly sided with the "suffering" of the "poor lamed Irish boy."[24] Devlin had also lost his job, perhaps because of his mental state, and in his words, "things looked hopeless."[25]

Sellers summarized Devlin's letter as "pathetic and inexpressibly pitiful."[26] Jane's excuse that she had a problem with Devlin's "moulding" of her children was subject to more chastising. Sellers wrote Jane, "How could you speak of your maternal joys in the midst of physical suffering and deny Devlin a share in the same joy," adding, "if you find life unbearable with Devlin, then it is your duty to sever the relationship, but in doing so, you certainly take into account the rights of the father."[27] As to another of Jane's excuses—that she "had released Devlin to follow his own revolutionary ambitions"—Sellers retorted, "You did not release him until you found his associations with you absolutely unbearable."[28] Knowing Jane as he did, he pressed Jane to face the facts: "You ran away from Devlin because you could not live with him any longer and not because you wanted to release him from the revolution."[29] Still, Devlin later explained to his daughter that "because of Jane's training and my training, and because of the fact that we were both wrapped up in the revolutionary movement, we were due for separate lives."[30] Now Jane awaited the birth of her third child—alone.

With most IWW leaders incarcerated, Jane no longer feared Bill Haywood's opposition to her leadership of the Housemaids' Union. She wrote Sellers, sharing a daring plan of action—she would present her case to the new GEB, at the same time asking for condemnation of Haywood's actions, while lauding Sellers's "brave, splendid actions" in assisting the Housemaids' Union.[31] Jane apparently failed to understand the enormity of the actions just taken by the United States government, as she openly began formulating her strategy at getting her name cleared. Within the Los Angeles IWW organization, Jane hoped to redeem herself and gain allies who could help her, ultimately beginning with an association with Los Angeles GRU secretary Warren O. Lamsa. Lamsa just happened to be under the Bureau of Investigation's surveillance.[32]

Jane also wrote Sellers with a "simple request." Would Sellers write to the provisional GEB, corroborating her statement about events in Denver? And while he was at it, could he get "the inside dope on the personnel of the IWW officialdom" and the relationships "swirling about in these groups?"[33] Jane needed to know who was in charge. In the meantime, Jane told Sellers, she had asked Devlin, to whom she was speaking again, to write about his experiences with Denver's mixed local and his Hotel and Restaurant Workers' local.[34] Despite the fact that a reorganized GEB now existed, Sellers wrote Jane back that her request was not "simple" at all.[35] In fact, he did not agree with her strategy.

Sellers reminded Jane of his earlier response to her in a lengthy letter months later, "With reference to the abuses of officialdom and the over centralization for the IWW that you mention, I shall maintain your policy for the correction of these weaknesses is wrong. . . . The top of every social structure, political state, IWW, or Salvation Army is a reflex of the intellectual condition of the bottom—the rank and file. You cannot improve on government in the IWW by tinkering with the top."[36] Sellers's advice continued:

> The only proper policy is to keep continually hammering the rank and file, these dark spots at the top will fade out. You will say that the Chicago crowd made it impossible for us to go ahead with education or anything else, even organization. They did, and we tried to get justice and failed. . . . If you try to bring charges against these fakirs now, with Lambert and Haywood in jail, with all the halo of the martyr that surrounds them, you will get nowhere. . . . If you ally yourselves with the old decentralizing element down there in any way, you are lost. You will be placing a weapon in the hands of our enemies that they will not hesitate to use against you with disastrous results.[37]

In 1913 at the IWW's annual convention, a Wobbly group had forced a vote to decentralize, in effect, reducing the power of the GEB. They lost, and to some, the scars of the division had remained. IWWs supporting this original decentralization attempt came mostly from the West, including California, from mixed locals.[38] Jane, put off by Sellers's words, struck back, replying that his "inferior ability to view the future" was "as inferior as Coler's [Kohler's]," who "sees the abuses of the organization."[39] Jane knew Sellers, still smarting from Grace's defection, detested Kohler and believed himself superior. Jane also disregarded Sellers's advice about condemning Bill Haywood and the old GEB.

While Jane ignored Sellers for his refusal to help her, she awaited her baby's birth in her boarding house room in San Diego. On June 21, 1919, she wrote Harriet Nillson in Los Angeles that she had felt the baby dropping into her pelvis a week earlier and now needed to make final arrangements for the birth. Jane wrote, "I feel pretty good now except I get tired easily."[40] Expecting the baby to be a girl, Jane added, "I expect Mary Jane to make her appearance any time—probably any time from Monday to Friday of next week."[41] Within her letter to Nillson, Jane also enclosed another letter to her friend Pete Aguilar of the Los Angeles GRU, advising him that she had written the GEB and that if they replied, they were to send the reply in his care. "Put it safely away. I may be in a hospital soon," Jane begged.[42]

But Aguilar had already received a letter dated May 27, 1919, not from the GEB, but from Ernest Holman, secretary-treasurer of General Recruiting Union No. 1100 in Chicago. After hearing from Jane and others, the provisional GEB had sent Holman a copy of *Haywood's Cross Examination*, with marked pages regarding Jane's misplaced patriotism as discussed in the trial testimony regarding Little's and Brazier's correspondence with Haywood. Holman was instructed to pass on the pages to Aguilar and the Los Angeles local, justifying why Jane had not received her charter.[43]

Holman, to his credit, wrote Aguilar: "I'll advise you to write the GEB and demand a full explanation of the charges against her. I am not in favor to drop this thing because I know the good work fellow worker Jane Street [has] been doing for the Domestic Workers, and I should like to see her vindicated."[44] It seemed while Jane's friends worked to help her with the powers in Chicago, her attempts at bringing down the old GEB had temporarily cost her recognition in the Los Angeles GRU, just as Sellers had predicted.[45] Jane could do nothing but wait.

Yet, three days after writing Nillson, and just days before her baby was due, Jane received welcome news from Lamsa, of the Los Angeles GRU. She had finally won. He detailed how Jane could get back into union organizing, receive new credentials, and organize in San Diego as part of the Los Angeles GRU until a San Diego GRU was solid. She would officially be a member of the Hotel, Restaurant and Domestic Workers Industrial Union No. 1100.[46]

Jane's journey for vindication was finally over, but the Denver Housemaids' Union was officially lost. She had shaken up the ladies of Denver's Capitol Hill, held off the employment agencies and their white slavers, defied the YWCA do-gooders, and combatted Phil Engle and his sexist attacks on her character. But unknown to her was a new enemy.

In Washington, D.C., newly appointed attorney general A. Mitchell Palmer was making plans to arrest remaining radicals, targeting mostly immigrants, with the help of his new Bureau of Investigation head—J. Edgar Hoover.[47] In California, Bureau of Investigation agents would now assist the state's judicial system in prosecuting a new criminal syndicalism act directly aimed at IWWs trying to effect change industrially or politically.[48] Wobblies, including Jane, were unprepared for the cat-and-mouse game that was about to ensue. Her efforts to connect with well-established IWW leaders effectively put her in California law enforcement's crosshairs.

*Chapter Eighteen*

# THE PRICE

No, little one, you cannot bring lives into the world and
stay with the revolution.

Calenal Sellers

J ane had a decision to make. She absolutely had to leave the
children so she could work and provide for her growing family.
Jane decided to ask Mrs. Geneva Ryan, her landlady, for help. The fifty-
year-old landlady had been intimately involved with the small family's
activities since Jane first arrived at the 1427 Market Street boarding
house in San Diego, six months pregnant. Married to an Irish saloon
keeper in a childless marriage, Mrs. Ryan, likely enjoyed keeping Jane's
toddler, Pat, from the time he arrived.[1] Now Jane had three children,
two of whom required watchful eyes. Dawn was ten years old and, if
necessary, could take care of himself at home. But the others?

Improvising a schedule that she believed could work for them all,
Jane would go to work in the morning after getting the children fed,
leaving the curly haired toddler with Mrs. Ryan, who had formed an
attachment to the child. Jane placed the baby in a contained area where
Dawn could keep an eye on her in their boarding house room. At noon,
Jane could return to the room to check on the children, feed them,
and nurse the baby.[2] Otherwise, during the day, there was Mrs. Ryan
to look in on them. Though not the best-case scenario for taking care
of her brood, Jane had no other options. Like so many other single
mothers, Jane could not afford to pay for childcare.

On July 14, 1919, Mary Jane Street had been born. Jane wired Devlin immediately about the birth, asking for the child's genealogical information, not because she was interested in recording family background but because she needed information to complete the child's birth certificate. Devlin, living in the Hotel Alexandria in Los Angeles, was now working for the Western Costumes Company, where he had a "good" job earning $86.30 a month.[3] He evidently had been sending money to Jane since her defection. His exuberance at being asked for family information and not money is almost palpable in his July 16, 1919, letter to Jane. He may have had no idea that Jane's request was for the birth certificate. In his postscript, Charles optimistically tells Jane that he "could get you and babies all kinds of picture [movie] work or stenography," if she would just return, adding, "Endless love for Mary Jane and you and Pat and Dawn."[4] Then, he blurts out an afterthought, "Tell me when to come to see Mary Jane and all." The Bureau of Information perused this letter, resealed it, and returned it to the mail. Agents determined that Charles Devlin, the "'common-law' husband of Jane Street," was no threat.[5]

When Jane originally completed birth certificate information on July 20, she does not name Devlin as the father of his child, instead providing a mix of Devlin's and Jack Street's names as the baby's father—*Charles Carroll Street*—on the birth certificate.[6] Evidently, the misnomer was deliberate and not a cavalier mistake on Jane's part. Perhaps she wanted total guardianship of her baby, a severance from Charles Devlin and future claims on his daughter. Yet on closer inspection of the document, an even more astonishing omission is Jane's name and personal information. Her information includes only a birth date, age, and number of children. Clearly, Jane wanted to conceal any personal information about both Devlin and herself from the government. Only later is a more complete birth certificate filed, yet Mary Jane Street's father is still misnamed, *Charles Devlin Street*. The mother is listed as Jane Tuttle.[7]

While Devlin "longed" for the baby Mary Jane, Sellers was livid about the third pregnancy.[8] After Jane wrote Calenal Sellers on July 17, 1919, announcing the child's birth, he predictably berated her for the decision to give birth to the baby at all, after expressing previously that having this child would bind her to "the chariot wheels of maternity."[9]

Sellers wrote Jane back on July 22, "It seems to me you should have had enough consideration to have at least avoided maternity this last time."[10] He reminded Jane that he had "protested so earnestly against bringing this little life into this awful world," but "was moved to refrain from it on account of [her] being the prospective mother."[11] Still, Sellers warned Jane, "When the awful times come, as come they will, in this country, when we are forced to choose the streets for a battle ground, you will have to skulk in the rear with the little ones."[12] He added, "No, little one, you cannot bring lives into the world and stay with the revolution. . . . You, with all your splendid abilities and magnificent revolutionary ardour [*sic*] are lost to the revolution," that is, the IWW's war to replace capitalism with economic socialism.[13]

Jane had historically listened to Sellers's rants with one ear, often dismissing his advice completely. Yet one statement from his July 22 letter seems to have resonated, especially since Jane had just received news she would receive the new IWW credentials: "If you would follow my advice, little one, it would be to get back into the revolution, as far as maternity will let you, and that will not be very far, and show 'by your fruits' that you are honest and true and a force for good in the IWW."[14] Sellers had finally gotten into Jane's head. She began looking for a way to mother three young children and contribute to the IWW's insurgency simultaneously. Perhaps she could even impress the rank and file, especially the men, and win back her good name.

Sellers's letter, considered "possibly important in case [of] any action in the future," was copied and filed.[15] With the Chicago trial—its verdict, sentencing, and appeals—and addition of the Sedition Act, Jane should have been more vigilant. Bureau agents now had carte blanche to read all suspicious mail, including that from a "C. W." Sellers.[16] Sellers, who had departed Denver for Seattle, immediately became wanted for theft of a woman's overcoat in June 1919. He had incurred a devastating injury beforehand, likely while working as a mechanic at a carnival company in Seattle, when his right hand became mangled. With a new criminal profile, the damaged hand became Sellers's most easily identifiable physical attribute, one that he had to hide in flight to first Salt Lake City and then Butte, Montana.[17]

In Butte, Sellers joined A. S. Embree, who was endeavoring to become the IWW's new secretary-treasurer. By his own admission,

Sellers intended to rise in the ranks himself, becoming a delegate from Metal Mine Workers Industrial Union (MMWIU) No. 800, bragging at the next general convention that it was the "biggest industrial union the IWW had."[18] In Butte, he claimed to be immune to endangerment since "none of their old enemies could get away with those old slanders and old lying charges."[19] He was also working with radical William Dunn, helping edit the *Butte Daily Bulletin*.[20] The Bureau of Investigation was surveilling and collecting all newspapers and correspondence sent out of Butte. Sellers's letters to Jane in July 1919 directly put her in a path for charges under not only the Espionage Act, but also the new California Criminal Syndicalism Act, if she chose to pursue IWW "outlaw" activities.[21]

Sellers wasted no time in abetting Jane's criminal activities in the face of the Sedition Act, even as the Bureau of Investigation surveilled his activities and mail. On July 26, 1919, from Butte, he mailed her MMWIU No. 800 bulletins, containing, according to the Bureau, "very rank IWW and Bolsheviki [*sic*] statements."[22] Also sent were a copy of the *New York Call* (socialist) newspaper; copies of *Industrial Worker*, *Rebel Worker*, *One Big Union Monthly*, and *The Truth*, and other IWW materials—remarkably all to Jane's home address in San Diego.[23] Agents noted that at times Jane now used an alias, including Jeanette Street, A. Coey, and Mrs. J. D. Warren, for receiving materials, albeit at the same Market Street address.[24]

While Jane was setting up her recruitment plan and waiting for her credentials, Charles Devlin traveled to San Diego on August 10 to pick up his son, Pat. He wanted to keep the boy for a while, and Jane allowed him to do so.[25] She wrote Harriet Nillson to check on the child because Devlin, just as Jack Street had done, depended on his landlady to look after the boy during the day. It did not take Devlin long to realize that he was out of this element. He quickly returned the child to Jane, realizing that the boy needed "a mother's care."[26] Devlin also wrote Jane that he was "sick of his job" and planned to quit.[27]

By August 15, the Bureau of Investigation was certain that "C.W. Sellers, now known as Calenal," was writing Jane from Butte.[28] The connection cemented the need to spy on Jane Street, and agents were doubly aware when Warren Lamsa finally sent Jane her IWW General Recruiting Union (GRU) organizer credentials, bills for literature and supplies, and her delegate credentials for the new Hotel, Restaurant and Domestic Workers Industrial Union No. 1100.[29] In detail, Lamsa explained how to recruit workers into various industries and complete membership documentation. The itemized bill contained item after item of what, according to the Sedition Act, were treasonous materials.

Two weeks later, Jane's own letter about guiding others in recruiting new members clearly established that she planned to organize a new local for the IWW. According to Jane, the new Hotel, Restaurant and Domestic Workers Industrial Union local would accept any worker engaged in feeding and housing others, with plans to include sanitation and health workers too.[30] She excitedly and immediately began soliciting new IWW members. Jane would show Sellers to his face that she could be part of the IWW movement—even with the children.

With Democrat U.S. attorney general A. Mitchell Palmer's initiation of a "Red Hunt," under Woodrow Wilson's Democratic administration, Wobblies became a favorite target. California Republican governor William Stephens reached out to Palmer, saying "Will you please at once take all steps possible to the end that America may be kept wholly American?"[31] In the coming months, Republican director J. Edgar Hoover of the Bureau of Investigation acquiesced, making deportation of all alien Wobblies automatic and mandatory.[32] In addition, men of the American Legion, an organization chartered by Congress as a patriotic veterans' service organization, willingly helped collect evidence for the Bureau of Investigation, even assisting making arrests of IWWs. It was a bipartisan effort. In California, the hunt was on in 1919.

Jane was working for Electric Cleaners at 1148 Sixth Street in San Diego when she approached new employee Mrs. Emerson, handing her a pamphlet and IWW card. Jane, after learning that the lady's husband worked at construction, pronounced that he is "the very man that ought to have one of our cards!"[33] The two were working together, canvassing the city in hopes of interesting people in purchasing new vacuum cleaners. Mrs. Emerson noticed that Jane also dropped IWW pamphlets at the homes and businesses where they stopped, including one fire station on 25th and Broadway Streets. Mrs. Emerson had felt uneasy. She knew about the IWWs, who were popularly called Reds. Surreptitiously keeping some of Jane's pamphlets, she turned them over to the local Bureau of Investigation office where Agent Walter A.

Weymouth was in charge. Emerson told Weymouth that she "expected to quit working for the firm in a few days as she did not want to be associated with Jane."[34] Instead of leaving her job, however, Mrs. Emerson turned informant and remained at Electric Cleaners.

On August 27, 1919, Agent Weymouth reported Jane's activities to the San Diego district attorney's office; to Bureau of Investigation offices in Los Angeles and San Francisco; and for good measure, to the Army Intelligence offices in San Francisco, Fresno, and Los Angeles. He noted, "If sufficient evidence is secured to warrant prosecution, then it will be submitted to the California District Attorney under the State Syndicalist Act."[35]

By late November the Bureau of Investigation was flummoxed. How was Jane Street acquiring all her IWW materials, especially the pamphlets? Agent Weymouth tasked Cato W. Holden, a member of the American Legion, to find out. He was to travel to Los Angeles and trace Charles Devlin, who, from reading personal correspondence, was apparently on "intimate terms" with Jane.[36] The Bureau of Investigation already knew that Devlin was an elevator pilot who could not do "hard labor" on account of having his leg amputated. Weymouth advised Holden that Devlin wore a prosthetic leg.[37]

On Holden's return, he reported that Devlin was not in Los Angeles, but he found that apparently every job Devlin had held was for no more than six weeks. Devlin was indeed a radical IWW, and the girls at Western Costume Company said that Devlin told them he was moving to a ranch near San Diego, where he was going to work "undercover" for the IWW. "Jane Street is absolutely in his power, as he is the father of her youngest child," Holden claimed, adding "I have a strong conviction that Jane is getting her pamphlets from him."[38]

The spy was incorrect. Charles Devlin had no power over Jane. It was Calenal Sellers who, after shaming her for years, had totally swept Jane up into what he called "the revolution." Recent events in Centralia, Washington, added to Sellers's fanatical diatribes. On Armistice Day, November 11, 1919, American Legionnaires, marching to commemorate the victims of World War I, allegedly initiated a conflict with the IWW in front of an IWW hall. Six people died during gunfire, and vigilantes viciously hanged Wobbly Wesley Everest, who had been captured and jailed. The incident, known as the Centralia Massacre, heightened the Red Scare across the country and inflamed the IWW. Sellers used the event to further radicalize Jane. He made certain that she had Centralia materials for recruiting.[39] Now American Legion raiding squads, including in San Diego, stoked the fire on both sides.[40]

Jane was pleased to meet Cato Holden. The short, dark-haired man with smiling hazel eyes set in a pleasant face introduced himself as a person interested in the IWW.[41] Holden, the American Legionnaire operative, was also a World War I veteran. He told Jane he had another friend, an army soldier named Frank Stein, who could be turned against the government in favor of helping the IWW. In reality, Stein had volunteered his services to the American Legion and agreed to be bait in a scheme to determine who was directing and supplying Jane. As for Jane, she was eager to initiate the new member, and especially one who could share IWW literature and spread the word with other soldiers in the area. Throwing caution to the wind, she fell for the ruse.[42]

Despite using an array of cloak-and-dagger methods—aliases, alternate addresses, streetcar meetings, secret notes—during November 1919, Jane instantly trusted Frank Stein when she first met him on December 6 at his home with his Swedish American in-laws, the Nilssons.[43] There, in front of family members, Jane openly shared seditious IWW membership materials, explaining that the purpose of the organization was to "take over the industries."[44] Jane added that the government was "only the toll over the capitalists and must be overthrown and a new industrial government take its place . . . a revolution was coming and very soon," quoting Sellers from his July 22, 1919, letter.[45] The IWW needed soldiers and sailors to join, Jane insisted. With Sellers's words in her head, Jane added that she "didn't like anyone belonging to the American Legion, primarily because of the events in Centralia where Legion men killed an IWW."[46]

The family, friends of American Legionnaires, struggled to show no emotion as they listened intently. When asked where she had acquired her materials (she had seven different titles), she informed the group that a Mr. Mahoney at the Oxford Hotel provided the literature now that she could no longer write Chicago for supplies. She smiled, confidentially explaining that the government was reading their Chicago mail.[47] Jane, while trying to prove herself worthy to Sellers and the IWW's rank and file, had walked into the trap.

With Jane now certain that she had a conduit to distribute materials to the soldiers and sailors on base in San Diego, Holden and Frank Harrison, also an American Legionnaire operative, had a conference on December 17, 1919, with Agent Weymouth and San Diego district attorney Utley regarding the advisability of prosecuting Jane Street under the California State Syndicalist Act. They agreed that they had plenty of evidence to justify her arrest, but Jane was the mother of three small children, all of whom they believed to be illegitimate, with the youngest only five months old. They worried that an arrest and prosecution during the holiday season would possibly create a sympathetic feeling for Jane in the city. Almost daily, newspapers recounted their raids on unsuspecting men and women, believed to be Bolsheviks, because of their ethnicities, political affiliations, or citizen status. Arresting an American-born woman with children would stir opposition as it was. Ultimately, they decided to wait and not take any action until after Christmas.[48]

Two days before Christmas, Mrs. Ryan opened her door to find a stout, nicely dressed man, about thirty-six years old, accompanied by another gentleman, oppositely slender, of about the same age. Agent Weymouth and Legionnaire operative Harrison were about to serve a warrant to search Jane Street's room while she was away at work.[49] When they inquired about her boarder, Mrs. Ryan gushed all she knew. She was disgusted with her tenant—she had discovered Jane was an IWW. There had been meetings late at night in Jane's room.

"Something should be done with Jane Street regarding her children," Mrs. Ryan complained. Jane was away all day, and when she could not leave them in her (Mrs. Ryan's) care, they received no attention at all! Mrs. Ryan told how Mary Jane, about six months old, was placed "in a pasteboard box on the back porch with a quilt up on one side as a shelter against the sun and wind."[50] The baby would remain there all day, except when Jane returned at noon to nurse her. Then there was the two-year-old, for whom Mrs. Ryan tried to care, and an older boy, about eleven years of age, left to take care of himself "the best that he could."[51] Harrison assured the woman that he would take this matter up with the county probation officer. Arrangements for the children's care would be made as soon as they were ready to make an arrest.[52] The men left without serving the search warrant they had procured earlier from the Justice Court. They doubted they would find anything after the interview with Mrs. Ryan.

Before she went to work that same day, Jane read the morning paper, as was her usual habit. Making front-page news was an American Legion raid and resulting arrest of J. A. Stromquist, an IWW delegate whom Jane had introduced to others, including Stein and Holden, in her boardinghouse room.[53] According to the *San Diego Union*, agents had collected a suitcase "full of red literature," and now had forty more subjects (people) to be examined.[54] Panicking, Jane rushed around her room, collecting all incriminating evidence she could find. Outside, she immediately burned all her IWW literature and letters— with Mrs. Ryan watching Jane as she set fire to the pile of papers.[55]

Agent Weymouth and Harrison had been part of the last evening's raids when the arrests were made. The newspaper also reported that though Stromquist claimed to be a "native-born citizen of the United States," Weymouth said that they had contrary evidence. Furthermore, the case against Stromquist would be "carried out under the new California syndicalism act," warning there would be more arrests to come.[56]

At 7:30 P.M., December 27, 1919, Jane met American Legion operative Stein at the corner of 6th and Laurel Streets in San Diego. She was worried about him, that he had been arrested with Stromquist and would face court-martial. With concern on her face, she asked the spy if he should flee to Tijuana or Mexicali, Mexico. Pulling ten dollars out of her purse, she offered Stein money she could not afford to give up to aid his escape. Stein brushed off her fears, saying that by leaving he would look guilty. He would wait a few days, thus expanding the small drama he was playing for the Bureau of Investigation. Suddenly Jane changed the subject and asked him if he happened to have a Yale key that would fit into a post office box. Jane claimed she had some letters of hers in the box that she had to get out. Even after incinerating all her correspondence with Wobblies and her collection of IWW publications, Jane apparently had loose ends of her own. Stein told her he had two or three keys at home but did not think they would fit.

Jane must have fretted all night about the letters, and rightfully so. She had no idea that Postmaster Barrows routinely called the Bureau of Investigation when he received suspicious letters or packages.[57] The next evening, Jane called Stein by phone and asked again to see him.

She had an important matter she wanted him to do for her. When he finally met her at 13th and E Streets, she told him she had changed her mind. She did not want to get Stein in trouble, again showing concern for him. Later, at 10:47 P.M., Jane reappeared on Broadway, between State and India streets, coincidentally running into Stein, who likely had been watching for her. Jane said, "I have been having a good time since I saw you."[58] She had something in her pocket. Stein suspected that Jane had gone to the post office and somehow gotten the mail. After leaving Jane, he went to the post office and discovered the glass to P.O. Box 680 shattered.[59] Surprisingly, the box belonged to J. A. Stromquist.[60]

On Tuesday morning, December 30, 1919, Jane arrived to work at her new job at the Butler Apartment Building. She probably was all but certain she had removed all incriminating evidence from her possession. What would Sellers do? Had she taken proper precautions? Had she protected Stein and others? The wait was surely miserable, a different kind of agony than when dealing with Bill Haywood and Phil Engle and his bunch. Mrs. Ryan was at the boarding house with her children, but there was tension, and Jane may have sensed that something had changed. Unbeknownst to Jane, Mrs. Ryan had asked Agent Weymouth to keep her from being involved in Jane's affairs in return for keeping her mouth shut while observing Jane.

When Agent Weymouth arrived after lunch at the Butler Apartment Building, along with the postmaster, sheer panic descended upon Jane. Weymouth asked her if she had broken into the post office box. Jane's instinct was to deny the crime vehemently, but it was to no avail. The agent then read Jane the charge—violation of the California Criminal Syndicalism Act. As Weymouth cuffed her, and a police matron stood ready to escort her to the San Diego County Jail, Jane begged to know what would happen to her children. Certainly, the only answer that she could be told—if she was indeed even answered—was that someone, certainly strangers, would now take care of Mary Jane, Pat, and Dawn.

Jane Street, the little rebel girl who placed motherhood above all other things, had just lost her children in her attempts to win IWW favor.[61] Sellers had been right—she could not bring lives into this world and stay with the IWW revolution.

# EPILOGUE

We have read in history books and other books about
slavery of long ago, but the way the housemaids must
work now from morning till night is too much for any
human being. I think we girls should get some consideration as every other labor class has, even though it is
housework.

"Fifteen weary housemaids" to
Mrs. Eleanor Roosevelt, February 1938

J ane sat for two weeks in the San Diego County Jail while the prosecution selected literature and subpoenaed witnesses to be used
for her first hearing beginning on January 7, 1920, in Judge Jennings's
Justice Court 1.[1] Mrs. Ryan, Jane's former landlady, contributed too.
She searched Jane's room and discovered Jane's original IWW membership card inside a mattress: Mixed Local No. 71, Branch GRU, February 1, 1915.[2] Jane had been a contrary prisoner, refusing even to
answer simple questions when a census enumerator visited her jail
cell. "If you can get me out of jail, I might remember something," she
teased the lady enumerator.[3]

After the defense presented its argument on February 20, 1920,
Jennings rather quickly rendered a surprising verdict. He found the
defendant not guilty and immediately released Jane from custody,
though almost everyone in the courtroom knew the case was suffi-
ciently strong to have warranted his holding Jane over for trial in the
superior courts. Bureau of Investigation agent Weymouth shared with
his colleagues, "I was confidentially informed that Judge Luce, Judge
of Superior Court for San Diego, used his influence to have this case
dismissed, and also that at various times he made remarks ridiculing

the idea of prosecuting the subject. This is probably true, as I know that Judge Luce also tried to handicap the fair price committee of this city in their work. He is an old 'Stand-Pat' Republican and apparently takes this stand from political motives."[4]

Weymouth, a Democrat, represented the Justice Department on San Diego's fair practice committee, part of a federal push to control merchants' pricing of their products in order to combat "profiteering" on essential goods. U.S. attorney general Palmer headed the federal committee whose goals had become a divisive political issue regarding free enterprise.[5] Remarkably, Jane had been acquitted despite evidence overwhelmingly supporting her guilt under the provisions of the California Criminal Syndicalist Act, and even the Sedition Act, because of politics. After sixty-one days, she was released, and her children were finally returned to her. Eight months later, the Sedition Act was repealed, but not until after hundreds of innocent people were persecuted and imprisoned for their words.

Jane continued to be a member of the IWW, even as federal agents sought her in connection with Sellers's activities in later years.[6] She had joined a new local in Kansas City, Missouri, in 1920, as evidenced from materials found in a March 1921 raid.[7] Otherwise, no mention of her becoming outwardly visible in labor agitation is apparent, which is no surprise, considering the political tenor of the country at the time and Jane's desire to avoid further criminal entanglement. Attorney General Palmer's raids, now under J. Edgar Hoover's leadership, had increased substantially beginning in January 1920, just prior to Jane's release, and had continued throughout the next months in cities across the country, including Los Angeles and San Francisco. As a result, Jane moved frequently and reinvented herself, while never allowing herself to become victimized. Still, Jane struggled.

I sat alongside Guy Leslie, Jane Street's seventy-nine-year-old grandson, at a kitchen table covered with a disheveled pile of photos and various papers, in Bullhead, Arizona, fall 2018. Nearby were Jack and Kathy Devlin, extended members of Charles Devlin's family, who had first reached out to Leslie. They chatted quietly with Loui, Leslie's wife, examining the collection of papers, which also included Devlin's letters to his children and his memoirs. Apparently, Jane had been a pack rat, saving all types of ephemera she must have considered sentimental or significant during her life. Certificates and diplomas, invoices and legal documents, birth and death certificates, her children's music programs, genealogy notes and newspaper obituaries, and other sundry newspaper clippings lay in piles in no chronological order.

A separate folder on the edge of the table bore Jane's creative side— her portfolio of compositions and even a fine pencil sketch she did as a child. Jane had saved Dawn's poetry and Grace Tuttle's writings, too, though Grace's modeling portfolio was missing. Leslie, fearing the nude photos were of his own mother, Mary Jane, and determining them to be too risqué, had tossed them in the trash a few years earlier, before realizing the photos had belonged to Grace. He also had thrown out the piles of notes that Jane made on herself each day. Still, there was much of Jane that her grandson had preserved.

Though her subsequent life is sometimes difficult to follow, perhaps due to fear of government surveillance or losing her children to Devlin, Jane's personal papers and conversations with Leslie help create cameos encapsulating Jane's struggle for stability while continuing to protest against injustices for herself and others. As in the past, her protests often got her into trouble, removing any normalcy for herself and her family. I often stopped Leslie to ask him what he recalled about Jane relating to each document and photo. When I did, he generally offered an anecdote. Still, he knew nothing about Jane's life prior to his birth in 1939.

Leslie chuckled when asked about Jane's directness. He had been on the receiving end often during his life, remarking that on one occasion, when he was a teenager, he had complained about taking an English class. "Why need it?" he whined. Jane responded, "One of these days you're going to want to tell a girl you love her and you won't know how!" He teased her, "What do you do when you run out of words?" Jane quickly reminded him, "I never run out of words."[8]

We sifted through each paper willy-nilly, examining its contents. Jane had retained two mysterious affidavits attesting to her work history and character, but their original purpose was unstated. The documents clearly illustrate her suffering after her release from jail. The first, signed by Mr. E. H. Gamble in Jackson County, Missouri, narrates how Jane worked for him as a stenographer from 1920 until 1922.

Gamble appears to be a benevolent employer who not only increased her salary to $27.50 a week but also offered Jane evening and Sunday work at the rate of one dollar an hour, to help her offset living expenses. He testified that Jane dressed very poorly and the condition of her hands was such as to indicate that she also did housework or laundry for a family. Jane's son Dawn frequently accompanied Jane to work, and Gamble noted that Dawn, too, was so poorly dressed that he was clearly in immediate need of clothing. Upon calling on Jane at her apartment in Kansas City, he noted that her apartment was in a very old house badly in need of repair.[9]

Perhaps Jane retained the affidavit as a character reference because Gamble testified to her strong work ethic and honesty, especially while taking care of three children through personal illness. She missed work only two times in the entire time she worked for him, and after staying home with a sick child, asked for work to make up the compensation she had lost, which he granted. On another occasion, Gamble describes how he knew Jane had been ill for days while still coming to work. She had chills and a bad cough, but she "stuck to the job" to the very last minute. He heard later that she had pneumonia. He clearly states that Jane was a

> serious-minded woman, with a quiet manner, and was a most
> efficient stenographer. I could never think of her without
> thinking of the responsibilities of her taking care of her three
> children and of the fortitude that she displayed in shoulder-
> ing this burden. If the father of her children ever contributed
> anything toward her or their support, it was not sufficient
> to prevent her from working no matter how bitterly cold the
> weather, how late the hour, or how unfavorable the state of her
> health whenever it was possible for her to do so; nor was it suf-
> ficient to enable her to clothe herself respectably, nor to live in
> comfortable quarters.[10]

As in the past, Jane said that her husband was deceased. Gamble had no idea that Jane's choice to support and live by herself was hers alone. After Jane suddenly quit work in 1922, an attorney in the same office suite as Gamble received a letter from Jane. In it, she said she left because Charles Devlin had taken Pat for a visit in Chicago but had refused to return the child to her. Jane had to travel to retrieve the boy but did not return to work because, as she said, she was "afraid to do so." The attorney presumed that Jane decided to disappear so that the father could not find the child again.[11] The trip and loss of work must have come at great cost to Jane.

The second affidavit, signed May 13, 1922, reveals similar circumstances except the witness was not as compassionate as Mr. Gamble. Kirk Harris, her former employer at the Golden Eagle Hotel in 1912, also testified to Jane's desperate circumstances. Several months after she was acquitted of charges in Sacramento in February 1920, Jane had sought him out at the Argonaut Hotel in San Francisco, where he was manager. Harris describes how Jane was broke and claimed to be the sole support for three children, including a nursing baby. Out of desperation, she had asked Harris for a loan, one that she promised to pay back on her next payday. Even a few dollars would help, Jane had implored. Harris had summarily turned her down, stating that he was not financially able to assist her. Harris allowed Jane one compliment, however. He said she had "a good reputation" with the men at her former job.[12]

Back at the kitchen table, Guy Leslie proudly recalled his grandmother's chutzpah when in 1928, a determined Jane, Leslie's mother—then nine-year-old Mary Jane—and eleven-year-old brother, Pat, boldly hitchhiked from San Francisco to New York City to join nineteen-year-old Dawn (Phil) Street. Dawn had obtained a job as a seaman on the *MacAbi*, a Panamanian naval vessel.[13] Supporting Leslie's anecdote was another document from Jane's personal papers, a certificate from the University of New York State, dated October 11, 1928. In anticipation of the upcoming presidential election between Republican candidate Herbert Hoover and Democratic candidate and New York City favorite Al Smith, Jane had to pass a literacy test at the university before voting for the first time in the state of New York. This was easily accomplished, and though Jane's Democratic candidate did not win, her New York voting registration was the first of many voting records throughout the remainder of her life.[14] Subsequent California records show Jane to have been a dedicated civic participant, registering every year to vote, and typically identifying with the Democratic Party. Deciding she did not care for New York, Jane and the children returned to California in the same manner as they had arrived—hitchhiking.

From the portfolio of writings on Guy Leslie's kitchen table came an autobiographical short story, "Something Like the Big House." It reveals intimate details about Jane's worries, physical health, and social conscience, especially during her experience with the New Deal's Civil Works Administration (CWA) and Works Progress Administration (WPA). At the same time, it documents her angry indignation at unfair treatment as an employee. (The short story is reproduced in full in the appendix.) Evidently, when jobs became scarce during the Great Depression, Jane registered to participate in federal employment programs. In 1933 she began working for a CWA sewing project, one of many temporary jobs for the unemployed during the winter of 1933–34 under President Franklin D. Roosevelt's administration. Four years later, in 1938, Jane had again entered a federal employment program, that time under the WPA. Though she was hired as a stenographer, she found herself in another sewing pool of five hundred women. Jane's candor, rebellious spirit, and demand for humane treatment almost caused her dismissal. By 1940 Jane finally gained a stenographer position within the WPA Art Project, leaving the "silent, subdued, slavish, inefficient, uninterested" women of the sewing project behind. The WPA Art Project ended in 1943.

At the same time, Jane was the primary caretaker for her young grandson. Leslie said that he received more love from his grandmother than from his mother, Mary Jane, who was about to enter her second marriage by way of a Mexican justice of the peace.[15] Jane always saw that he was fed and clothed while Mary Jane's attention was obligatory.[16] Jane had also loaned money to Pat (David), who struggled as a music teacher and musician before serving in the United States Army during World War II.[17] She quipped to Leslie, "You should always do what you say and say what you do," adding, "You only need to pay back the money if the person needs it; otherwise don't pay it back."[18] Jane knew that her children might not be able to pay her back, though much later they sometimes helped support her.

When asked for more stories about his grandmother that might describe her personality and later life, Leslie smiled and then told of her being fired from regular clerical and stenography work in Los

Angeles sometime in the 1940s. Leslie said when she was let go from one stenographer pool for her outspokenness, Jane overheard other women murmuring, "Poor, Jane, poor Jane. She got fired," as she walked out of the office. Leslie said Jane spunkily told him that she didn't mind because she didn't have to work anymore![19] Despite her bravado, Jane needed the work. Yet her young grandson only recalled Jane's words of proud defiance, not her defeat.

Leslie said his grandmother retained her intrepidness during the 1940s. While living with Jane in Los Angeles near a military base, he said, a practice bomb inadvertently found its way through the roof of their two-story house, plunging all the way through to the ground under the house's subfloor. Jane raced outside, got on her hands and knees under the house, and searched for the bomb. Once she found it, she hurriedly used her bare hands to cover the projectile with sand.[20] She must have feared fire.

Documents in Jane's personal papers yielded further information about changes in her life. In 1948, at sixty-one years old, Jane went back to school and earned another certification. She qualified under the State of California Department of Professional and Vocational Standards Board of Examiners for a license to practice psychoanalysis as a consultant in social work. Such work hearkened back to the years she first began making notes on her own dreams and sensed something wounded in Calenal Sellers.[21] Successive city licenses show she worked in this field for several years.

Jane never overcame loneliness, however. She spent her final years living in a one-room studio apartment in an old office building in Los Angeles.[22] Furnishings were sparse. Still, she had a table and chair, where she composed on an old black Underwood, overcoming a lone typewriter key that did not quite work. Her words record a life of loss, regret, and redemption in the portfolio of writings. About two dozen poems, several short stories, a dozen or so witty "fillers" (as Jane called them), and more serious protest articles reveal a passionate woman with social empathy, humorous insight, and an unbounded love for her children and grandchildren. Jane died with her family surrounding her in Los Angeles on April 25, 1966. Though her body was cremated at David Street's expense on the same day as her death, it was later that an airplane "respectfully" dispersed Jane's ashes off the Santa

Monica coastline at 3:30 P.M. on September 19, 1971, perhaps as part of Jane's last wishes.[23]

Though no gravestone permanently memorializes Jane Street's life, her story lives on, a testament to the spirit of at least one defiant woman, no doubt among many others, who would have liked to change what she saw as an unfair world. Jane's narrative illustrates how, despite gendered oppression and discrimination, women of the lowest class did make headway—in fact, a documented progress, debunking early-twentieth-century "just a housewife" views of women. In very few instances historically have domestic workers been able to organize successfully with so little support. Yet rebel girl Jane Street defied male syndicalism not only in an organization famous for its equity, but also among western society women who benefited from a nearly feudal class system within their homes. Still, Jane's work came at great personal cost, including financial hardship, isolation, dysfunctional children, and lack of enduring relationships.

The fight continues, though seemingly in slow motion and fraught with discrimination along the way. In 2010, almost a century after Jane Street's housemaid rebellion, a Domestic Worker's Bill of Rights, supported by the National Domestic Workers Alliance, a relatively new labor advocacy group, became the first legislation in the country to protect domestic workers.[24] Since the bill's inception, nine states have passed laws to extend labor protections to domestic workers, including eight-hour workdays with time and a half for overtime, vacation time every seven days of work, some paid vacation, and time for breaks. Workers' Compensation Insurance and certain disability benefits are afforded to full-time domestic workers in some states. New York has gone even further, protecting domestic workers from harassment due to gender, race, sex, religion, or origin, and employers making any unwanted sexual advances, both physical and verbal—all actions Jane endured. Currently (2020), a National Domestic Workers Bill of Rights is in discussion on Capitol Hill.[25]

One female Colorado politician reminds us that "when women support women, women win!"[26] On March 20, 2019, women marched to prove they can harness the political power of diverse women and their communities to create transformative social change. In the city where

Jane fought the powerful and elite, today's annual Denver's Women's March is committed to dismantling systems of oppression through nonviolent resistance and building inclusive structures guided by self-determination, dignity, and respect.[27] Ironically, the 2019 march began in front of the site where once stood the mansion belonging to society leader Ellen Van Kleeck, one of Jane's Capitol Hill adversaries.

But what about the other men and women in Jane Street's story?

Capitol Hill mistress Louise Sneed Hill thought Colorado guardsman and playboy Bulkeley Wells would marry her after her husband Crawford Hill died in 1922. Instead, Wells eloped with a twenty-three-year-old strawberry-blonde just weeks later, whom his accountant described as "a beautiful woman, how intelligent, I could not say."[28] Louise, who was later heard to say, "I'll break him!" strongly encouraged her social and political contacts, and her financial backers to drop Wells.[29] On May 26, 1931, Wells, on the verge of bankruptcy, fatally shot himself. Circulating was a rumor that representatives from the Western Pacific Railroad had been waiting outside in the lobby, prepared to offer him an executive position paying $20,000 a year.[30]

Louise continued as the "The Dowager Queen of Denver Society," entertaining much the same schedule as before. When her "faithful and revered" maid Cora Cowan became ill and died suddenly on April 30, 1930, Louise staged a spectacular funeral in the stately drawing room of her Sherman Street mansion. Dignitaries and Denver's high society attended the event, noting that Cora's casket was a pall of Easter lilies, Louise's favorite flower. Inside the casket, the maid was dressed in a pile of blue tulle, the elegant gown certainly nothing she ever would have worn in life. Most attendees had known Cora in her capacity as secretary and maid, and likely sincerely honored her. *Denver Post* owner Fred Bonfils was a pallbearer, along with other business leaders, and his favorite reporter, Pinky Wayne, covered the affair.[31] What they did not know was that Cora had been passively rebelling against her controlling mistress, including secretly investing her money and planning her own estate with Louise's financial accountant.[32] When Louise discovered that Cora's personal business had been made behind her back, she had Cora's estate and family repay her for paltry items. After Cora's ashes were interred in the Hill family plot in Denver's Fairmont

Cemetery, the Cowan family had her removed to Ohio per Cora's original wishes.[33]

Rebel girl Elizabeth Gurley Flynn, after her dismissal from the IWW, joined the Communist Party in 1936, becoming arrested in 1951 under the Smith Act.[34] She served two years in prison, all the time writing essays and making notes for her memoir. She continued to be a strong advocate of women's rights, often speaking and writing on women's issues, and was a founding member of the American Civil Liberties Union. After becoming chairwoman of the United States Communist Party in 1961, she traveled to the Soviet Union often. It was there that she died in 1964. Her lover, Carlo Tresca, who opposed fascism, was gunned down on a New York street, in 1943, likely ordered by a mob boss, a fascist sympathizer. Tresca had criticized Benito Mussolini and later the Stalin regime.[35]

William "Big Bill" Haywood also died in the Soviet Union in 1928, where he had fled seven years earlier after his release on bail during an appeal of the Chicago IWW mass trial verdict and shortly afterward, a guilty judgment for criminal conspiracy to overthrow the United States government. He had borrowed heavily from his supporters and friends to finance two $15,000 bonds, leaving several people bereft. One supporter, Mary Marcy, having lost everything, was so devastated that Haywood had selfishly betrayed her, that she committed suicide.[36] Ironically, Haywood had not been a "paragon of virility" either, as his iconic image had portrayed. After his arrest in 1919, prison doctors found him under six feet tall, overweight, diabetic, and suffering from ulcers.[37]

IWW Charles Lambert's twenty-year sentence, along with the sentences of other imprisoned IWWs, was commuted by President Harding. In April 1923 Lambert was deported to Scotland, his home country. He worked diverse jobs—baker, diamond prospector in British Guiana, oil field roustabout in Curacao, and finally a runner for a London bookmaker. Interestingly, the rest of his extended family remained in America, and his nephew Jack Lambert became a well-known character actor.[38] Charles Lambert never married and died in London in 1962. He would be a passing note in history except for the "open" letter he wrote to President Harding in 1923 describing the infamous mass IWW trial with remarkable detail and color.

Phil Engle evaded arrest until the Red Scare subsided. In 1924 he tried his hand at playwrighting, publishing "The Stool Pigeon, a Drama in Two Acts," in a labor newspaper.[39] Three years later, on September 28, 1927, Engle was hit by a car crossing the street in Minneapolis, where he was working as a "religious lecturer."[40] He had purchased a life insurance policy the day before. After the Wobblies honored him with a fine funeral, Engle was buried in Detroit near his younger brother Benjamin and mother, Dora.[41]

Grace Tuttle, Jane's sister and the "Girl in Red," lived with Albert Kohler in Denver, employing her creative talents to run the Lincoln Studies Music Studio on 1916 Lincoln Street until 1919.[42] She never married again, choosing to remain with Kohler, who worked as a cook. Grace died on February 3, 1925, at the age of forty-two years old, reportedly the result of alcohol and drug use.[43] She is buried at Fairmount Cemetery.[44]

After Grace's death, Albert A. Kohler and Calenal Sellers apparently reconciled. Kohler relocated to Chehalis, Washington, and was briefly married in 1926 to Ruth A. Bush, Sellers's niece.[45] Later, when Kohler registered for World War II enlistment, he named "Mrs. Jane Tuttle" as his contact. At the time, Jane was living in Philadelphia, Pennsylvania.[46] The date of Kohler's death is unknown.

According to the Bureau of Investigation, Claude (Calenal) Welday Sellers's activities marked him the most intemperate advocate of violence and sabotage in the history of the IWW organization.[47] Two months after Jane's release, Sellers took part in the Anaconda Road Massacre, where outside the Neversweat Mine in Butte, Montana, Anaconda Copper Company mine guards opened fire on union picketers, hitting sixteen miners in the back as they tried to flee and killing miner Thomas Manning. Sellers, dubbed "a strike promoter," testified as a witness for the inquest into Manning's killing.[48] Afterward, Sellers's Butte speeches were so rabid, that copies were sent to J. Edgar Hoover to read personally.[49] A month later, in May 1920, Sellers was arrested for organizing IWWs and acting as a Centralia Massacre accomplice by raising a defense fund for men accused of killing American Legionnaires. He burned his way out of jail and escaped, becoming one of J. Edgar Hoover's most wanted men as he evaded arrest.[50] Over the years, Sellers often appeared at Jane's home in California, so much so that Jane's grandson Leslie recalls her friend "Colonel." Sellers died December 29, 1960, in Seattle. He was eighty-three years old.[51]

Herbert R. Bumpass, alias Jack Street, was arrested one more time. On March 20, 1918, over a year after his alleged crime, Bumpass was charged for violation of the Reed Amendment by an overzealous Arkansas police chief, who was backed by a determined district attorney. Arkansas had a "bone-dry" liquor law, which outlawed the transportation, delivery, and storage of liquor in an attempt to eliminate alcohol sales in the state. It did not prevent individuals from crossing into the state with their personal alcohol, however, and Bumpass had brought whiskey into Pine Bluff, Arkansas, from Monroe, Louisiana, in February 1917. The Reed Amendment, passed July 1917, exacted a $1,000 fine for transporting liquor into a dry state. The chief of police and district attorney tried to pin the Reed Amendment on Bumpass, but after learning that Bumpass brought the liquor into the state before the law was in effect, Bureau of Investigation agents had the charges dropped.[52] Bumpass had avoided criminal prosecution yet again.

Using the name John Street, Bumpass married once more, this time to divorcee Winona Nicodemus Wright in 1927. The couple lived out their lives in De Soto, Missouri, where Bumpass worked as a printer.[53] Just as in the past, he used nicknames. Instead of "Horse," Winona called him "Bear," and she was his "Cat."[54] Though Winona's Wright family suspected John Street had a dubious past, the family reports that Bumpass apparently explained that he had dropped his last name during World War I because "it sounded German."[55] Herbert R. Bumpass died on June 13, 1954.[56] His ashes are interred in Valhalla Cemetery in Bel-Nor, Missouri. As for Jane Street, she never mentioned Jack Street to her grandson.

Not long after Mary Jane's birth, Charles Devlin headed back east, where he opened his own business in Chicago, though still working for labor's interests. He rarely saw the children, but never disparaged Jane, telling his children years later, "I still hold her in the highest esteem. She has been a wonderful Mother to you children. She has done more than her share. I hold myself solely responsible for all of this."[57] In 1927 he met and married Ida Zelenke in Chicago. Afterward, the couple lived alternately between California and Chicago while Devlin tried to run businesses. In California, he took on politics, actively participating in the State Democratic Speakers' Bureau and forming a Disabled Persons Club, a social organization supported by his local Lions' Club for the physically handicapped.[58]

Though Devlin worked hard to become close with his children after years of separation, he never achieved the intimacy he desired. His letters to Pat (David) and Mary Jane are poignant with detail and love as he tries to give fatherly advice and explain his absence in their lives. Jane's grandson remarked that Ida Devlin later blocked his children and grandchildren from getting in touch with their father and grandfather.[59] Devlin died on September 7, 1950, in San Bernardino, California.[60] He is buried in Mountain View Cemetery in San Bernardino.

Not surprisingly, Jane Street's children's lives ebbed and flowed with tragedy and disappointment. Though the children inherited their mother's talents, they also bore her damaging proclivities. Dominant in all three children's lives is artistic creativity. Dawn Philander Street, who went by Phil as an adult, was not only musically inclined but wrote beautiful poetry. He was also jailed for being a conscientious objector.[61] Mary Jane Street, married at least three times, possessed a superb contralto-soprano voice but could not raise her son without Jane's help. And it was Patrick Charles Devlin, who later changed his name to stage name David Street, whose public life exposed family talents and self-destruction.

David Street played seven musical instruments, performed in a big band, and acted in Hollywood as a "B" actor between 1949 and 1962. The paparazzi followed his activities intently, furnishing black-and-white glossies for Hollywood rags, generally because he was usually in the company of well-known, glamorous leading ladies, including Jayne Mansfield, Ava Gardner, and Marilyn Maxwell. He married multiple times—to Mary Beth Hughes; Mary Francis Wilhite; Cathleen Gourley, stage name Lois Andrews; and Elaine Perry. Probably the most famous of his wives was Debralee Griffin, stage name Debra Paget.[62] Some of these marriages lasted mere days, some divorces due to addiction and spending problems.

Jane Street in 1948.
*Courtesy of Guy Leslie, Jane Street
Family Papers*

Did Jane's personal relationships and care differ among her children because of her life experiences? Probably. Yet, her constant love for them extended to her grandchildren even as their parents struggled. When her first grandchild was born, she reflected her joy through verse.

> I have always wanted
> To be free
> To do something—
> Some special, sacred
> Something
> For which I was born.
> And guiltily
> I've stopped
> And become
> Enmeshed in
> Strange and intricate

> But common-place relationships.
> And then my first grandchild is born.

Jane, who prized motherhood, felt redeemed through the birth of her grandchildren.

A small boy clutched the hand of a short, plump woman as they walked toward MacArthur Park. He noticed her hair was black this day, not the iron-streaked curls of the day before. She explained to the child that when she changed her diet, she could grow new black hair over her gray instantly. He did not question her—his "Dommie" (she did not want to be called Grandmother) had been the center of his life since he was born five years ago, and he believed everything she said. Sometimes she took him on the tram to Angel's Point, and other times they went to a movie. But walking to MacArthur Park was almost a daily occasion. There they listened to groups playing guitars and singing, and sometimes the old woman would join them, her voice true. She loved music, as did his uncles and mother Mary Jane.

Later his grandmother would tell him about her lost love, Hamilton-something, and wondered that if she lost some weight, she might get him back. How she missed Hamilton! This confused him. Dommie had lots of men friends, Old Jim, Kohler, and someone called "Colonel." In fact, almost all her friends were men. Afterward, on the streetcar ride home, Dommie would nod off, and he would have to nudge her gently to wake her up before their stop. When he helped her with her Victory Garden, she never told him she had been a radical.[63]

Years later, he brought his new baby girl to his grandmother for an introduction. The old woman peered down at the child, and then looked up into her grandson's face, her black eyes unwavering. "Don't ever let her spirit be broken," she cautioned, "She's a feisty girl!"

Just like her great-grandmother, Jane Street.

# APPENDIX
## *Something Like the Big House*
### Jane Street

*This piece was written circa 1938. Where necessary for clarity, I have taken the liberty of adding punctuation.—JLB*

This story is more or less about me. It isn't a bit of fiction or a psychological study, an economic treatise, a political trick, a series of research notations, or propaganda exposé—although I realize it possibly might be regarded from any of these viewpoints. But it is, in truth, a very human document.

I am writing about what I feel and know of a government sewing project. I don't know just what the other women feel except as indicated by their words and actions, which are restricted. (The very restrictions are everywhere apparent and indicate a lot!) No, I am not going to write from sympathy and understanding of their problems, which, I confess, I am tempted to do; but for which I might be accused of drawing too much upon my imagination. No, I'll write about myself.

In the first place—no, not the first place, for I was in a sewing project in the CWA back in 1933, where I was placed a few days after it opened up, before we could be properly assigned. I'll refer to this CWA project later. Anyway, the second time I found myself in a sewing project was when I had asked for a better paying job. I am an office worker. Under the WPA, it was announced that stenographers were to receive $94. Therefore, when paid $55, I protested.

"You squawk too much," shouted the supervisor who transferred me. "You know we always get rid of anyone who squawks!"

He was a stupid, ignorant, petty tyrant—a man at the head of an educational project who didn't know how to spell! He told me that no stenographer was worth $94!

I was not only angry. I was wounded deeply.

For years a sense of inferiority had been growing on me. All my life I had been liked by people—men and women both. I really never disliked anyone. I just sized them up and took them for what they were. This uncultured brute of a boss—I didn't dislike him. How could he hate me? It was an awful thing for him to throw me into a sewing project for $55! Other people managed somehow to get along with him. Evidently, he didn't want me around. What was the matter with me?

It seemed funny, in fact impossible, for me to believe that I had been liked all my life because I was young. Perhaps my personality had changed. Perhaps I was at fault and was too egotistical to see it. I had definitely begun to doubt myself.

And when I went to appeal to those higher up and got outside their office, I found that I couldn't keep my chin from twitching. I couldn't go blubbering in there!

Working in that office was painful at best. Maybe other jobs like that were too. Why should I fight for something I didn't want? I only wanted the extra money.

So, I decided not to appeal my case but to take my jolt. I went to the sewing project.

It was on the third floor of a fairly modern factory building, was well lighted and well ventilated. There were about 500 or 600 of us, about half negro, or perhaps more, and we sat at long narrow tables, one after another throughout the length and breadth of the big room. The toilet was boarded up in the far corner, with the nurse's department nearby, containing six cots. The white-collar aristocracy occupied the corner near the entrance and were separated from us by a low railing.

Under the old CWA sewing project on which I had worked, we had gone pretty far with the cooperative principle. We had "assembly" for a few minutes every morning, which included an open airing of grievances and answering of inquiries and community singing; we had dancing to the radio and other forms of entertainment at our recess periods, occasional banquets, and always an abundance of flowers. We used to visit and report about our sick, and sing "Happy Birthdays" daily. In our room, we really didn't have a boss but cooperated on a voluntary basis. Our "newspaper," which was read at assembly, contained shop notes, some good laughs to start the day with and some gripping cooperative propaganda.

In the Art Room, they made layettes lovingly for some baby of the unemployed. And we made dresses and quilts, as well as our supplies and equipment would permit, eagerly and industriously, with which to cover our sisters and brothers in poverty. Back in 1933, we used to hope, and say in our paper, that in time the unemployed could clothe all the unemployed. We knew that the garment factories wouldn't like it. But we figured that industry and devotion such as ours would win out against their sabotage. And when in the last days of the CWA setup, the quota was reduced and some of our members obliged to leave, we used to cry and sing farewells with the enthusiasm of a revival camp meeting; and some of the members who were laid off used to come back and work for nothing!

Well, here I was walking into a WPA sewing project, to which I had been transferred.

Over the tables in the large factory room, suspended at intervals from the rafters or ceiling boards were hanging baskets, which, through someone's loving care, had been filled with ivy and put there to add to our cheer. But the water was evaporated and the ivy was almost dead. So, at recess, I stood upon a chair or table and poured some water in several of the painted cans. But I didn't get to the rest. The monitor came around and ordered me to quit. Afterward, every one of the baskets was taken down.

Although there were 500 to 600 people, there were only about 75 machines—ordinary electric machines, there being only two power machines, such as used in garment factories.

On these the girls were supposed to "learn so that they might sometime get a job in private industry." The rest of us did hand work. We hemmed sheets, pillow cases, towels, and diapers by hand. Sometimes they threw a big box of scraps at us with which to make quilts. But no individual choice of color or artistic design was permitted. We were forced to sew multicolored blocks together in monstrous hap-hazard that would injure the eyesight and impoverish the soul of anyone of artistic leanings, of which there were many.

At one time, my foul-mouthed Italian monitor (a female imitation of the movie Italian gangster) gave me a few small pieces of blue and white cotton goods and said I could do anything I wanted to. I appliqued a flower of blue on a background of white. It was a very bad piece of needlework but fairly good design. It made the top of a crib quilt. As I remember it, it cost the government about $22.50—which is expensive in money, which is bad, but more expensive in human suffering, which is worse!

We were forced to make handkerchiefs—untold numbers of them—out of flimsy lawn, with what I measured to be 1/32 of an inch hem. One old lady over 60 was compelled to take it out and do it over four times!

"What yuh doin' sittin' there, starin' into space?" cracked out a floor woman whom we called Paul II in preference to other names less refined. The report was that she used to be a matron in a woman's prison.

"Resting my eyes."

"Yes, you are. Well, git yuh some glasses. Quit talkin' now, you girls, and go on to work."

My own eyes were streaming water. I thought I had some foreign particle in one but nothing of that sort could be found. Evidently, it was the strain. Of course, I rebelled. But I felt sorry for some of the others, and sometimes did their work for them.

One woman, a negress weighing over 200 lbs., who sat beside me, couldn't sew as well as a man who has never tried. She could never use a thimble and couldn't do the folding of the hems on the sheets. Her name was Mattie. Her hair was a kinky mat. Her big eyes looked out at me with childish simplicity and won my heart. I think she was a good cook.

"You all come and see me sometime. I'll cook you a nice meal. . . . It'll be clean," she added. Poor Mattie. She had an inferiority complex too.

(I have been in a sewing project within the last few weeks, where I was transferred from the timekeeping department just after I joined the CIO office workers' union. They aren't making handkerchiefs by hand any more. They make them by machine! Nor do they make quilts any more. But they shift around the hand sewers to the machines and vice versa; they try to tell you how long you can stay in the toilet, they make you quit talking, tell you where you can sit, turn around the clock so you can't see it and a display bulletins which prohibit organization on the job.)

Well, when I was back there in the big sewing project—the Big House, we often called it—one day a bird flew in through an open window and became frightened in an effort to get out. "Poor bird," I thought. "It is in prison too." A wave of superstitious awe passed over the group. There were sighs and hushed whispers. "Some one of us will die," said one of the negroes. No one dared to move to help the bird escape.

The windows were frosted squares of light covering three sides of the room. They were too high to see through unless one stood up. At recess time, many of us used to crowd around an open window and look out. There were iron bars there. I'm sure there were iron bars. Maybe they were from the fire escape. It was a prison cell all right—only we went home every day. We only worked five hours but it seemed an endless day. One counted every minute of the time.

How hard it was to make oneself come every day! We filed up the stairs and past the timekeeper, who checked us in. If we were one minute past the allotted time, we were docked an hour! And many a one was docked too, women with whole families, some of them, with unavoidable causes for being late, women who actually suffered at the loss of 45¢ from a $55 paycheck!

One time I got the intestinal flu. I didn't know what it was. I am never sick. I would have thought it was ptomaine poisoning if I had eaten anything else except a boiled potato and some bread. I fasted, thinking I would be able to work the next day. I was deathly sick on the street car, but managed somehow until I was nearly there when I had to vomit from the car window, the diarrheal discharge soiling my underwear. The project nurse was on the car and took me in hand.

"It's the water," she told me. "There have been over a hundred sick here. They're sick all the time with it. . . . My, I was afraid something would happen to you on the stairs," she added sympathetically.

I just stuck it out that day, and the next and the next fasting and keeping on the job.

One out of every five people, at least, that I talked to had had it, most of them thinking they had ptomaine poisoning.

There were long lists of absences called every day. I don't know how many had it. I don't know how many died. Two day's absence meant a discharge from the project.

Why didn't they do something about it? I didn't know of anybody at all outside the project who had the disease. Why didn't they give us bottled water? Or at least analyze the water, or examine the plumbing. An epidemic in a hotel once had been traced to a dead rat which had crawled into a pipe during plumbing repairs. With such a big percentage of cases there must be a local cause.

So, when a head official came into the project, I suggested the matter to her. I thought that maybe she, like myself, although in the midst of it, might not have known anything about it. I asked her if she would like for me to take her around and have her talk with others who had been sick in the same way. She said no, for me to give her a list of their names. I gave her a list of ten. She called them up to her desk one at a time, and then she called me up. She sat me down and started in on me.

"Don't you know that it's against the rules of the project to collect lists of names? I have talked with every one of these girls and there's simply nothing to it at all. There isn't any epidemic and it would best for you not to cause any more trouble."

[I responded,] "If you brought them up here and started in by threatening them, as you have me, it is no wonder that they have denied ever being sick. If women, sick enough to die, drag themselves here, too poor to even lay off a day or an hour, what do you expect them to do in order to keep you from firing them altogether? It is no wonder they denied it. I should think you would want to do everything possible to check this thing. If you want to prove you're sincere, just ask the girls who have been sick in this way to stand up against that wall over there. You wouldn't have room for all of them."

But she wouldn't do it. I insisted that something be done. I told her that it was a loathsome and dangerous disease and that no steps at checking it should be neglected.

The next day, I inquired of the supervisor in charge as to what had been done. She replied, "See here, I want you to quit interfering with the project."

They whitewashed the toilets! And they put a partition up around the cots. The supervisor used to come and stand in front of them and threaten people who came to the toilets. In this way, she intimidated them from seeing how sick some of the women really were. The epidemic continued to rage. The list of absentees continued to be very long. I demanded again to know whether or not anything had been done. I never received from anyone anything but indignity and insult. The supervisor announced from the platform—steps near the middle of the room—that there was no epidemic and that the water was perfectly safe. Many of the women brought their own water, and most of us went all the hot day without water.

Evidently from their standpoint, we must be given to understand that it was none of our business. We were merely inmates.

However, as time went on, filtered water was supplied, a new supervisor was shoved into place on the project, the hot water abated and the epidemic had subsided.

Some of the girls whose names I had turned in shunned me after that. But some of them told me that they had not denied being sick but that, of course, they were unable to say that it was the water that caused their sickness. No, it wasn't cowardice on their part but duplicity on hers.

I approached the new supervisor once while we were waiting for a car. "Do you have any ideals for the sewing project?" I asked. "Ideals?" she inquired. "Why, yes, I want to be as kindly as possible to the girls." We had a new matron in the institution. She always high-hatted me—didn't even speak to me when she came and went on the same car. She was from the relief ranks, just as we were. But she had to maintain her authority.

The girls continued to be switched from the machines after they had become more or less proficient and the hand workers shoved into their places. This might be sabotaging the project, but, anyway, the girls had to learn to function in private industry! Many of them were over 50 years of age.

There were rebels on the job, however, who blazed out in unexpected directions. Someone would start writing letters, to Washington, to state officials, the public press—"to everybody." They would expose the inadequate toilets, the unauthorized search for stolen articles, etc. It always did a little good. Officialdom, fearing the voters' disapproval, always made a gesture at reform.

There never was one moment that I didn't feel the weight of the thing on my spirit. "If I stay here another day," said one of the girls, "I'll go to pieces. I don't know what it is. But it seems to me I just can't stand it."

"Look at it," every day I would whisper to myself in agony. "But I can't put my shoulder into trying to change it! . . . There is something else that I must do."

Over and over again, day after day—I knew personally almost every one of them—I searched the faces to find what they were thinking. In some degree perhaps they all felt as I did. Like me, they all had something else which they must do somewhere. Perhaps each nursed her secret daydreams as she sewed—the drunks, the tellers of dirty stories, the cultured, the poetic, the studious; the negroes, the Mexicans, the lady from Turkey, and the four corners of the earth! The young, the middle-aged, the old—perhaps each had loved a man once and from that love, tributaries of pain and hope would keep trickling down to irrigate whatever might grow in their lives until the very last day!

But seeds, of social worth, can be planted, and be watered by these tributaries.

I still wondered about myself. What hadn't I done more? Why didn't anyone else among them do something?

Suppose we were organized. Suppose the "project" was *our* project—our project on which to follow our initiative, to create a cooperative industry, to clothe, and not merely the unemployed, but all of our fellow workers—ours to regulate and operate to unimagined success!

Who are these straw bosses and their higher-ups who oppress us? Do we work *for* them, or *under* them? If we work under them, they are the servants of many. We could make it so.

Is there no spirit to the thing? Can't the whole project be a thing alive in itself?

All those women—silent, subdued, slavish, inefficient, uninterested—working only, for their $55 a month! And those back of the small wooden railing, the white-collar ones, despising the others, also holding jobs, demoralized even with puny authority, also doing what they are told, for whatever their price is!

Couldn't someone wake them up? Couldn't we have a real cooperative?

I organized women once. I saw them build something. But I loved them enough to do it. I loved the women of the project, but not enough to try. I didn't love the union, nor the project, or the cooperative enough. But someone else with love in their hearts and spirit and faith can do it. That's what it takes. It isn't hopeless.

A bird flying through the window caught them in a wave of fear. Sometime, light flying through the window will catch them in a wave of hope.

Courtesy of Guy Leslie, Jane Street Papers

# NOTES

### *Prologue*

1. Matt Masich, "The Colorado Coalfield War and the Children of Ludlow," *Colorado Life Magazine*, n.d., http://www.coloradolifemagazine.com/The-Colorado -Coalfield-War-and-the-Children-of-Ludlow/; "33 Known Dead at Ludlow; Mothers and Babies Slain," *Denver Rocky Mountain News*, April 22, 1914, p. 5. For an excellent overview of the Ludlow Massacre, see Caleb Crain, "There Was Blood," *New Yorker*, January 19, 2009. The Colorado Coal Field Wars, 1912–14, occupied northern Colorado from Louisville southward to Ludlow. It was in the latter community where the worst of the fights occurred. Mostly immigrant miners, led by the United Mine Workers of America (UMWA), fought for economic, legal, and political independence from their employers, primarily the Colorado Fuel and Iron Company. Tent No. 58, the largest tent in the colony, was used for an infirmary and maternity ward.

2. *The Military Occupation of the Colorado National Guard, 1913–1914* (Denver: Press of the Smith-Brooks Printing Company, 1914), 46.

3. Robert Knight, "Fighting to Win Colorado," *International Socialist Review* 14, no. 6 (December 1913): 333. Mother Jones, as she was commonly called, was Mary Harris Jones, a prominent labor activist and widow of a coal miner, who antagonized Colorado mine owners, operators, and state militia. Miners adapted the song, "She'll Be Coming Around the Mountain," in honor of Mother Jones.

4. H. Marcy, "In Colorado," *International Socialist Review* 14, no. 11 (May 1914): 710, 714. The number of residents in the Ludlow tent colony varies in different accounts.

5. Frances Wayne, "Coroners' Verdict Names [Karl] Linderfelt and Maj. [Patrick] Hamrock," *Denver Post*, May 2, 1914, p. 1; Clara Ruth Mozzor, "Ludlow," *International Socialist Review* 14, no. 11 (May 1914): 723.

6. Marcy, "In Colorado," 710, 717; Walter H. Fink, *The Ludlow Massacre* (United Mine Workers Association, 1914), 11.

7. Mozzor, "Ludlow," 724. Killed were Mrs. Charles Costa, her children Lucy, age four, and Onafrio, age six; Mrs. Petra Valdez, her children Elvira, age three months, Mary, age seven, Eulalia, age eight, and her nephew Rodolfo, age nine; Cloriva Pedregone, age four months, and Rodgerio Pedregone, age six; Lucy Petrucci, age two, Joe Petrucci, age four, and Frank Petrucci, age six months. Mrs. Petrucci, though also in the Costa cellar, survived despite early reports.

"14 Bodies Found in Ludlow Ruins," *Denver Post*, April 23, 1914, p. 17. A monument of a man, woman, and child, in memory of the miners and their families who died that day, looms over the cellar where the women and children died at Ludlow. Although the United Mine Workers of America owns the site, the Ludlow Massacre, a watershed event in labor history, has been designated a National Historical Landmark.

8. "Colorado Workers Hear E. G. Flynn," *Solidarity*, May 15, 1915, p. 1. The topic of Flynn's address was "War: Can Labor Be Neutral?" Hugh O'Neill, "Most Magnetic Woman in America in Denver to Preach Her Message," *Denver Post*, May 3, 1915, p. 4.

9. O'Neill, "Most Magnetic Woman," 4.

10. Ibid.

11. "Women Close Session to End Ludlow Clash," *Denver Rocky Mountain News*, May 6, 1914, p. 3; "Law and Order League Women Offer Sympathy to Ammons and Militia as Victims of Press," *Denver Rocky Mountain News*, May 8, 1914, p. 9; "33 Known Dead at Ludlow," 5; "Militia and Mine Guards Are Blamed for Ludlow Battle," *Colorado Springs Gazette*, May 3, 1914, p. 1. A vast number of newspaper articles continued to appear in Colorado Springs and Denver for months as conflicting stories appeared and efforts to place blame continued. Helen Grenfell made a report to President Woodrow Wilson giving the league's view of the Ludlow Massacre, that is, that the strikers were at fault.

12. "Law and Order League Women Offer Sympathy," 9; Marcy, "In Colorado," 710, 712–13, 717.

13. Editorial, *Denver Rocky Mountain News*, May 18, 1914, p. 6. Dr. John Chase specialized in diseases of the eye and ear. He helped found Gross Medical College, which later became Denver Medical College. He also commanded the National Guard during the 1903–4 Colorado labor wars as a brigadier general, another conflict with sullied history.

14. "Thousands of Denver Women to March to Capitol and Demand of Ammons Withdrawal of Militia," *Denver Post*, April 24, 1914, p. 1. "Women Close Session," p. 3. Gail M. Beaton, *Colorado Women: A History* (Boulder: University Press of Colorado, 2012), 151. None of the women in the Women's Peace Association were members of labor unions. See Fink, *Ludlow Massacre*, 27, 53.

15. Editorial, *Denver Rocky Mountain News*, May 18, 1914, p. 6.

16. Elizabeth Gurley Flynn, *The Rebel Girl: An Autobiography*, rev. ed. (1973; New York: International Publishers, 1994), 188–89. Colorado Fuel and Iron Company was a Rockefeller Corporation subsidiary.

17. Joe Hill, "Letter to Editor," *Solidarity*, November 29, 1914, p. 4.

18. Joe Hill, "The Rebel Girl," *IWW Songs to Fan the Flames of Discontent*, 9th ed., Joe Hill Memorial Edition (Cleveland: IWW Publishing Bureau, 1916), 35. Elizabeth Gurley Flynn first wrote Joe Hill and then visited him as he sat in a Utah prison accused of murder, generally believed to be unjustly. Hill was executed on November 19, 1915. Flynn, *The Rebel Girl: An Autobiography*, 191–94.

See discussion of Joe Hill's case in Jane Little Botkin, *Frank Little and the IWW: The Blood That Stained an American Family* (Norman: University of Oklahoma Press, 2017); and William M. Adler, *The Man Who Never Died* (New York: Bloomsbury, 2012).

19. Flynn, *The Rebel Girl: An Autobiography*, 65.

### Chapter 1

1. "Ask That Show Be Suppressed," *Plain Dealer*, July 18, 1906, p. 2. "Girl in Red Critically Ill Dancer Whose Tent Was Attacked by Newburg Mob Suffers Relapse," *Plain Dealer*, August 13, 1906, p. 3. Part of Ohio's Newburgh Township became Newburgh Heights in 1904. At the time of this event, locals still called the area Newburgh and a neighboring area Woodland Hills. See *Encyclopedia of Cleveland History*, Case Western University, https://case.edu/ech/articles/n/newburgh.

2. "Luna Park," Center for Public History, Cleveland State University, https://clevelandhistorical.org/items/show/259. Trolley parks, originally started in the nineteenth century, were picnic and recreation areas along or at the ends of streetcar lines, later adding amusement parks. Frederick Ingersoll, owner of the Ingersoll Construction Company, got his start building vending machines, roller coasters, and other amusement park rides. By 1901 his company was building entire amusement parks. The first two Luna Parks opened in Cleveland and Pittsburgh in 1905. At its peak, Ingersoll's company ran over forty amusement parks across the country and in such exotic locales as Mexico City and Berlin, Germany.

3. "Luna Park," Center for Public History, Cleveland State University.

4. "Women Storm Girl in Red," *Plain Dealer*, July 20, 1906, p. 1. The production of "The Girl in Red" reportedly first appeared in New York City in 1901. See "Girl in Red Critically Ill," 3.

5. "Women Storm Girl in Red," 1.

6. Ibid.; "Girl in Red Critically Ill," 3. Grace Tuttle suffered a nervous breakdown and was hospitalized. Though newspaper articles reveal several women assuming the name "La Neta" between 1901 and 1911, hiding the actual identities of the women was part of their allure. See "Sees Burlesquers Trip," *Plain Dealer*, May 1, 1911, p. 19.

7. Grace Tuttle, "True Experiences of an Artist Model," Guy Leslie, Jane Street Family Papers, n.d., 1. Guy Leslie is Jane Street's grandson. "Society Notes," *Jersey City Evening Journal*, August 1, 1905, p. 8. Grace worked as a pianist as well.

8. Tuttle, "True Experiences," 1.

9. Guy Leslie, personal interview by the author, September 28, 2018.

10. Tuttle, "True Experiences," 2.

11. Ibid.

12. "Continuous Vaudeville That Never Stops," *Cincinnati Post*, August 10, 1907, pp. 1, 5. Exotic "cooch" dances, ostensibly Syrian in origin, were brought

into American burlesque in the early twentieth century with increasing focus on female nudity. National circuits of burlesque shows competed with the vaudeville circuit, both including comedic routines, soubrettes with singing and dancing, and eventually striptease in a free-flowing alcohol atmosphere.

13. "Girl in Red Critically Ill," 3.

14. Frank (Francis) Tuttle died November 13, 1905, in Hot Springs, Garland County, Arkansas. "Clark Strong Tuttle Diary," Leslie, Jane Street Family Papers; *Hot Springs, Arkansas, 1909 City Directory*, 341.

15. Leslie, personal interview, September 28, 2018. See also "Request for Registration as Provided in Section 2933.5 of the Business and Professions Code," Dept. of Professional and Vocational Standards, Medical Examiners, State of California, 1948, Leslie, Jane Street Family Papers.

16. Leslie, personal interview, September 28, 2018.

17. Leslie, Jane Street Family Papers.

18. Ibid.; Guy Leslie, personal interview by the author, May 30, 2019.

19. 1900 Federal Census, Harrison, Vigo, Indiana, Roll 409, Page 14A, Enumeration District 0124.

20. *California Death Index, 1940–1997*; US Social Security Application for Account Number, March 18, 1939, Leslie, Jane Street Family Papers; *U.S., Find A Grave Index, 1600s-Current* (database online), Provo, UT, Ancestry.com, 2012.

21. "Read Daughter's Name on List of Dead," *Indianapolis Journal*, January 3, 1904, p. 2.

22. "His Daughter Grace Not Victim of Fire," *Indianapolis Journal*, January 4, 1904, p. 2. Grace Tuttle went to Chicago on December 28, 1903, to study music.

23. *Terre Haute, Indiana, 1904 City Directory*, 562.

24. National Archives and Records Administration, Washington, DC (NARA) M233, Registers of Enlistments in the United States Army, 1798–1914, Roll MIUSA1798_102910, Roll No. 51, p. 78.

25. "Happy Hollow, aka: McLeod's Amusement Park." http://www.encyclopedia ofarkansas.net/encyclopedia/entry-detail.aspx?entryID=1206. The site of McLeod's Amusement Park was known as Happy Hollow before the park was created. African Americans living in the mountains around the 1870s ventured down to the springs to do their wash, and as they worked, they sang songs of praise. Because of the rejoicing that took place, the vale became known as Happy Hollow. Happy Hollow began as a picture studio for tourists who sent home postcards poking fun at themselves and Arkansas. Other famous visitors to the park included Billy Sunday, Carry Nation, and Al Capone. The amusement park complexes gradually developed from McLeod's vision. Today, all that remains are the Happy Hollow Springs on the southeast slope of North Mountain, and the Happy Hollow Motel has the "happy" distinction of preserving the name.

26. Mildred Morris, "Girl of 17, Forbidden to Wed Militia Lieutenant, Ends Life," *Denver Rocky Mountain News*, August 16, 1916, p. 3.

27. "Transport Egbert Arrives Off Port with Smallpox on Board," *San Francisco Call*, May 7, 1901, p. 7; NARA M233 p. 78. Herbert R. Bumpass (Jack Street) originally enlisted in Company G, Second Arkansas Infantry, in Brownsville, Arkansas, on February 2, 1899. See also NARA M871; Indexes to the Carded Records of Soldiers Who Served in Volunteer Organizations During the Spanish-American War, compiled 1899–1927, documenting the period 1898–1903, p. 1; Missouri Death Certificate #19418. Bumpass mustered in as a private from Searcy, Arkansas on May 29, 1899. "Second Arkansas Volunteer Infantry, Mustered In May 25, 1898, for Two Years; Mustered Out February 25, 1899, Company G," Report of the Adjutant General of the Arkansas State Guard, U.S., Adjutant General Military Records of Arkansas, 1631–1976, p. 91.

28. NARA M233, p. 78. A search in NARA records for Bumpass's criminal actions produced no other information.

29. Herbert Bumpass was born August 22, 1875, in Lonoke, Lonoke County, Arkansas, to Augustin and Virginia Kirk Bumpass. Missouri Death Certificate #19418. See *Hot Springs, Arkansas, 1903 City Directory*, 103.

30. Jack Street photo, undated, Leslie, Jane Street Family Papers. In Jack Street's final marriage to Winona Nicodemus Wright, he went by "Bear" and Winona was "Cat." Phil Wright, email to author, September 17, 2018. Wright is Jack Street's step-grandson.

31. Gertrude Riske (pseudonym for Jane Street), "A Lover's Prayer," Leslie, Jane Street Family Papers.

32. *Hot Springs, Arkansas, 1908 City Directory*, 137.

33. "Arkansas County Marriages, 1838–1957," Index, FamilySearch, Salt Lake City, Utah, 2009, 2011.

34. *Hot Springs, Arkansas, 1906 City Directory*, 131; Birth Record No. 98552, City of St. Louis, State of Missouri in Devlin Family Papers. Jane lived at 2634 Locust Street, St. Louis, Missouri.

35. 1910 Federal Census, Hot Springs Ward 6, Garland, Arkansas, Roll T624_50, Page 11A, Enumeration District 0069. Herbert Bumpass married Dollie in 1906, while he was simultaneously courting Jane Tuttle.

36. William Franz moved back with his mother. *Hot Springs, Arkansas, 1910 City Directory*, 145.

37. "Lieut. Street Pleads Not Guilty to Crime Charge Against Him," *Denver Post*, August 27, 1916, p. 21.

38. Birth Record No. 98552, City of St. Louis, State of Missouri, Leslie, Jane Street Family Papers. The baby is buried in an unmarked grave in Saints Peter and Paul Catholic Cemetery in St. Louis.

39. Missouri State Archives, Marriage Records, 127.

40. Registry of Births—City of St. Louis, 472.

41. Gertrude Riske (pseudonym for Jane Street), "To Her Husband," Leslie, Jane Street Family Papers.

42. Leslie, Jane Street Family Papers.

43. By late 1909, Herbert R. Bumpass would become part of a forgery case. See "Fortner's Case Continued," *Arkansas Gazette*, November 24, 1909, p. 1; "Bumpass Seeks Protection," *Arkansas Gazette*, December 21, 1909, p. 1; "Trial of Fortner Postponed Sixth Time," *Arkansas Gazette*, December 21, 1909, p. 1. In 1912 Herbert and his brother Robert H. were indicted for arson. See "Love Cult Secrets Told, Dr. Bumpass Acquitted," *Denver Post*, March 21, 1913, p. 5.

## *Chapter 2*

1. Hadar Laskey, "The Rise of Women in the Workforce in the 19th and 20th Century," https://historicalgeographiesofthecity581.wordpress.com/2017/10/30/the-rise-of-women-in-the-workforce-in-the-19th-and-20th-century/.

2. Kirk Harris was arrested for a backroom poker game in April 1913 at the Golden Eagle Hotel, where he was proprietor. "Seven Gamblers Confess Guilt," *Sacramento Bee*, April 22, 1913, p. 4.

3. California State Library, Sacramento, Great Register of Voters, 1900–1968, Accession No. 162169, vol. 1912–1914; "Golden Eagle Sold to Harris," *Sacramento Bee*, January 22, 1912, p. 3.

4. Kirk Harris sworn affidavit, State of California, May 13, 1922, Leslie, Jane Street Family Papers.

5. Ibid.

6. Ibid. The affidavit was later used to prove Jane Street's work history after she was arrested for criminal syndicalism. Jane retained the affidavit, perhaps fearing future arrests during the roundup of Industrial Workers of the World (IWW).

7. "Hotels Are Filled by Tourists," *Sacramento Bee*, March 29, 1912, p. 16.

8. Kirk Harris sworn affidavit.

9. California Voter Registration, Sacramento County, CA, 1912–1914.

10. Jane Street, from "Mommie, Mommie," n.d., Leslie, Jane Street Family Papers.

11. Philip S. Foner, *Women and the American Labor Movement* (New York: Free Press, 1979), 275.

12. Ibid.; Kim England and Kate Boyer, "Women's Work: The Feminization and Shifting Meanings of Clerical Work," *Journal of Social History* 43, no. 2 (Winter 2009): 312–13.

13. Foner, *Women and the American Labor Movement*, 275; England and Boyer, "Women's Work," 313.

14. See Laskey, "Rise of Women"; Roslyn L. Feldberg, "'Union Fever': Organizing Among Clerical Workers, 1900–1930," in *Workers' Struggles: Past and Present*, ed. James Green (Philadelphia: Temple University Press), 155.

15. Ruth Milkman, *On Gender, Labor, and Inequality* (Chicago: University of Illinois Press, 2016), 93. See Alice Kessler-Harris, "Where Are the Organized Women Workers," *Feminist Studies* 3, no. 112 (Fall 1975): 96–98, for further discussion.

16. E. H. Gamble affidavit, State of Missouri, draft copy, 1922, Leslie, Jane Street Family Papers.

17. Milkman, *On Gender*, 94.

18. Ibid., 95; Anne F. Mattina, "Corporate Tools and Time-Serving Slaves: Class and Gender in the Rhetoric of Antebellum Labor Reform," *Howard Journal of Communications* 7 (1996): 155.

19. James K. Bartram, "I Can't Speak: Social Control and the IWW Free Speech Movement" (master's thesis, California State University, 2018), 37.

20. Some believe that *Los Angeles Times* owner and editor Harrison Grey Otis is credited with first publishing the word "Wobbly," while others, such as IWW Mortimer Downing, reported that Chinese speakers said "I Wobbly Wobbly" instead of "IWW."

21. Flynn, *The Rebel Girl: An Autobiography*, 108–9.

22. "Shots Fired in the Textile Strike Rioting Today," *Sacramento Bee*, February 26, 1912, p. 8.

23. Foner, *Women and the American Labor Movement*, 429.

24. "Important Figure in Strike," *Sacramento Bee*, October 16, 1912, p. 6. The Lawrence Strike also became known as the Bread and Roses Strike, named after a political slogan introduced in 1911 by feminist leader Rose Schneiderman following the March 25, 1911, Triangle Shirtwaist Factory fire. In December 1911 James Oppenheim wrote a poem, "Bread and Roses," first published in the *American Magazine* with the attribution line "Bread for all, and Roses, too," a slogan of the women in the West. The poem immediately became a popular folk song. See Ardis Cameron, "Bread and Roses Revisited: Women's Culture and Working-Class Activism in the Lawrence Strike of 1912," in *Women, Work & Protest*, ed. Ruth Milkman (New York: Routledge, 1985), 43–46, for an analysis of the Lawrence Strike and the emergence of feminist labor leaders.

25. *Sacramento Bee*, January 25, 1913, p. 1.

26. "Hotel Workers Take Notice," *Solidarity*, February 14, 1914, p. 1; "IWW and the Hotel Workers," *Solidarity*, February 21, 1914, pp. 1, 4. Hotel and Restaurant Workers No. 112 formed in New York City by 1915. See "IWW History Project," University of Washington, http://depts.washington.edu/iww/.

27. "Hotel Workers Take Notice," 1.

28. "Unemployed Riot; Destroy Property," *Sacramento Bee*, March 5, 1914, p. 1; "Solving Unemployment in San Francisco, California," *Solidarity*, January 24, 1914, p. 1.

29. "Let California's Capital City Show Her Proper Spirit," *Sacramento Bee*, March 7, 1914, p. 2.

30. "Sacramento's Brutal Treatment of Hungry Army of Unemployed," *Solidarity*, March 21, 1914, pp. 1, 4; "Solving Unemployment in California," *Solidarity*, March 21, 1914, p. 4; "Unemployed Riot; Destroy Property," 1.

31. Melvyn Dubofsky, *We Shall Be All*, abridged ed. (Chicago: University of Illinois Press, 2000), 171. IWW attorney Austin Lewis is credited with the quote.

Both Ford and Suhr were indicted, convicted, and imprisoned. See "The Wheatland Riot and What Lay Back of It," *Solidarity*, April 21, 1914, p. 3, for the IWW's position.

32. Paul Frederick Brissenden, *The IWW: A Study of American Syndicalism* (New York: Columbia University, 1919), 331.

33. *Solidarity*, April 28, 1914, p. 2.

34. *Solidarity*, August 15, 1914, p. 4. Sacramento Local 71 ordered 350 copies of *Solidarity* weekly.

35. *Industrial Worker*, July 17, 1913, p. 2.

36. *Industrial Worker*, July 17, 1913, p. 2. Plaza Park is now named Cesar E. Chavez Memorial Park.

37. Charles Ashleigh, "Women Wage Workers and Woman Suffrage," *Solidarity*, April 14, 1914, p. 2.

38. John M. Foss, "'Hello Girls' in the West," *Solidarity*, May 9, 1914, p. 1. Foss was a member of the IWW General Executive Board in 1914.

39. *Solidarity*, April 11, 1914, p. 4.

40. *Proceedings of the Tenth Convention of the Industrial Workers of the World, Held at Chicago, Illinois, November 20 to December 1, 1916* (Chicago: Industrial Workers of the World, 1917), 134.

41. Nigel Sellars, *Oil, Wheat & Wobblies* (Norman: University of Oklahoma Press, 1998), 20. Frank Little was unsuccessful in his endeavors.

42. "Exposition and Hotels in Unity," *San Francisco Chronicle*, March 26, 1914, p. 5.

43. "'Dolores' Will Be Presented Here in Two Months and at 1915 Exposition," n.d., Leslie, Jane Street Family Papers. The Panama-Pacific International Exposition ran February 20 through December 4, 1915.

44. California Voter Registration, San Francisco County, CA, 1913.

45. A return address is written on the poem itself. Gertrude Risk, "A Lover's Prayer," n.d., Leslie, Jane Street Papers.

46. Jane Street, from "Office Workers," n.d., Leslie, Jane Street Papers.

47. California Voter Registration, San Francisco County, CA, 1913; California Voter Registration, Sacramento County, CA, 1912–1914.

48. California Voter Registration, Sacramento County, CA, 1912–1914.

49. "IWW History Project." Charles L. Lambert took the helm of Sacramento's Recruiting Union, Local No. 71, away from Andy Barber sometime in 1914, likely due to growing membership and the local's leadership in the Wheatland Hops strike defense of two men, Ford and Suhr. "I.W.W. Activities," Case #368973:68, Roll #810, Investigative Reports of the Bureau of Investigation 1908–1922, Old German Files (OGF), 1909–1921, FBI Case Files, National Archives Microfilm Publication M1085, NARA, Washington, DC.

50. "I.W.W. Activities," Case #368973:68. The card was discovered under or in Jane's mattress after her 1920 arrest.

51. Jane Street, "The People's Forum," *Sacramento Union*, July 11, 1914, p. 4.

52. Ibid.

53. Ibid.

54. Flynn, *The Rebel Girl: An Autobiography*, 191–93. See discussion of Joe Hill's case in Botkin, *Frank Little*, and Adler, *The Man Who Never Died*.

55. The "Rebel Girl" sheet music was published in 1915.

56. "Elizabeth Gurley Flynn Lectures," *Solidarity*, May 1, 1915, p. 4.

57. Elizabeth Gurley Flynn, "Women on the Picket Line," *Solidarity*, May 1, 1915, p. 4.

58. "Oakland News," *Solidarity*, June 19, 1915, p. 4.

59. Elizabeth Gurley Flynn, "The IWW Call to Women," *Solidarity*, July 31, 1915, p. 9.

60. "Composer Is Suicide; Body Guarded by Dog," *San Diego Union*, July 9, 1916, p. 2.

61. "Woman's Work—Other News and Views," *Solidarity*, February 27, 1915, p. 4.

62. Ibid.

63. Melvyn Dubofsky, *We Shall Be All*, 183–84. Twenty thousand members were reported to have joined the AWO in 1916.

### Chapter 3

1. Rosemary Fetter, "From Tragic to Scandalous, Tales Endure Ages," *Denver Post*, February 11, 2001, https://extras.denverpost.com/life/love0211.htm. See also Rosemary Fetter, *Colorado's Legendary Lovers* (Golden, CO: Fulcrum, 2004).

2. Leigh A. Grinstead, *Molly Brown's Capitol Hill Neighborhood* (Denver: Historic Denver, 2002), 72. Louise Hill unveiled the statue to announce the beginning of Denver's social season every year. Later the statue was sold to pay for the mansion's restoration. The actual address of the Hill mansion should have been 150 10th Street, but the state capitol was on Sherman, so the Hills moved the main entrance to 969 Sherman Street.

3. Ibid. Louise Hill ruled Denver's social scene until 1942.

4. Ella Miriam Sullivan, "Limousine at Last Wins Mrs. Hill Away from Spirited Span of Bays," *Denver Post*, October 22, 1916, p. 1.

5. "Information Concerning Denver's Most Superb and Charming Residence Addition, New Capitol Hill," New Capitol Hill Realty Co., Denver, 1900.

6. Phil Goodstein, *The Ghosts of Denver* (Denver: New Social Publications, 1996), 12.

7. "Information Concerning Denver's Most Superb and Charming Residence."

8. Ibid.

9. Ibid.

10. Grinstead, *Molly Brown's Capitol Hill Neighborhood*, 7. H. C. Brown, developer of Capitol Hill, later became the owner and builder of the Brown Palace. See Debra B. Faulkner, *Ladies of the Brown: A Woman's History of Denver's Most Elegant Hotel* (Charleston: History Press, 2010), 12–13.

11. About seventy-five miles northeast, a struggling prospector named John H. Gregory discovered a tremendous gold vein in a gulch that was to bear his name in 1859, establishing the rich Central City–Black Hawk mining district in Gilpin County, Colorado. For a history of this mining camp, see Caroline Bancroft, *Gulch of Gold: A History of Central City, Colorado* (Denver: Sage Books, 1958).

12. Charlotte A. Barbour, "Vanished Neighborhood on Capitol Hill, Denver," *Colorado Magazine* 37, no. 4 (October 1960): 254–61. Capitol Hill's politically connected residents included George W. Baxter, referred to as "Governor" because of his political experiences, including one month as Wyoming's territorial governor. Baxter escaped to Denver with his large family after extensive involvement in an infamous Wyoming invasion by hired henchmen and murders of small cattlemen, known as the Johnson County War. See also John W. Davis, *Wyoming Range War: The Infamous Invasion of Johnson County* (Norman: University of Oklahoma Press, 2010), 78, for the history of Baxter's involvement in the Johnson County War. Willard Teller, brother of Henry M. Teller, former United States secretary of the interior, was a powerful Central City lawyer. Charles J. Hughes served on the senate beginning in 1909. Colorado governor James H. Peabody, who rented the Whitehead mansion, lived on Capitol Hill during his tumultuous office term. He earned disdain primarily because of his decision to call in Colorado's National Guard to put down the 1904 Cripple Creek–Victor mining district strike. More than a hundred men died, and even more were injured and arrested or deported from Colorado. See Goodstein, *The Ghosts of Denver*, 76, 79.

13. Tom Noel and Barbara Norgren in *Denver: The City Beautiful* (Denver: Historic Colorado, 1993), 8, state that half of Denver's banks failed in 1893, and thousands of properties were sold to anyone able to pay the delinquent taxes. More than half of the 600 realtors in business in the 1893 city directory were out of business two years later. While 2,338 building permits had been granted in 1890, only 124 permits were issued in Denver in 1894.

14. The Swansea process, developed in Wales, involves mixing gold and silver ore with copper sulfide ore. Since the copper matte acts as a vehicle to hold the gold and silver, larger quantities of the ore could be recovered.

15. *Representative Women of Colorado* (Denver: Alexander Art, 1911), 15. Alice Hale Hill came to Colorado in 1868 and immediately became the center of hospitality in Gilpin County, where her husband's smelter was located. In 1878 Hill moved to Denver, where she became a charter member of the Denver Women's Club. She served eight years as the YWCA president, raising a large part of money for the institution's site and construction. Alice died in 1908.

16. Louise Bethel Sneed Hill was born March 28, 1862. She deducted three years from her age in the 1900 federal census. *U.S., Find A Grave Index, 1600s–Current* (database online), Provo, UT, Ancestry.com, 2012. See also 1900 United States Federal Census, Denver, Arapahoe, Colorado, Roll 119, Page 4A, Enumeration District 0067. William Morgan Sneed's estate was estimated to be

about $64,000 in 1860. See 1860 Slave Schedule, Wm M. Smid (Wm. M. Sneed), Nutbush, Granville, North Carolina, accessed December 13, 2018, https://wc .rootsweb.com/cgi-bin/igm.cgi?op=GET&db=dwilliams%2D1&id=I27; Samuel Thomas Peace, "Zeb's Black Baby," *Vance County, North Carolina: A Short History* (Henderson, NC: Seeman Printery, 1955), 216. Sneed died in 1892. See https:// www.findagrave.com/memorial/49497665.

17. William Morgan Sneed was of slight physical stature with unusually small feet in which he reportedly took great pride. He became clerk of the county court and an officer in the Civil War. At the close of the Civil War, the county was in chaos, and lawlessness was at a high. When Mr. James Madison Bullock's slain body was found alongside a Granville road, distinct footprints of a small man were found near the body. Initially, the crime was assumed to have been committed by a traveling vagrant or recently freed slave, but eventually suspicion was placed on Sneed, who had begun courting Bullock's widow. Sneed, who was known to have been infatuated with James's wife Sarah, married her within weeks of the murder. Because of Sneed's prominence in the community, suspicions were discussed quietly, and with a subsequent cover-up of the crime, the law never acted. Months later, William was seen in public wearing a watch similar to one imported from Europe by the deceased James Bullock. The marriage was received coolly by Granville Society. Peace, "Zeb's Black Baby," 216.

18. "Hill-Sneed Nuptials," *Denver Rocky Mountain News*, January 16, 1895, p. 1. Louise and Crawford Hill were both thirty-three years old when they married, with Louise the elder.

19. Fetter, "From Tragic to Scandalous." Louise Sneed Hill changed her birth year at first to portray herself younger than her husband. Afterward, with Louise's input, most governmental documents report various birth years, some as many as eight years later than her actual birth year.

20. See Ellis Meredith, "Women Citizens of Colorado," *The Great Divide*, February 1894, Meredith Collection MSS.427, Carton 2, Stephen H. Hart Library and Research Center (SHL), for a brief overview of Colorado's suffrage movement one year after its success. Ms. Meredith was a prominent leader in the Colorado Women's Suffrage Association. Also see *Strong Sisters: Elected Women of Colorado*, Documentary, Directed by Laura Hoeppne and Meg Froelich, StrongSisters .org, 2016, http://www.strongsisters.org/ and https://www.youtube.com/watch?v =kgtaICe0Wvg&feature=youtu.be.

21. *Strong Sisters: Elected Women of Colorado.* Three women were elected: Clara Cressingham, Carrie C. Holly, and Frances Klock.

22. Colorado state senator Nancy Todd in *Strong Sisters: Elected Women of Colorado.*

23. Mildred Morris, "Mrs. Hill Discusses Politicians, She's Delegate Now and Glad," *Denver Rocky Mountain News*, August 10, 1916, p. 7.

24. Frances Wayne, "Training for Women as Nation's Reserves Shown in Germany," *Denver Post*, January 26, 1916, p. 10.

25. "Mrs. Verner Z. Reed Hailed Society's Queen, Contests Leadership of Mrs. Crawford Hill," *Denver Rocky Mountain News*, August 4, 1913, p. 1.

26. "Law and Order League Women Offer Sympathy," 9.

27. "Bancroft Correspondence," Crawford and Louise Sneed Hill Collection, MSS.309, Carton 6, FF66, File 1, SHL.

28. Louise S. Hill to Mrs. Claude K. Boettcher, July 27, 1937, and August 17, 1935, Crawford and Louise Sneed Hill Collection, MSS.309, Carton 6, FF90, SHL; Louise S. Hill to Mrs. Robert Chase, August 17, 1932, Crawford and Louise Sneed Hill Collection, MSS.309, Carton 6, FF121, File 23, SHL.

29. Louise S. Hill to Mrs. Grace Cabot, April 13, 1935, Crawford and Louise Sneed Hill Collection, MSS.309, Carton 6, FF112, File 23, SHL. Louise S. Hill to Mrs. Robert Chase. A sample of Louise Hill's calendar can be found in "Frederick G. Bonfils," Crawford and Louise Sneed Hill Collection, MSS.309, Carton 6, FF94, File 15, SHL. A review of all Hill correspondence in MSS.309, Carton 6, reveals a universal dictated response to friends and acquaintances alike.

30. Louise S. Hill to Mrs. N. P. Hill (Elinor), January 4, 1928, Crawford and Louise Sneed Hill Collection, MSS.309, Carton 7, FF316, File 1, SHL.

31. "Molly Brown, the Sacred 36 and Louise Hill," *Denver Post*, April 10, 2012, http://blogs.denverpost.com/library/2012/04/10/molly-brown-sacred-36-louise-hill/1016/.

32. Faulkner, *Ladies of the Brown*, 45; "Sacred Thirty-Six: Notes," Caroline Bancroft Collection, Western History Collection, Series 2, Box 12, File 45, Denver Public Library (DPL). The name "Sacred Thirty-Six" was adopted in 1902.

33. "Sacred Thirty-Six: Notes." See also Grinstead, *Molly Brown's Capitol Hill Neighborhood*, 78. Alice Hill created the first social directory.

34. "Sacred Thirty-Six: Notes."

35. Ibid.

36. Fetter, "From Tragic to Scandalous." Of note, Margaret Brown ran for a Colorado state office in 1910. She lost.

37. "High Society and the Mining Hall of Fame," *Colorado Central Magazine*, September 1, 2005, https://coloradocentralmagazine.com/high-society-and-the-mining-hall-of-fame/. Of note, Denver's millionaire Capitol Hill speculator Dennis Sheedy was Irish.

38. Tom Morton, "Louise Sneed Hill and Denver's 'Sacred Thirty-Six,'" Fairmount Foundation, April 23, 2013, http://fairmountheritagefoundation.org/louise-sneed-hill-and-denvers-sacred-thirty-six/.

39. "Denver Diary," *Contemporary* insert, *Denver Post*, April 15, 1962, p. 5.

40. Fetter, *Colorado's Legendary Lovers*.

41. "Bancroft Correspondence." Letters and cards within this collection illustrate the relationship between Louise S. Hill and Caroline Bancroft, Hill becoming Bancroft's patron by the 1930s. Both women delivered gifts of compliments, flowers, and promises of social introductions to each other. Later Bancroft

became a member of the Sacred Thirty-Six, in part for her journalism and her prominent ancestry.

42. Barbour, "Vanished Neighborhood," 264. Data came from homes owned by the Bergers, Fullertons, Newtons, Baxters, Hughes, Boettchers, Tellers, and Woods families.

43. 1910 United States Federal Census, Denver Ward 10, Denver, Colorado, Roll T624_116, Page 5A, Enumeration District 0126.

44. "Work in Denver Is Called to the Attention of all Citizens of State," *Denver Rocky Mountain News*, January 30, 1916, p. 29.

## *Chapter 4*

1. "Storage Eggs Purchased for Society's Servants, Cook Served Ancient 'Hen Fruit' to Family," *Denver Rocky Mountain News*, March 27, 1916, p. 3; "Rich Women's Ears Burn When Housemaids' Union Prepares Blacklist," *Denver Post*, March 27, 1916, p. 4; "How a Cold Storage Egg Started the Servant Girls Union," *Washington Post*, September 24, 1916, p. 8.

2. "Rich Women's Ears Burn," 1.

3. "Housemaids' Union Will Train Model Mistresses in Denver," *Denver Post*, March 20, 1916, p. 4.

4. "Storage Eggs Purchased for Society's Servants," 3.

5. "Rich Women's Ears Burn," 1.

6. Ibid., 1, 4.

7. "Society Women's Ears Tingle as Maids' Union Fixes Blacklist," *Denver Post*, March 27, 1916, p. 4.

8. Ibid.

9. Ibid.

10. "Rich Women's Ears Burn," 1.

11. William D. Haywood, "How to Organize," *Solidarity*, April 21, 1916, p. 1.

12. Morris, "Girl of 17, Forbidden to Wed," 3.

13. "Mrs. Mary Ann Tuttle Found Dead," Leslie, Jane Street Family Papers. The obituary names Grace Franz instead of Grace Tuttle. Mary Ann was found dead in her home. See also Arkansas Death Index, 1914–1923.

14. Grace is a music teacher living at 1128 Acoma, Denver, Colorado. *1916 Denver City Directory*, 1756. This building still stands (2018) near Denver's Civic Center and Public Library.

15. Jane Street to Mrs. Elmer S. Bruse, 1917, NARA, Department of Justice, Record Group 60, File 18701–28, https://archive.iww.org/history/library/Street /letter/. The letter was discovered in the National Archives in 1976, where it had been stored after having been intercepted by the Bureau of Investigation. Mrs. Bruse, an Oklahoma IWW organizer, never received the letter. This letter is rich with detail describing Jane Street's efforts to organize and maintain DWIU Local 113 and combat virile syndicalism.

16. Street to Mrs. Elmer S. Bruse.

17. Ibid.

18. Frances Wayne, "Housewives' Assembly Decided on Golden Rule as Best Way to Treat New Housemaid Union," *Denver Post*, March 26, 1916, p. 10.

19. Street to Mrs. Elmer S. Bruse.

20. "Housemaids' Union Will Train," 4.

21. Phyllis Palmer, *Domesticity and Dirt* (Philadelphia: Temple University Press, 1989), 146–47.

22. Ibid., 147.

23. Ibid.

24. Street to Mrs. Elmer S. Bruse.

25. Ibid.; "Housemaids' Union Will Train," 4.

26. "Housemaids' Union Opens War to Train Society Women of Denver to Know Their Place," *Denver Post*, March 20, 1916, p. 1.

27. Ibid.

28. Ibid.

29. Ibid.

30. Frances Wayne, "Housewives' Assembly Decided on Golden Rule as Best Way to Treat New Housemaid Union," *Denver Post*, March 26, 1916, p. 10. The women's eight-hour workday law, also known as the "Laundry Girls Law," passed overwhelmingly in 1912. It stated that employment of females in any and all manufacturing, mechanical, and mercantile establishments, and laundries, hotels, and restaurants for more than eight hours during any twenty-four hours of one calendar day would be illegal. House servants were the exception. Helen Ring Robinson, the first woman elected to the Colorado state senate, helped pass the bill. "Here in Brief Are Proposed Laws on Which You Are to Vote at the November Election," *Denver Post*, October 20, 1912, p. 7; "Twelve Amendments Carry; Women's and Miners' Bills Obtain Greatest Majorities," *Denver Rocky Mountain News*, November 10, 1912, p. 8.

31. Wayne, "Housewives' Assembly Decides on Golden Rule," 10.

32. "Housemaids' Union Opens War," 1, 4; "Storage Eggs Purchased for Society's Servants," 3.

33. "Housemaids' Union Will Train," 4.

34. "Housemaids' Union Opens War," 1.

35. Passport Applications, January 2, 1906–March 31, 1925, Roll 2103, Vol. 2103, Certificates 219976–220349, September 20–21, 1922, NARA, Washington, DC.

36. Frances Wayne, "Member of Household of Mrs. Crawford Hill Paid Honor at Funeral," *Denver Post*, May 4, 1930.

37. Otto Liese to Nathaniel Hill, May 3, 1930, Cora Cowan Estate, MSS.309, Carton 12, File 1, Crawford and Louise S. Hill Collection, SHL.

38. Robert Huysman, Huysman Family Papers; James O'Hare, email to author, January 16, 2016.

39. Robert Huysman, Huysman Family Papers; James O'Hare, email to author, January 16, 2016; *1887 Dayton, Ohio, City Directory*, 161.

40. 1900 U.S. Federal Census, Chicago Ward 4, Cook, Illinois, Roll 248, Family History Film 1240248, p. 12A, Enumeration District 0094.

41. Wayne, "Member of Household"; New York, Passenger Lists, 1820–1957, Year 1904, Arrival New York, New York, Microfilm Serial T715, 1897–1957, Microfilm Roll 0497, Line 7, Page 148; James O'Hare, email to author, January 16, 2016.

42. Mark O'Hare, email to author, January 16, 2016. Mark is the grandson of Ethel Bertling O'Hare, Cora Cowan's niece. James O'Hare, Mark's father, told a story about how Samuel Clemens, a guest next door to the Hills, walked over to visit them at their home without a coat. Someone mentioned that Clemens was not properly attired for a visit. After the visit, Clemens sent a coat to the Hill home, asking that it be draped over a chair so he could fulfill his social obligations whenever he visited.

43. "Fine of $300 of Mrs. Crawford Hill for Smuggling Gowns," *Denver Rocky Mountain News*, June 24, 1913, pp. 1, 7.

44. "Fine of $300 of Mrs. Crawford Hill," 1; "Mrs. Crawford Hill Fined $300 on Charge of Smuggling Gowns," *Denver Post*, June 24, 1914, p. 1.

45. Wayne, "Member of Household."

46. Frederick Bonfils Biography, BMSS.1664, SHL.

47. John Moore, "Extra, Extra! A Look Back at Denver's Own 'Newsies' Past," March 16, 2016, https://www.denvercenter.org/news-center/extra-extra-a-look -back-at-denvers-own-newsies-past/. The *Rocky Mountain News*, founded in 1859, published its last edition on February 27, 2009, partly because of losses incurred while trying to compete with the *Denver Post*, still in publication (2019).

48. Moore, "Extra, Extra!"; "The *Rocky Mountain News* at the Denver Public Library," https://history.denverlibrary.org/rocky-mountain-news-denver-public -library.

49. David Wallechinsky and Irving Wallace, quoted in "History of Newspapers: The *Denver Post*," https://www.trivia-library.com/a/history-of-newspapers -the-denver-post.htm.

50. "Fine of $300 of Mrs. Crawford Hill," 1, 7; "Mrs. Crawford Hill Fined $300," 1. The *Post* published opinions of Sacred Thirty-Six members who refused to believe that eastern dispatches were true, citing confusion in names or the incident itself. One person is quoted, "She has too much money to take a chance of being arrested on a smuggling charge just to save a few dollars."

51. Louise S. Hill to Mr. Frederick G. Bonfils, October 29, 1931, Crawford and Louise Sneed Hill Collection, MSS.309, Carton 6, FF94, File 13, SHL.

52. "Storage Eggs Purchased for Society's Servants," 3.

53. "Society Women's Ears Tingle," 4.

54. Ibid.; "Storage Eggs Purchased for Society's Servants," 3.

55. "House Maids Union Has Blown Up on Shoal of Debts," *Denver Post*, July 26, 1916, p. 4.

## Chapter 5

1. The residence, still standing (2019), is 1401 North Gilpin, Denver, Colorado. See 1910 and 1920 *Denver City Directories*. Frances Wayne, "Housewives' Assembly Decided on Golden Rule as Best Way to Treat New Housemaid Union," *Denver Post*, March 26, 1916, p. 10.

2. "Ms. Campbell, Aristocrat of Colorado, Dies," *Denver Post*, August 7, 1937, p. 2.

3. *Representative Women of Colorado*, 123.

4. "The National Society of the Colonial Dames of America in the State of Colorado," 1916, Title Page, National Society of the Colonial Dames of America in the State of Colorado Collection, 1896–1990, MMS.1580, FF36, SHL.

5. "Law and Order League Women Offer Sympathy," 9. See "To the Historian of the National Society of the Colonial Dames of America, Report of the Colonial Dames in the State of Colorado, from 1914–1916," National Society of the Colonial Dames of America in the State of Colorado Collection, 1896–1990, MMS.1580, FF135, SHL.

6. "Law and Order League Women Offer Sympathy," 9.

7. Mabel Mann Runnette, *A History of the Monday Literary Club, 1881–1939*, vol. 1 (January 1939), 48, SHL.

8. Ibid.

9. All information on the women of the Housewives' Assembly taken from *Representative Women of Colorado*, and the 1900, 1910, and 1920 Federal Censuses, Denver, Colorado.

10. *Representative Women of Colorado*, 135.

11. 1900 Federal Census, Eau Claire Ward 3, Eau Claire, Wisconsin, Page 8, Enumeration District 0025.

12. 1900 Federal Census, Denver, Arapahoe, Colorado, Page 3, Enumeration District 0077; 1920 Federal Census, Denver, Denver, Colorado, Roll T625_162, Page 9B, Enumeration District 237.

13. Wayne, "Housewives' Assembly Decided on Golden Rule," 10.

14. Dick Kreck, "She Covered Addiction, Immigration, Health, Abused Women, and Orphaned Children—A Century Ago," *Denver Post*, October 15, 2017, https://www.denverpost.com/2017/10/15/frances-pinky-wayne-denver-post/. Wayne had joined the *Denver Post* in 1909 after a short stint at the *Denver Rocky Mountain News* from 1906 to 1909. Wayne left the *Post* in 1946.

15. Ibid.

16. Rosemary Fetter, "Colorado History: How Denver Became the Christmas Capital of the World," *Colorado Gambler*, December 18, 2013. Frances Wayne was the daughter of Judge James B. Belford, a United States congressman, and Frances McEwen Belford.

17. Kreck, "She Covered Addiction."

18. Ibid.

19. Wayne, "Housewives' Assembly Decided on Golden Rule," 10.

20. Ibid.

21. Ibid.

22. Ibid.

23. Ibid.

24. Ibid.

25. C. W. Sellers, "The Domestic Workers' Union," *Solidarity*, May 13, 1916, p. 2.

26. "How a Cold Storage Egg Started the Servant Girls Union," 8.

27. Wayne, "Housewives' Assembly Decided on Golden Rule," 10.

28. "How a Cold Storage Egg Started the Servant Girls Union."

29. See Bancroft, *Gulch of Gold*, 11, 14–42, for a narrative of John H. Gregory's gold discovery.

30. George G. Suggs, *Colorado's War on Militant Unionism: James H. Peabody and the Western Federation of Miners* (Norman: University of Oklahoma Press, 1991), 152. See also Botkin, *Frank Little*, 55, for discussion of ethnicity and class in Colorado's Cripple Creek mining district, a WFM union camp.

31. Katie Klocksin, "Tensions and Torches after the Great Chicago Fire," WBEZ 91.5 Chicago, https://www.wbez.org/shows/curious-city/tensions-and-torches-after-the-great-chicago-fire/23056033-9387-4d4b-a398-ab0431419279. Historians examine how the decision to rebuild Chicago in a new fire limits zone affected ethnic areas and a strong community spirit.

32. Ibid. See also "Chicago Fire of 1871," *History*, https://www.history.com/topics/19th-century/great-chicago-fire. For an eyewitness description of the Chicago Fire, see "The Chicago Fire," *Daily Rocky Mountain News*, October 14, 1871, p. 1.

33. "A Suggestion," *Daily Rocky Mountain News*, October 11, 1871, p. 1.

34. Ibid.

35. "The Servant Girl Question," *Daily Rocky Mountain News*, October 12, 1871, p. 2.

36. Ibid.

37. "The Servant Girl Matter," *Daily Rocky Mountain News*, October 13, 1871, p. 1.

38. Ibid.

39. Ibid.

40. "Wailings from a 'Wictim,'" *Daily Rocky Mountain News*, October 15, 1871, p. 1.

41. Ibid.

42. Ibid.

43. "A Servant Girl's Defense," *Daily Rocky Mountain News*, October 17, 1871, p. 1.

44. Ibid.

45. Donna L. Van Raaphorst, *Union Maids Not Wanted: Organizing Domestic Workers, 1870–1940* (New York: Praeger, 1988), 23. Irish in America came in large numbers after the potato famine began in 1845. Between 1851 and 1892, arrivals averaged between 50,000 and 75,000 per year. Almost half of these immigrants, 49 percent in the 1800s, were women classified as unskilled workers.

46. 1910 Federal Census, Denver Ward 15, Denver, Colorado, Roll T624_118, Page 1A, Enumeration District 0191.

47. Van Raaphorst, *Union Maids Not Wanted*, 32. The author's Scandinavian and orphaned grandmother, Louise Peterson Little, was employed as a housemaid in a Boulder, Colorado, mansion in 1916.

48. 1900 Federal Census, Denver, Arapahoe, Colorado, Page 13, Enumeration District 0083.

49. Rosalyn Terborg-Oenn, "Survival Strategies Among African-American Women," in *Women, Work & Protest*, ed. Ruth Milkman (New York: Routledge, 1985), 140–41.

50. 1910 Federal Census, Shreveport Ward 1, Caddo, Louisiana, Roll T624_510, Page 4B, Enumeration District 0036.

51. 1910 Federal Census, Denver Ward 14, Denver, Colorado, Roll T624_117, Page 4B, Enumeration District 0180.

52. "A Six-Day Week," *Denver Rocky Mountain News*, November 2, 1901, p. 5. The Housemaids' Union of Denver organized with sixty charter members. See also *Denver Rocky Mountain News*, November 1, 1901, p. 3.

53. "Labor Leaders are in Session," *Denver Rocky Mountain News*, November 7, 1901, p. 6.

54. For an analysis of the first Housemaids' Union of Denver, see David Kirkpatrick, "Jane Street and Denver's Rebel Housemaids: The Gender of Radicalism in the Industrial Workers of the World" (master's thesis, Princeton University, 1992), 17. Kirkpatrick is the only journalist-historian to have previously delved into Jane Street's housemaid rebellion.

55. *Rocky Mountain News*, January 20, 1916, p. 5.

56. "Three Plays Written in Denver Make Big Hits at Women's Club," 1911, Denver Women's Club Collection MSS.1059, Box 1, FF128, SHL.

57. "In the World of Books," *Colorado Springs Gazette*, June 18, 1916, p. 4.

58. L. Elizabeth Moyer, "The Perfect Servant Girl," *Denver Rocky Mountain News*, July 6, 1902, p. 42.

59. "Study Class," *Colorado Springs Gazette*, October 8, 1916, p. 22.

60. "Teagowns Again Become Fashionable through Revival of Afternoon Teas," *Denver Rocky Mountain News*, October 5, 1902, p. 2.

61. Ibid.

62. "Boy Scouts as Nurse Maids, England's Plan," *Colorado Springs Gazette*, March 19, 1916, p. 7.

63. Wayne, "Housewives' Assembly Decided on Golden Rule," 10.

64. Ibid.

65. "How a Cold Storage Egg Started the Servant Girls Union." The quote is clearly Louise Hill's, as shown in the later story.

66. "Preamble to the IWW Constitution."

### *Chapter 6*

1. "Denver House Maids Join IWW," *Solidarity*, April 22, 1916, p. 1, reprinted from *Denver Times*, April 10, 1916.

2. "I.W.W. Activities," Case #368973:7, Roll #810, Investigative Reports of the Bureau of Investigation 1908–1922, OGF, 1909–1921, FBI Case Files, National Archives Microfilm Publication M1085, NARA, Washington, DC.

3. World War I Selective Service System Draft Registration Cards, 1917–1918, Denver County, Colorado, September 12, 1918, National Archives Microfilm Publication, Roll #1561844, NARA, Washington, DC; "Various," Case #373702:1, Roll No. 821, Investigative Reports of the Bureau of Investigation 1908–1922 (OGF), 1909–1921, FBI Case Files, National Archives Microfilm Publication M1085, NARA, Washington, DC.

4. "Various," Case #373702:10,12.

5. Ibid., 12, 17. Claude Sellers lived with his father, Jackson Sellers, next door to his brother Leroy Sellers, in Ozawakee, Kansas, in 1915. Kansas State Census Collection, 1855–1925, Kansas State Historical Society, Topeka, Kansas, Roll ks1915_110, Line 22.

6. "I.W.W. Activities," Case #368973:7.

7. From 1896 until 1900, Claude Sellers worked as a stenographer. See *1896 Leavenworth City Directory*, 106, and *1898 Leavenworth City Directory*, 222. In 1900 Sellers worked as a hotel clerk, still living in his parents' home. 1900 United States Federal Census, Leavenworth Ward 3, Leavenworth, Kansas, Roll 486, Page 12A, Enumeration District 0094, FHL microfilm 1240486. Sellers is reported to have installed an engine and dynamo on a farm in Jewell City, Kansas, in 1907. *Topeka State Journal*, April 20, 1907, p. 9.

8. "Various," Case #373702:10; 1940 United States Federal Census, Denver, Denver, Colorado, Roll T627_484, Page 8A, Enumeration District 16-11.

9. "I.W.W. Activities," Case #368973:7; "Various," Case #373702:10.

10. "Various," Case #8000–291596:15–16, #709, Investigative Reports of the Bureau of Investigation 1908–1922, OGF, 1909–1921, FBI Case Files, National Archives Microfilm Publication M1085, NARA, Washington, DC; "Various," Case #373702:17; *Anaconda Standard*, June 8, 1919, p. 5.

11. "Charge He Stole Woman's Overcoat," *Seattle Star*, June 28, 1919, p. 10.

12. "Fire at Tacoma Prison," *Seattle Star*, June 1, 1920, p. 1.

13. "Various," Case #373702:10. The Bureau of Investigation agent's report was dated October 1920. Sellers actually left Denver after September 1918 after registering for the draft. "Various," #373702:12, 21–23; World War I Selective

Service System Draft Registration Cards, 1917–1918, Denver County, Colorado, September 12, 1918, National Archives Microfilm Publication, Roll #1561844, NARA, Washington, DC.

14. "Various," Case #373702:10.

15. "I.W.W. Activities," Case #368973:20.

16. "Various," Case #373702:10, The Bureau of Investigation (BOI), founded in 1908, would later change its name to the Federal Bureau of Investigation (FBI).

17. Ibid., 16.

18. "IWW History Project," University of Washington, http://depts.washington .edu/iww/map_locals.shtml. Of the five Denver IWW locals organized before 1916, only three were for specific trades. For the Denver free speech fight, see Philip Foner, *Fellow Workers and Friends: IWW Free-Speech Fights as Told by Participants* (Westport, CT: Greenwood Press, 1981), 145–56. See also "Nineteen IWW Men Jailed in Denver," *Industrial Worker*, February 13, 1913, p. 1; "Recruits Needed for Denver Fight," *Industrial Worker*, March 6, 1913, p. 1. Peter Murray was the secretary-treasurer of Local 26 at the time.

19. "Denver House Maids Join IWW," 1.

20. "Housemaids' List Is Increased—60 Attend Meeting of Union," *Denver Rocky Mountain News*, April 17, 1916, p. 7.

21. "Denver House Maids Join IWW," 1.

22. Ibid.

23. "There's Trouble a-Brewing Between Mistress and the Cook, Bridget Says 'Look Out' While Madam Cries 'the Very Idea!'" *Denver Rocky Mountain News*, April 13, 1916, p. 6.

24. "There's Trouble a-Brewing," 6.

25. Ibid.

26. Want-Ad Section, *Denver Post*, April 16, 1916, col. 4, 2.

27. "To IWW's Everywhere," *Solidarity*, April 22, 1916, p. 4.

28. "Housemaids' List Is Increased—60 Attend Meeting of Union," *Denver Rocky Mountain News*, April 17, 1916, p. 7.

29. Ibid.

30. "To All IWW Locals, Take Notice!" *Solidarity*, April 15, 1916, p. 4. A *scab* is an individual who crosses strike lines to work.

31. "Housemaids' List Is Increased—60 Attend Meeting of Union," *Denver Rocky Mountain News*, April 17, 1916, p. 7.

32. "Denver House Maids Join IWW," 1.

33. Ibid.

34. Other IWW strike leaders included Joseph Ettor and Arturo Giovanitti, both arrested and charged with inciting a riot three miles away, leading to loss of life. They were acquitted in November 1912. See Elizabeth Gurley Flynn's account of their trial in *The Rebel Girl: An Autobiography*, 146–51.

35. Ibid., 137–38. A second group of children was prevented from exiting Lawrence when troopers surrounded the railroad station, clubbing parents and

children alike. This vicious act drew general American interest to the actions of the troops and police in Lawrence.

36. See Jane Addams Hull House, https://janeaddamshullhouse.org.

37. Louise W. Knight, *Spirit in Action* (New York: W. W. Norton & Company, 2010), 23. See Jane Addams's war on garbage collection in a female sphere in Jean Bethke Elshtain, *Jane Addams and the Dream of American Democracy* (New York: Basic Books, 2002), 169.

38. Robin K. Berson, *Jane Addams: A Biography* (Westport, CT: Greenwood Press, 2004), 102. Patricia Daniels, "Jane Addams, Social Reformer and Founder of Hull House," https://www.thoughtco.com/jane-addams-1779818.

39. Jane Addams, *Twenty Years at Hull-House* (Chicago: Addams Publications, 2011).

40. Knight, *Spirit in Action*, 246–47. DAR canceled Addams's membership in 1928 because of Addams's pacifist views. Not all DAR women agreed with the move, thoughtfully supporting Addams's "peace issues as well as with their own revolutionary heritage" through a committee of protest. See Berson, *Jane Addams*, 106.

41. "Colonial Dames of America Board Members," April 18, 1916, Colonial Dames of Colorado Collection, MSS.1580, File 135, p. 63, SHL; "Colonial Dames of America Board Members," October 17, 1916, Colonial Dames of Colorado Collection, MSS.1580, File 135, p. 69, SHL; "Colonial Dames of Colorado General Meetings," March 14, 1916, Colonial Dames of Colorado Collection, MSS.1580, File 136, p. 23, SHL.

42. "Colonial Dames of America Board Members," October 17, 1916, Colonial Dames of Colorado Collection, MSS.1580, File 135, pp. 71, 73, SHL.

43. "Historian," *Semi-Annual Report of the Colonial Dames of Colorado*, June 7, 1916, Colonial Dames of Colorado Collection, MSS.1580, File 55, p. 2, SHL.

44. "Mrs. Grenfell to Tell Wilson Ludlow Story," *Denver Rocky Mountain News*, May 22, 1914, p. 7.

45. "Awful Story from Ludlow, Jane Addams Weeps over Story Told by Refugees—Is Like Tale from Balkans," *Riverside Daily Press*, May 19, 1914, p. 1.

46. Ibid.

47. "Order League Backs Strike," *Denver Rocky Mountain News*, May 29, 1914, p. 14.

48. "Housemaids Ask Butlers to Aid," *Denver Rocky Mountain News*, April 24, 1916, p. 10.

49. Ibid.; "Mrs. Grenfell to Tell Wilson Ludlow Story," 7.

50. "Housemaids Ask Butlers to Aid," 10.

### Chapter 7

1. "I.W.W. Activities," Case #368973:9. Calenal Sellers wrote Jane Street from Butte, Montana, on July 22, 1919, giving his views about children and the IWW.

The Bureau of Investigation opened the letter, copied and resealed it, and placed it back in the mail.

2. Charles Devlin to Mary Jane Devlin, November 1938, Jack and Kathy Devlin, Devlin Family Papers.

3. "Bumper Crops Certain throughout Colorado as Result of Storm," *Denver Rocky Mountain News*, May 1, 1916, p. 5.

4. Frances Wayne, "Women Must Keep City from Clutches of Speer Vice Rings, Says Mrs. Costigan," *Denver Post*, May 1, 1916, p. 1. Known as "Boss Speer," Republican Robert Speer was reelected as Denver's mayor for a third term in office in 1916. He had a past history of assigning patronage jobs as he built his political base as well as collecting graft from Denver's red-light district on Market Street. Yet he set out to make Denver a "City Beautiful," doubling the city's park spaces, paving streets, planting trees, and generally cleaning up the city. Mabel's lawyer-husband, Edward Prentiss Costigan, was a recently turned Democrat who had represented the UMWA at the conclusion of Colorado's coal wars. The couple was intimately involved with both local and national politics. The Costigans moved to Washington, D.C., in 1917, to serve under Woodrow Wilson, after E. P. Costigan's appointment to the United States Tariff Commission.

5. Wayne, "Women Must Keep City from Clutches," 1.

6. Flynn, *The Rebel Girl: An Autobiography*, 114.

7. Archie Green, David Roediger, Franklin Rosemont, and Salvatore Salerno, eds., *The Big Red Songbook* (Oakland: PM Press, 2016), 16.

8. Charles Devlin, "Denver Booms Once More," *Solidarity*, August 12, 1916, p. 4.

9. "The Maids' Defiance," in *The Big Red Songbook*, 297.

10. Devlin, "Denver Booms Once More," 4.

11. C. W. Sellers, "The Domestic Workers' Union," *Solidarity*, May 6, 1916, p. 2.

12. Street to Mrs. Elmer S. Bruse.

13. Ibid.

14. Ibid.

15. "IWW Street Meeting Interrupted by Police," *Denver Rocky Mountain News*, July 22, 1916, p. 3.

16. *Proceedings of the Tenth Convention*, 35; "I.W.W. Activities," Case #368973:37–38.

17. Leslie, personal interview, September 28, 2018. After Jane Street's death, Guy, her grandson, discovered hundreds of daily snippets and, finding them so personal, destroyed the notes.

18. Ibid.

19. Ibid.

20. Ibid.

21. Sellers, "The Domestic Workers' Union," 2.

22. Ibid.

23. Ibid.

24. Ibid.

25. Ibid.

26. Ibid.

27. Ibid.

28. Ibid.

29. Ibid.

30. "I.W.W. Activities," Case #368973:9. This incident is chronicled in a July 22, 1919, letter that Calenal Sellers wrote Jane Street from Butte, Montana. The Bureau of Investigation opened the letter, copied and resealed it, and placed it back in the mail.

31. Ibid.

32. Ibid.

### *Chapter 8*

1. Devlin to Mary Jane Devlin, ca. November 1938.

2. Ibid.

3. Ibid.

4. Ibid.

5. Kirkpatrick, "Jane Street and Denver's Rebel Housemaids," 26; Street to Mrs. Elmer S. Bruse.

6. *International Socialist Review*, November 1914, p. 319. It should be noted that Philip S. Foner in *Fellow Workers and Friends: IWW Free-Speech Fights as Told by Participants* does not discuss either of these two free speech fights. Devlin claims to have been in numerous strikes and riots while in the IWW. Devlin to Mary Jane Devlin, ca. November 1938.

7. For a description of the Adam Forepaugh and Sells Brothers Circus event in Washington, D.C., see "Circus in Town, Little Ones Happy," *Washington Times*, May 1, 1902, p. 9.

8. The Adam Forepaugh and Sells Brothers America's Greatest Shows Consolidated—Kilpatrick's famous ride, ca. 1900, Buffalo: Courier Litho Co. Photograph, https://loc.gov/item/97502487/. The performance in New York City's Madison Gardens began April 3, 1900, and ended April 21, 1900. Adam Forepaugh and Sells Brothers Circus Ad, *New York Daily Tribune*, Apr 15, 1900, p. 13. "Circus Reaches Jersey City," *New York Daily Tribune*, March 31, 1900, p. 8.

9. Charles Devlin, "Memoirs," no date, Leslie, Jane Street Family Papers.

10. Ibid.

11. Ibid.

12. Charles Devlin to Charles Patrick "Pat" Devlin (David Street), ca. April 1944, Jack and Kathy Devlin, Devlin Family Papers.

13. Ibid.; Devlin, "Memoirs." Specific details from Devlin's memoirs provide description. The little-known M. L. Clark Circus was owned by M. L. Clark from 1883 to 1901. The name was then changed to M. L. Clark & Sons with M. L. Clark & Lee Clark as the owners. The name remained unchanged from 1902 until 1929.

Floyd and Howard King used the title of M. L. Clark & Great Sangor Circus in 1922. E. E. Coleman then took out the M. L. Clark & Sons Circus in 1930. He revised the same title again in 1943, 1945, and 1946. See Q&A Board, https://circushistory.org/questions/question/m-l-clark-sons.

14. Devlin, "Memoirs."

15. Ibid.

16. Jack and Kathy Devlin, *Descendants of Patrick Devlin and Bridget Henry of Londonderry, Ulster, Ireland*, 2016, Devlin Family Papers. Mary McCloud Devlin died from blood poisoning, possibly relating to the birth and death of a baby boy in 1893.

17. Devlin to Charles Patrick "Pat" Devlin (David Street), ca. April 1944.

18. Ibid.

19. 1900 United States Census, Little Grant, Grant, Wisconsin, Roll 1790, Page 1A, Enumeration District 0042, FHL microfilm 1241790. The farm belonged to Jacob Henry, Charles Devlin's uncle.

20. Devlin to Charles Patrick "Pat" Devlin (David Street), ca. April 1944.

21. Ibid.

22. Fred W. Thompson to Joel W. Watne, June 12, 1967, Fred Thompson Collection, Subseries A, Box 9, File 18, Walter P. Reuther Library, WSU.

23. "The Accident That Befell Charley Devlin," *Guttenberg Press*, 1901; Devlin, *Descendants of Patrick Devlin*. Louis Devlin reportedly filed suit against the city of Chicago for not enforcing an ordinance requiring a watchman to be on site.

24. Devlin, "Memoirs."

25. Ibid.

26. Ibid.

27. Ibid.

28. Ibid. In hobo slang, a "Johnson" is a thief or some other sort of criminal. A "punk" is a young hobo.

29. Devlin, "Memoirs."

30. Ibid.

31. Ibid.

32. Ibid.

33. Ibid.

34. Charles Devlin performed a high-wire act in Hagenback's Wild Animal Show. *Brooklyn Eagle*, October 2, 1912, Jack and Kathy Devlin, Devlin Family Papers.

35. Ibid. No mention of this wager is found in Waco newspapers. Members of the Devlin family believe that Charles told the story in his memoirs to help promote himself. He did, however, go on a world tour.

36. Devlin, "Memoirs."

37. Ibid.

38. Brooklyn Eagle.

39. Brissenden, *The IWW*, 365. Brissenden calculates twenty-six free speech fights overall, the earliest beginning in 1906.

40. Devlin, "Memoirs." The *New York Call* was associated with the Socialist Party of America.

41. Ibid.

42. Ibid.

43. Charles Devlin traveled through Western Europe and points through the South Pacific, including Australia.

44. The union was later called the Hotel, Restaurant and Domestic Workers Industrial Union.

45. *Proceedings of the Tenth Convention*, 35.

46. Sellers, "The Domestic Workers' Union," 2.

47. Jane Street, "Denver Domestics," *Solidarity*, June 10, 1916, p. 2. This lengthy article provides enormous detail on the way Jane organized the union local and at what costs. She directly asks for financial help.

48. Devlin to Mary Jane Devlin, ca. November 1938. Charles Devlin had been living in San Diego in early 1916. See also Devlin to Charles Patrick "Pat" Devlin (David Street), ca. April 1944.

49. On May 10, 1916, DWIU Local 114 in Salt Lake City organized. *Proceedings of the Tenth Convention*, 35. By November 1916, Domestic Industrial Workers locals had organized in Chicago and Duluth. See Mort E. Warshawsky, "The Domestic's Industrial Union," *Solidarity*, November 18, 1916, p. 2. It should be noted that no Chicago Domestics Industrial Union is listed on the University of Washington IWW History Project map. See http://depts.washington.edu/iww/map _intro.shtml. Jane is reported to have gone to Chicago to organize a domestics' union in the *Denver Rocky Mountain News*, July 13, 1916, p. 4. The latter event could not be corroborated.

50. Devlin to Mary Jane Devlin, ca. November 1938.

51. Ibid.

52. "IWW Activities," Case #368973:7.

53. *1918 Denver City Directory*, 1208.

54. "IWW Activities," Case #368973:7.

55. Ibid.

56. Ibid., 6.

57. "IWW Street Meeting Interrupted by Police," *Denver Rocky Mountain News*, July 22, 1916, p. 3.

58. The building served as the home for Denver's Chamber of Commerce from 1910 to 1950. Still standing (2019), it is now a residential building called Chamber Lofts.

59. Devlin, "Denver Booms Once More," 4.

60. John Aller (Alar), a Croatian miner and family man, had been shot several times in the back and neck by an Oliver Mining Company gunman early Thursday

morning, June 22, 1916, while standing in a picket line just outside his own home. "Iron Ore Strikers in Deadly Grapple with Steel Trust," *Solidarity*, July 1, 1916, p. 1. See Leslie H. Marcy, "The Iron Heel on the Mesaba Range," *International Socialist Review* 17, no. 2 (August 1916): 74–78, for an account of the murder. Robert M. Eleff, "The 1916 Minnesota Miners' Strike against U.S. Steel," *Minnesota History* 51, no. 2 (Summer 1988): 68. The name *Aller* may have originally been *Alar*, although censuses record "Aller." See Botkin, *Frank Little*, 222–24, 237–43.

61. "IWW Inquiry Begins Before Smallwood," *Duluth News*, July 22, 1916, p. 6. *Proceedings of the Tenth Convention*, 134.

62. "Penury May Put End to Strike of IWW," *Duluth News Tribune*, August 2, 1916, p. 5.

63. Flynn, *The Rebel Girl: An Autobiography*, 152. Elizabeth Gurley Flynn and Carlo Tresca had a thirteen-year-long relationship, although they were married to others. "Tresca and Others Held After Infamous Hearing," *Solidarity*, August 5, 1916, p. 1; George P. West, "The Mesaba Strike," *International Socialist Review* 17, no. 3 (September 1916): 160.

64. "IWW Street Meeting Interrupted by Police," *Denver Rocky Mountain News*, July 22, 1916, p. 3.

65. Devlin, "Denver Booms Once More," 4; "IWW Street Meeting Interrupted by Police," *Denver Rocky Mountain News*, July 22, 1916, p. 3.

66. Devlin, "Denver Booms Once More," 4.

67. "IWW Street Meeting Interrupted by Police," 3.

68. Ibid.

69. Ibid. No mention of a man named "Skay" was included in the report. Elevator pilots or operators were required to manually operate elevators prior to the 1970s. Charles Devlin would have known how to regulate the elevator's speed based on a good sense of timing.

70. Devlin, "Denver Booms Once More," 4.

71. "Deputy Sheriff J. C. Myron of Duluth and T. Ladvalla Hit by Strikers' Bullets," *Duluth News Tribune*, July 4, 1916, p. 1.

72. "Ashurst Denounces IWW: Says Initials Really Mean Imperial Wilhelm's Warriors," *Evening Star*, August 17, 1917, p. 2.

### Chapter 9

1. Two attorneys were a Mr. Vogel and Mr. Whitehead of the Free Speech Defense League. Devlin, "Denver Booms Once More," 4.

2. Ibid.

3. Ibid.

4. Ibid.

5. Ibid.

6. Ibid.

7. Ernest Riebe created Mr. Block for IWW publications beginning in 1912.

8. Kirkpatrick, "Jane Street and Denver's Rebel Housemaids," 33.

9. Devlin, "Denver Booms Once More," 4.

10. Kirkpatrick, "Jane Street and Denver's Rebel Housemaids," 34.

11. *Solidarity*, July 22, 1916, p. 4.

12. Ibid.

13. Ibid. In Wobbly-speak, a "scissorine" is the female counterpart to the male "scissorbill," a person who identifies with a boss and not the working class.

14. Joe Hill, "Stung Right" (1912), in *The Big Red Songbook*, 119–20. According to the editors of *The Big Red Songbook*, the last line of the song is thought to be a reference to Upton Sinclair's 1906 novel *The Jungle* about the meatpacking industry. Another perhaps more accurate origin that predates Sinclair's novel was the 1898 military "beef scandal." The United States Army contracted for beef products from three Chicago packinghouses, including Armour & Company. The meat was poor quality, and worse, so heavily packed in chemicals, that Spanish-American commanding general Nelson A. Miles called the products "embalmed beef." An enormous number of soldiers died from food poisoning as a result.

15. Devlin, "Denver Booms Once More," 4.

16. Ibid.

17. World War I Registration Colorado, Denver, Roll 1561844, Draft Board 8.

18. Street to Mrs. Elmer S. Bruse.

19. Melanie Rosenberg, email to author, August 26, 2019, Engle Correspondence. Melanie's husband Steve is the great-grandson of Phil Engle's sister Lottie.

20. Certificate of Death, State of Minnesota, #20420–3327; 1910 Federal Census, Denver Ward 2, Denver, Colorado, Roll T624_114, Page 5A, Enumeration District 0051, FHL microfilm 1374127. Phil Engle's father, Benjamin, was a grocer in New York City's lower east end when he died unexpectedly in 1885. Phil's widowed mother, Dora Monsky Engle, remarried Meyer Wartellsky in Detroit, Michigan, in 1887, resulting in Engle's half siblings. The Engles (Engels) and Monskys were Polish Jews who escaped the "Pale of Settlement," Russian controlled territories, where Jewish inhabitants were persecuted in their daily lives. Rosenberg, email to author, August 26, 2019.

21. *1909 Denver City Directory*, 475; *1917 Denver City Directory*, 824.

22. Foner, *Women and the American Labor Movement*, 400; David D. Kirkpatrick, email to author, May 10, 2020.

23. Phil Engle, "What's the Use?" *Industrial Worker*, February 12, 1913, p. 3.

24. Street to Mrs. Elmer S. Bruse.

25. Ibid.

26. Ibid.

27. Guy Doty, "Recruits Needed for Denver Fight," *Industrial Worker*, March 6, 1913, p. 1.

28. David D. Kirkpatrick, emails to author, February 6, 2018, and May 10, 2020.

29. Foner, *Women and the American Labor Movement*, 398.

30. Botkin, *Frank Little*, 54. See also Clara Stiverson, interview by Elizabeth Jameson, July 29, 1975, as quoted in Elizabeth Jameson, "Imperfect Unions, Class, and Gender," *Frontiers: A Journal of Women Studies* 1, no. 2 (Spring 1976): 91.

31. Francis Shor, "'Virile Syndicalism' in Comparative Perspective: A Gender Analysis of the IWW in the United States and Australia," March 14, 1998, https://iww.org/history/library/misc/Shor1998.

32. Kirkpatrick, "Jane Street and Denver's Rebel Housemaids," 5.

33. Devlin, "Denver Booms Once More," 4. A previous free speech fight in 1913 caused headaches for city fathers. Apparently, they did not want a repeat, especially with the optics of arresting women.

34. Ibid.

35. "House Maids Union Has Blown Up on Shoal of Debts," *Denver Post*, July 26, 1916, p. 4.

36. Ibid.

37. Ibid.

38. Ibid.

39. Ibid.

40. William D. Haywood, Testimony before U.S. District Court of Illinois, August 12, 1918, Transcript available from U.S. vs. Haywood et al., 1917–1918, Series 5: Legal Problems, Trials, and Defense, File 3, 11394, Box 117, Subseries B. Walter P. Reuther Library, WSU.

41. Kirkpatrick, "Jane Street and Denver's Rebel Housemaids," 33. More women were organizing, and *Solidarity*, recognizing the momentum, honored them with a special women's issue on July 1, 1916.

42. Mildred Morris, "Look Out for Soft 'Sabotagers,'" first published in *Denver Rocky Mountain News*, July 13, 1916, p. 7, reprinted in *Solidarity*, July 29, 1916, p. 4.

43. Ibid.

44. Ibid.

45. Ibid.

46. Kirkpatrick, "Jane Street and Denver's Rebel Housemaids," 29.

47. As an example, see "Sabotage Cooks' Scheme to Make Mistress Kind," *Chicago Daily Tribune*, July 14, 1916.

48. Elizabeth Gurley Flynn, "Sabotage," originally published as "Sabotage, the Conscious Withdrawal of Industrial Efficiency," October 1916, www.iww.org/history/library/Flynn/Sabotage.

49. Ibid.

50. Kirkpatrick, "Jane Street and Denver's Rebel Housemaids," 29; Foner, *Women and the American Labor Movement*, 409.

51. *The Truth about the IWW Prisoners* (New York: American Civil Liberties Bureau, 1922), 1.

52. Devlin, "Denver Booms Once More," 4.

53. Ibid.

54. Ibid.

55. At the *Proceedings of the Second I. W. W. Convention in Chicago, Illinois* (1906), 287, the following clause was added to the constitution: "Mixed locals. No member of a trade that is organized in his locality is qualified for admission into a mixed local in the same locality, and no member of a mixed local can remain a member of the same after his trade has been organized in that locality." See Brissenden, *The IWW*, 276–88, for problems with mixed locals. The earlier Denver mixed local was No. 26, dissolved after 1915. See "IWW History Project," University of Washington, http://depts.washington.edu/iww/map_locals.shtml.

56. Devlin, "Denver Booms Once More," 4.

### *Chapter 10*

1. Mrs. Jane Street, Domestic Workers' Industrial Union, 404 Charles Building, *1916 Denver City Directory*, 775. See also "IWW Activities," Case #368973:9. The Bureau of Investigation, under the terms of the 1918 Sedition Act, opened Jane Street's mail, copied the letters, and resealed them. Calenal Sellers describes attempting sex with Jane in one letter, dated July 22, 1919. The five-page letter—full of Sellers's personal beliefs, pledges of support, recriminations, excuses, and self-contradictory statements—reveals an unusual history between Jane Street and Calenal Sellers. A second letter, written one week later, expresses Sellers's remorse for his words and actions toward Jane. See "IWW Activities," Case #368973:19–21.

2. "IWW Street Meeting Interrupted by Police," *Denver Rocky Mountain News*, July 22, 1916, p. 3; "IWW Activities," Case #368973:9.

3. "IWW Activities," Case #368973:10.

4. Ibid.

5. Ibid.

6. Ibid.

7. Ibid.

8. Ibid.

9. Ibid.

10. Ibid.

11. Ibid.

12. "Various," Case #373702:17, Roll #821, Investigative Reports of the Bureau of Investigation 1908–1922, OGF, 1909–1921, FBI Case Files, National Archives Microfilm Publication M1085, NARA, Washington, DC.

13. Ibid.

14. "IWW Activities," Case #368973:9.

15. Ibid.

16. Ibid.

17. Margaret Sanger, "Voluntary Motherhood," Speech, National Birth Control League, March 1917.

18. Emma Goldman, "Marriage and Love," in *Anarchism and Other Essays* (New York: Mother Earth Publishing, 1910), https://www.marxists.org/reference /archive/goldman/works/1914/marriage-love.htm.

19. Ibid.

20. Ernest Griffith, "Free Love and the Home," *Industrial Worker*, June 5, 1913, p. 3.

21. Matilda Rabinowitz, *Immigrant Girl, Radical Woman* (Ithaca: Cornell University Press, 2017), 109, 138. IWW Matilda Rabinowitz (Robbins) organized in the East, becoming one of only two female general organizers before 1920. She helped lead the 1912 Lawrence Textile Strike.

22. Claudio L. Goldin, "The Work and Wages of Single Women, 1870–1920," *The Journal of Economic History* 40, no. 1 (March 1980): 83.

23. Ibid.

24. Foner, *Women and the American Labor Movement*, 41.

25. Kaite Mark, "Domestic Workers: An Ongoing Fight for Human Rights, Respect, and Dignity at the Workplace," http://archives.evergreen.edu/webpages /curricular/2010-2011/ageofirony/aoizine/kaite.html.

26. "Domestic Workers, Fight for Your Rights!" (Chicago: IWW, n.d.). In the pamphlet, the IWW claims that employers sexually assault domestic servants.

27. There were exceptions. In New Orleans, the IWW organized a union of prostitutes to resist madams who increased the rent on the "cribs" where they worked. In Butte, Montana, prostitutes, who enjoyed the patronage of IWW miners, boycotted scabs and militiamen in solidarity with the IWW. Kirkpatrick, "Jane Street and Denver's Rebel Housemaids," 31–32.

28. Ibid., 32.

29. Heather Mayer, *Beyond the Rebel Girl* (Corvallis: Oregon State University, 2018), 3.

30. Kirkpatrick, "Jane Street and Denver's Rebel Housemaids," 32.

31. Foner, *Women and the American Labor Movement*, 400.

32. *Proceedings of the Tenth Convention*, 134–35.

33. Ibid. Later editions of *Solidarity* posted articles for women readers, but the periodical never incorporated a weekly women's section.

34. Mayer, *Beyond the Rebel Girl*, 63.

35. See Mayer, *Beyond the Rebel Girl*, 83–88 for discussion of Lillian Larkin's case.

36. See Mark, "Domestic Workers."

37. Note how the term "white slavery" elevated the concerns of white women over women of color regarding prostitution. See Mayer, *Beyond the Rebel Girl*, 66.

38. "White Slave Cases Will Be Decreased by New Decision," *Denver Post*, February 7, 1915, p. 28.

39. Market Street, in Denver's red-light district, was well known throughout the West. Originally named McGaa Street, Market Street was renamed Holladay

Street in 1866. But, by 1880, the prostitution business was so prevalent, that the Holladay family requested to have their name removed from the street and the reputation that came with it. The city obliged and renamed it Market Street. In 1909 Police Commissioner George Creel stated that the women who worked as prostitutes were victims, not criminals, who could be reformed. He worked to send prostitutes to a municipal farm for reformation. Efforts such as his and other city reforms forced the madams of Market Street to go underground by 1915.

40. Beaton, *Colorado Women*, 69–70.

41. Ibid., 70.

42. Ibid., 69–70.

43. Jack Carney, "Prostitution and Wage Slavery," *Solidarity*, September 23, 1916, p. 3.

44. Hon. W. B. Wilson, "Results of the First Scientific Investigations Ever Carried on by a Nation into Occupations Most Hazardous to Spiritual Welfare and the Causes for Their Downfall and Degradation," *Denver Post*, July 19, 1917, p. 58–59.

45. The five most hazardous occupations in order of their danger were domestic service, hotel or restaurant worker, low-grade factory trades, trained nursing, and last, stenographic positions. A. R. Pinci, "No. 1—The Perils That Beset the Girl Who Does Housework," *Denver Post*, July 19, 1917, p. 58; Charles Patrick Neill, *United States Bureau of Labor, Report on Condition of Woman and Child Wage Earners in the United States*, 19 Volumes (Washington, DC: Government Printing Office, 1910–13). Volume 15 discusses findings concerning occupation and criminality of women.

46. David Katzman, *Seven Days a Week: Women and Domestic Service in Industrializing America* (Champaign: University of Illinois Press, 1981), 104. Frances Keller provided the study.

47. Foner, *Women and the American Labor Movement*, 401.

48. Street to Mrs. Elmer S. Bruse.

49. Kirkpatrick, "Jane Street and Denver's Rebel Housemaids," 17.

50. C. W. Sellers, "Denver Housemaids' List Stolen," *Solidarity*, November 11, 1916, p. 1.

51. Ibid.

52. "Press Committee," *Solidarity* August 26, 1916, p. 4.

53. Local 614 Press Committee, "Rebel Girl Defenders," *Solidarity*, November 25, 1916, p. 3.

54. Kirkpatrick, "Jane Street and Denver's Rebel Housemaids," 31–32.

55. Ibid., 32.

56. "IWW Activities," Case #368973:9.

57. Street to Mrs. Elmer S. Bruse.

### Chapter 11

1. "Prophet of New Cult Is Kicked Out of House by Husband of 'Affinity,'" *Denver Post*, December 2, 1912, p. 2.

2. At the end of 1909, the year in which Jane Street divorced Henry R. Bumpass, Bumpass became a "material witness" in a forgery case. He was with the forger, real estate operator Dwight Fortner, when a $12,000 check suddenly bore an unauthorized endorsement. Bumpass was pressed on all sides, a St. Louis court demanding his appearance to testify for the defendant, while at the same time, Bumpass claimed private detectives were threatening the "third degree" if he testified. The proceedings were temporarily dropped, and Bumpass avoided any criminal connection to Fortner. "Fortner's Case Continued," *Arkansas Gazette*, November 24, 1909, p. 1; "Bumpass Seeks Protection," *Arkansas Gazette*, December 21, 1909, p. 1; "Trial of Fortner Postponed Sixth Time," *Arkansas Gazette*, December 21, 1909, p. 1; "Bumpass Goes to St. Louis," *Arkansas Gazette*, December 22, 1909, p. 14.

3. "A Weird Tale from Municipal Court," *Chicago Day Book*, November 30, 1912, p. 28.

4. Ibid.

5. "Prophet of New Cult Is Kicked Out of House," 2.

6. "A Weird Tale from Municipal Court," 28; "Prophet of New Cult Is Kicked Out of House," 2.

7. "Prophet of New Cult Is Kicked Out of House," 2.

8. "A Weird Tale from Municipal Court," 28.

9. "Prophet of New Cult Is Kicked Out of House," 2; "Love Cult Secrets Told, Dr. Bumpass Acquitted," *Denver Post*, March 21, 1913, p. 5.

10. "Love Cult Secrets Told, Dr. Bumpass Acquitted," 5.

11. *Chicago Day Book*, December 13, 1912, p. 8. Anna Hoffman and Nick Marcella were also indicted for arson by a grand jury. *Chicago Day Book*, December 17, 1912, p. 7.

12. *Chicago Day Book*, December 17, 1912, pp. 6–7.

13. "Love Cult Secrets Told, Dr. Bumpass Acquitted," 5.

14. "Cannot Bind Wife to Leave Mother," *Illinois State Journal*, August 1, 1913, p. 1.

15. Ibid.

16. Ibid. Bumpass continued to live in Chicago until departing for Denver in 1915. Mrs. Virginia C. Bumpass Obituary, *Arkansas Gazette*, May 29, 1914, p. 13.

17. Major Patrick J. Hamrock commanded Colorado National Guard companies A, B, and K, and he was responsible for bringing in the Gatling guns and first firing them into the Ludlow tents. At his court-martial, Hamrock was found guilty. See "33 Known Dead at Ludlow; Mothers and Babies Slain," 5. Many of the members of these companies had been replaced with mine guards and general thugs, and not regularly enlisted guardsman. "Major Hamrock at Head of List and 18 Others Are Named but All in His Command Accused," *Denver Post*, May 13, 1914, pp. 1–2.

18. Between June 1915 and June 1916, Villa's raiders attacked people on American soil thirty-eight times by some reports. As a result, using powers granted by

passage of the National Defense Act of 1916, which established the United States National Guard, President Woodrow Wilson fully mobilized National Guard units from all states and the District of Columbia for duty on the southern border on June 18, 1916. For an overview of what would be called the Mexican Expedition, see James W. Hurst, *Pancho Villa and Black Jack Pershing: The Punitive Expedition in Mexico* (Westport, CT: Praeger, 2007). The Punitive Expedition officially ended on February 5, 1917. See also Fred Greguras, "1916 State Mobilization Camps," rev. June 2015, https://dmna.ny.gov/historic/reghist/wwi/, accessed February 2, 2018.

19. "These Are the Denver Men Who Are Going to Mexico," *Denver Post*, June 15, 1916, p. 4. The location is also where the 1914 Ludlow court-martial hearings were held. See Greguras, "1916 State Mobilization Camps." Originally called the Colorado State Rifle Range, the military camp at Golden was later renamed Camp George West.

20. "Scott Asks Wilson What to Do in Last Conference with Mexico," *Denver Rocky Mountain News*, May 1, 1916, p. 3.

21. "Feeding 1,000 Mules and Horses Puzzle for State Guard Head," *Denver Post*, July 20, 1916, p. 4.

22. Ibid.

23. Ibid.

24. Ryley Cooper, "Girl of 18 Chooses Death When Marriage is Denied and Shoots Self in Head," *Denver Post*, August 15, 1916, p. 1; Morris, "Girl of 17, Forbidden to Wed," 3.

25. Morris, "Girl of 17, Forbidden to Wed," 3.

26. Ibid.

27. Ibid.

28. "Judge Sends Back Street Jury for Another Effort," *Denver Post*, September 29, 1916, p. 4.

29. Morris, "Girl of 17, Forbidden to Wed," 3.

30. Cooper, "Girl of 18 Chooses Death," 2.

31. Morris, "Girl of 17, Forbidden to Wed," 3.

32. Ibid.

33. Cooper, "Girl of 18 Chooses Death," 1.

34. Ibid., 2.

35. Ibid.

36. "Lieut. Street Detained in Jail," *Denver Rocky Mountain News*, August 17, 1916, p. 3.

37. Cooper, "Girl of 18 Chooses Death," 2; Morris, "Girl of 17, Forbidden to Wed," 3.

38. Cooper, "Girl of 18 Chooses Death," 2.

39. Ibid., 1.

40. Ibid., 2.

41. Ibid., 1.

42. Morris, "Girl of 17, Forbidden to Wed," 3.

43. Cooper, "Girl of 18 Chooses Death," 2.

44. "Girl of 17, Forbidden to Wed," 3; "Lieut. Street Detained in Jail," 3. John Rush became a Colorado state senator in 1917.

45. "Lieut. Street Detained in Jail," 3.

46. Morris, "Girl of 17, Forbidden to Wed," 3.

47. Ibid.

48. "Lieut. Street Pleads Not Guilty to Crime Charge Against Him," *Denver Rocky Mountain News*, August 27, 1916, p. 9.

49. Ibid.

50. "Lieut. Street Detained in Jail," 3.

51. See the *Cheyenne Record*, August 24, 1916; and the *Ordway New Era*, August 25, 1916.

### Chapter 12

1. Devlin to Mary Jane Devlin, November 1938.

2. Press Committee, *Solidarity*, August 26, 1916, p. 3.

3. "Housemaids' Dope on 'Bosses' Stolen, Union Is Dismayed," *Denver Rocky Mountain News*, November 1, 1916, p. 4.

4. Press Committee, "Denver Unity Brings Results," *Solidarity*, September 16, 1916, p. 1.

5. "IWW Activities," Case #368973:10.

6. "Lieut. Street Detained in Jail," *Denver Rocky Mountain News*, August 17, 1916, p. 3.

7. "Soldier Deserts to Shield Friend," *Denver Post*, September 25, 1916, p. 11.

8. Ibid.; "Housemaids' Dope on 'Bosses' Stolen," 4.

9. "Lieutenant Found Not Guilty by Jury," *Denver Rocky Mountain News*, September 30, 1916, p. 12.

10. "Troop A's Picnic at Lakeside Ends with Order to March to Rifle Range and Possible War," *Denver Post*, July 19, 1916, p. 14; "Colorado Guard Officer Born to War Traditions," *Denver Rocky Mountain News*, August 20, 1916, p. 12.

11. Vernon H. Jensen, *Heritage of Conflict* (Ithaca, NY: Cornell University Press, 1950), 130.

12. Ibid.

13. Tim Blevins, Chris Nicholl, and Calvin P. Otto, eds., *The Colorado Labor Wars 1903–1904* (Colorado Springs: Pikes Peak Library District, 2006), 9–10.

14. Jensen, *Heritage of Conflict*, 130.

15. Ibid.; Blevins, Nicholl, and Otto, *Colorado Labor Wars*, 9–10.

16. Beaton, *Colorado Women*, 126. See Emma Florence Langdon, *The Cripple Creek Strike 1903–1904* (Victor, CO, 1904), for Langdon's narrative.

17. Jensen, *Heritage of Conflict*, 131.

18. Ibid., 132–33. Both Brigadier General Chase and Adjutant General Bell defied the judge's orders and the rule of law. Later warrants were sworn out for

the unlawful detention and false imprisonment of the four miners, all WFM union men. The United States Supreme Court ultimately supported the state of Colorado's methods of military intervention and repressive measures *in times of crisis*, and Governor James Peabody was vindicated (*Charles H. Moyer v. James H. Peabody, Sherman M. Bell, and Bulkeley Wells,* 212 U.S. 78 [1909]). See Suggs, *Colorado's War on Militant Unionism*, 159–77.

19. James A. Crutchfield, *It Happened in Colorado* (Helena, MT: Two Dot Press, 2008), 109.

20. "Aggie Trustees Oppose Battery of College Men," *Denver Post*, December 11, 1915, p. 5.

21. Editorial, *Denver Rocky Mountain News*, June 10, 1915, p. 6.

22. "Judge Sends Back Street Jury for Another Effort," *Denver Post*, September 29, 1916, p. 4; "Soldier Deserts to Shield Friend," 11.

23. "Verdict Expected Today in Guardsman's Trial," *Denver Post*, September 28, 1916, p. 8.

24. "Lieut. Street Detained in Jail," 3.

25. "Street, Vindicated, To Be Reinstated in State Militia," *Denver Post*, September 30, 1916, p. 4; "Lieutenant Found Not Guilty by Jury," 12.

26. "Lieutenant Found Not Guilty by Jury," 12.

27. "Judge Sends Back Street Jury," 4.

28. Ibid.

29. Morris, "Girl of 17, Forbidden to Wed Militia Lieutenant, Ends Life," 3.

30. "Judge Sends Back Street Jury," 4.

31. "Lieutenant Found Not Guilty by Jury," 12.

32. "Judge Sends Back Street Jury," 4.

33. "Street, Vindicated, To Be Reinstated," 4.

34. Ibid.

35. Sellers, "Denver Housemaids' List Stolen," 1.

36. Ibid.

37. "Housemaids' Dope on 'Bosses' Stolen," 4.

38. Ibid.

39. Ibid.

40. Sellers, "Denver Housemaids' List Stolen," 1.

41. Street to Mrs. Elmer S. Bruse.

42. Sellers, "Denver Housemaids' List Stolen," 1.

43. Ibid.

44. Ibid.

45. Ibid.

46. Ibid.

47. "Housemaids' Dope on 'Bosses' Stolen," 4.

48. The ads emphasized *healthy* because Denver was considered a health resort city. Employers did not want to hire people who had moved to the city to improve their health because these employees tended to be transient workers.

"Survey of Employed Women of Denver, Colorado, Made Under Direction of the Central Field Committee," February 18, 1917, p. 1, YWCA Denver Manuscript Collection, MSS.1254, Carton 6, FF107, SHL.

49. See this ad in the *Denver Post*, October 25, 1916, p. 18. There is a total of fifteen employment-seeking ads beginning August 22, 1916, and ending October 25, 1916, in the *Denver Post* and *Denver Rocky Mountain News* tied to 1614 Franklin Street, Denver, Colorado.

50. The earliest ads for "Wanted Situations Female" and male began August 22, 1916, in the *Denver Post*. These ads continued until the week Domestic Workers Union Local No. 113 moved into the boarding house at 1614 Franklin, with the last ad on October 25, 1916, in the *Denver Post*. After the union took over the residence, all ads of this nature ceased.

51. Jane never stated that she had married Charles Devlin, and no marriage record exists in the state of Colorado. However, in making renewed contact with their daughter, Mary Jane, in 1938, Devlin stated he had married Jane before their travel to Arizona during the 1917 summer. This is highly doubtful, as evidence suggests otherwise. Devlin to Mary Jane Devlin, ca. November 1938.

52. *Denver Post*, October 25, 1916, p. 18.

53. Sellers, "Denver Housemaids' List Stolen," 1; Street to Mrs. Elmer S. Bruse.

54. The residence at 1614 N. Franklin Street is located in what is described today as the City Park West neighborhood in Denver. The house is about a mile away from the park.

55. A 2018 Zillow real estate ad provided all details regarding 1614 North Franklin Street. The house has been on the market several times. See https://www.zillow.com/homedetails/1614-N-Franklin-St-Denver-CO-80218/13321690_zpid/. The author also visited the address in person. Street to Mrs. Elmer S. Bruse.

56. Street to Mrs. Elmer S. Bruse.

57. See a representative ad in the *Denver Post*, August 11, 1916, p. 11.

58. Sellers, "Denver Housemaids' List Stolen," 1.

59. Street to Mrs. Elmer S. Bruse.

60. "Housemaids' Union Rents House in Franklin Street," *Denver Rocky Mountain News*, November 8, 1916, p. 6.

61. Street to Mrs. Elmer S. Bruse.


### Chapter 13

1. "1916 Minutes of the Regular Meeting of the Board of Directors of the YWCA," YWCA Denver Manuscript Collection MSS.1254, Carton 1, FF2, SHL.

2. "A Brief History, Denver Young Women's Christian Association, 1886–1917," Colorado Historical Society, YWCA Denver Manuscript Collection MSS.1254, Carton 6, FF111, SHL.

3. Ibid.

4. "Background Material for Use in Sermons, Talks, or Programs for YWCA Week," YWCA Denver Manuscript Collection MMS.1254, Carton 43, FF1046, SHL, 1.

5. *Representative Women of Colorado*, 52.

6. Sullivan, "Limousine at Last," 1.

7. Ibid.

8. Ibid.

9. Ibid.

10. Ibid.

11. Fetter, *Colorado's Legendary Lovers*.

12. Ibid. According to Fetter, the Smuggler-Union mine produced $50 million between 1902 and 1923.

13. E. B. Adams, "My Association with a Glamourous Man, Bulkeley Wells," privately published, 1961. E. B. Adams was the Smuggler Mine's attorney in Telluride from 1908 until 1923.

14. MaryJoy Martin, email to author, June 16, 2017. See MaryJoy Martin, *The Corpse on Boomerang Hill* (Montrose, CO: Western Reflections, 2004).

15. See Wilbur Fiske Stone, *History of Colorado* (Chicago: S. J. Clarke, 1918), 113–14, for a whitewashed biography of Bulkeley Wells.

16. Sellers, "The Domestic Workers' Union," 2.

17. Fetter, *Colorado's Legendary Lovers*; Martin, *The Corpse on Boomerang Hill*, 273; Polly Pry, "General Bulkeley Wells," *Telluride Journal*, May 18, 1905, p. 6.

18. See Martin, *The Corpse on Boomerang Hill*, for a fine narrative of the Telluride labor wars. Dubofsky, *We Shall Be All*, 30.

19. "Moyer Files Suit," *Delta Independent*, April 7, 1905, p. 1. WFM president Charles H. Moyer claimed that he was subjected to the deprivation of rights, privileges, and immunities secured to him by the Constitution and laws of the United States. Moyer v. Peabody, et al, 212 U.S. 78, argued in 1909, is a decision by the United States Supreme Court that held that the governor and officers of a state National Guard, acting in good faith and under authority of law, may imprison without probable cause a citizen of the United States in a time of insurrection and deny that citizen the right of habeas corpus. Associate Justice Oliver Wendell Holmes Jr. delivered the opinion for a unanimous court. See Charles H. Moyer, Plaintiff in Error, v. James H. Peabody, Sherman M. Bell, and Bulkeley Wells, 212 U.S. 78 (1909).

20. Dubofsky, *We Shall Be All*, 32.

21. Fetter, "From Tragic to Scandalous."

22. Fetter, *Colorado's Legendary Lovers*; "Molly Brown, the Sacred 36 and Louise Hill," *Denver Post*, April 10, 2012, http://blogs.denverpost.com/library/2012/04/10/molly-brown-sacred-36-louise-hill/1016/.

23. Fetter, *Colorado's Legendary Lovers*.

24. Ibid.; Tom Morton, "Louise Sneed Hill and Denver's 'Sacred Thirty-Six,'" Fairmount Who's Who," April 23, 2013; Fetter, "From Tragic to Scandalous"; Adams, "My Association with a Glamourous Man." See Martin, *The Corpse on Boomerang Hill*, 317.

25. Fetter, *Colorado's Legendary Lovers*.

26. Ibid.

27. Ibid.

28. Mildred Morris, "Housewives Are Declared Failure," *Denver Rocky Mountain News*, November 19, 1916, p. 5.

29. See Morris, "Look Out for Soft 'Sabotagers,'" 7, *Solidarity*, July 29, 1916, p. 4; and Morris, "Girl of 17, Forbidden to Wed Militia Lieutenant," 3.

30. Mike Peters, "100 Years Ago: Former Tribune-Republican Reporter Arrested at Washington, D.C. Protest," *Greeley Tribune*, January 21, 1919, https://www.greeleytribune.com/news/100-years-ago-former-tribune-republican-reporter-arrested-at-washington-d-c-protest/.

31. Mildred Morris, "Housewives Discard Sentiment, Learn Justice! Then Maids Will Stay on Jobs, Declares Expert," *Denver Rocky Mountain News*, November 16, 1916, p. 5; Palmer, *Domesticity and Dirt*, 92.

32. Morris, "Housewives Discard Sentiment," 5.

33. Ibid.

34. Ibid.

35. Ibid.

36. Mayer, *Beyond the Rebel Girl*, 66. Gail Writer, who probably suggested the speaker to the ladies, was a member of the field committee representing the west-central states of the same YWCA commission, besides being a member of the Housewives' Assembly. "1916 Minutes of the Regular Meeting of the Board of Directors of the YWCA," YWCA Denver Manuscript Collection, MSS.1254, Carton 1, FF2, SHL.

37. Fetter, *Colorado's Legendary Lovers*. See also "Molly Brown, the Sacred 36 and Louise Hill."

38. "Preamble to the IWW Constitution."

39. Flynn, "The IWW Call to Women," 9.

40. Mort E. Warshawsky, "The Domestic's Industrial Union," *Solidarity*, November 18, 1916, p. 2.

41. Sellers, "The Domestic Workers' Union," 2.

42. Hinah Shah and Marci Seville, "Domestic Worker Organizing: Building a Contemporary Movement for Dignity and Power," *Albany Review* 75, no. 1 (January 2012): 421–22.

43. Henrietta Roelofs, as quoted in Palmer, *Domesticity and Dirt*, 92.

44. Ibid. Roelofs backed the National Society for the Promotion of Industrial Education (NSPIE)'s position and endeavor to gain congressional funding for state education programs to prepare youth for the complicated skills needed in an industrial society, i.e. vocational home economics.

45. Palmer, *Domesticity and Dirt*, 92.

46. Ibid. Palmer notes that the American Home Economics Association was averse to making home economics "industrial." On the contrary, Roelofs's hope was that vocational education would clarify the industrial status and improve the labor standing of domestic workers. In much of the United States, vocational home economics became equated with a woman's keeping her own house.

47. Following recommendations from Frederick W. Taylor's 1911 book, *Principles of Scientific Management*, many factories implemented sped-up assembly line operations that required less skill from easily replaceable labor.

48. Warshawsky, "The Domestic's Industrial Union," 2.

49. Jane Street, "Job-ites," Leslie, Jane Street Family Papers. Jane writes that "job-ite" is a term used in the IWW meaning someone who cares for nothing but his job.

50. Jane Street, "Job-ites," *One Big Union Monthly* 2, no. 6 (June 1938): 15.

51. Mrs. Junius Flagg Brown (Mary Louise Brundige) was born in 1844 in Tallmadge, Ohio, and died on April 20, 1937, in Denver at the age of ninety-two.

52. "Denver Art Museum Now Open Sundays," *Camp Hale Ski-Zette*, May 5, 1944, p. 1. The house at 933 Pennsylvania Street (now Avenue) was known as the Henry Wise Hobson–Junius Flagg Brown House. Hobson had been a U.S. Colorado state attorney. The structure was demolished in 1974 for a suburban-style condominium project. Goodstein, *The Ghosts of Denver*, 273.

53. "Untitled," *Colorado Golden Transcript*, December 24, 1908, p. 3.

54. "Denver Needs Home for Art Treasure Donated to City by Heirs of Brown," *Denver Post*, December 10, 1916, p. 47. J. F. Brown had made his money early along with his partner-brother, John S. Brown, in the mercantile business after arriving in Denver by way of an oxcart.

55. Ibid. The Brown collection became a permanent lease to guarantee the paintings could never be sold and to ensure the foundation for an art gallery for Denver. A new art building and art institution to house the collection and others was built on 14th and Bannock Streets.

56. Ibid.

57. Morris, "Housewives Are Declared Failure," 5.

58. Attending were Mrs. Jasper Writer, Mrs. James D. Whitmore, Mrs. William Shaw Ward, Mrs. Junius F. Brown, Mrs. Anna Wolcott Vaile, Mrs. Charles B. Kountze, Mrs. Charles Graham, Mrs. E. A. Peters, Mrs. Kate Hallack, Mrs. Henry Warren (wife of the late Bishop Warren), Miss Rosalie Venable, Mrs. Will Iliff, Mrs. John Campbell, Mrs. Fred Dick, Mrs. William Tebbetts, Mrs. Theodore Holland, Mrs. Henry Winter, Mrs. David H. Lehmann, Mrs. James H. Teller (wife of Justice Teller of the Colorado supreme court), Mrs. Ray S. David, Mrs. William E. Sweet, Mrs. Margaret R. Millar, and Mrs. James H. Baker (wife of the former president of the University of Colorado).

59. "Biographical Note," Rhoda Elizabeth McCulloch Papers, 1884–1978, Sophia Smith Collection, Five College Archives & Manuscript Collections, Smith

College Archives, South Hampton, MA. Henrietta Roelofs earned a BA from Lake Erie College in 1906 and then attended the YWCA precursor organization's Secretarial Training Institute. She joined the YWCA of the USA Home Department staff in 1908. From then until her retirement in 1939, Roelofs worked in various capacities for the National Association. She died January 26, 1942, at age 63. *New Canaan Directory* (Stamford, CT, 1943), 358.

60. *Central Reformed Church, Members, 1850–1874*, Hope College, Thiel Research Center, Holland, Michigan. Henrietta Roelofs was born in Grand Rapids, Michigan, to George and Mary Dykema Roelofs. Henrietta Roelofs worked with the YWCA to sponsor the Women's Committee of the Council of National Defense during World War I. Roelofs was a prime player in helping women achieve their characterization as the "second line of defense." See Lynn Dumenil, *The Second Line of Defense* (Chapel Hill: University of North Carolina Press, 2017).

61. Morris, "Housewives Are Declared Failure," 5.

62. Ibid.

63. Ibid.

64. Ibid.

65. Ibid.

66. Ibid.

67. Ibid.

68. Ibid.

### Chapter 14

1. Street to Mrs. Elmer S. Bruse.

2. "Wanted Female Help," *Denver Rocky Mountain News*, December 14, 1916, p. 13. The ad read "DOMESTIC WORKERS' UNION, employment office and room house. 1614 Franklin."

3. Street to Mrs. Elmer S. Bruse.

4. Ibid.

5. Ibid.

6. Ibid.

7. Rabinowitz, *Immigrant Girl*, 121; Melvyn Dubofsky, *"Big Bill" Haywood* (New York: St. Martin's Press, 1987), 3.

8. Ralph Chaplin, *The Rough-and-Tumble Story of an American Radical* (Chicago: University of Chicago Press, 1948), 199. Chaplin was elected *Solidarity*'s new editor during the Tenth Annual IWW Convention. The Agricultural Workers Union (AWO) changed its name to the Agricultural Workers Industrial Union (AWIU) in 1917.

9. Ibid.; Dubofsky, *"Big Bill" Haywood*, 94.

10. Chaplin, *Rough-and-Tumble Story*, 199.

11. Rabinowitz, *Immigrant Girl*, 121; Ellen Doree Rosen, *A Wobbly Life: IWW Organizer E. F. Doree* (Detroit: Wayne State University Press, 2004), 26.

12. William D. Haywood, *Bill Haywood's Book: Autobiography of Big Bill Haywood* (New York: International Publishers, 1929), 13; Kirkpatrick, "Jane Street and Denver's Rebel Housemaids," 45.

13. "Haywood's arrival always caused a sensation among strikers." See Rabinowitz, *Immigrant Girl*, 121. "'He had a personal and physical magnetism nobody could resist,' one woman-Wobbly recalled." See Kirkpatrick, "Jane Street and Denver's Rebel Housemaids," 44. Haywood, speaking in the heat of bitter struggle to strikers who adored him, made the workers feel that he was a comrade and fellow worker, one of their very own. See James Cannon, "The Champion from Far Away," in *Notebook of An Agitator* (New York: Pathfinder Press, 1958), 169, first published in *Labor Action*, January 16, 1937.

14. Dubofsky, *"Big Bill" Haywood*, 4, 14; Kirkpatrick, "Jane Street and Denver's Rebel Housemaids," 44.

15. Dubofsky, *"Big Bill" Haywood*, 14.

16. Rabinowitz, *Immigrant Girl*, 121; Kirkpatrick, "Jane Street and Denver's Rebel Housemaids," 45; Dubofsky, *"Big Bill" Haywood*, 1.

17. Haywood, *Bill Haywood's Book*, 13. Haywood did not lose his eye in a mining accident as some have claimed. Instead, he accidentally gouged his eye with a knife while trying to make a slingshot.

18. Rabinowitz, *Immigrant Girl*, 121.

19. William D. Haywood was a member of the Socialist Party of America (SPA) until 1913 when the SPA voted him out because of his militant views and rhetoric. Haywood supported direct action instead of using the vote for change. "Result of Referendum D, 1912: Vote Closed February 26," *Cleveland Socialist*, March 15, 1913, p. 4.

20. In Minnesota, twenty thousand miners were on strike after one of their own had been murdered during a peaceful protest and others jailed. In retaliation, mining company gun-thugs, along with local law enforcement, attempted to arrest Montenegrin strike leaders, killing several men in the process. The Montenegrin miners were blamed for the deaths though they fired no weapons. Bill Haywood wired IWW organizers Elizabeth Gurley Flynn and Joseph Ettor and GEB chairman Frank Little to go to the Iron Range on July 7, 1916, to assist the strikers and their families. Flynn's lover, Carlos Tresca, along with Frank Little, Joseph Schmidt, and Sam Scarlett, were arrested for "constructive presence," a legal twist where there is an alleged commission of crimes, but the person charged is not actually present. Authorities claimed their speeches incited the deaths at the Montenegrin's home. Later, Frank Little was released, but the others were held over for a grand jury. Flynn began working furiously for the prisoners' releases and called for contributions to strike funds. See Botkin, *Frank Little*, 222–43, for a detailed account of this event.

21. Haywood, *Bill Haywood's Book*, 292; Botkin, *Frank Little*, 243.

22. Haywood, *Bill Haywood's Book*, 292.

23. Ibid.

24. Ibid.

25. Ibid.

26. Haywood was rumored to have been leaving a brothel at the time of the arrest. Dubofsky states that Haywood was arrested at Denver's railway depot, where he had gone to see Moyer off. Dubofsky, *"Big Bill" Haywood*, 31.

27. Ibid.

28. *Official Proceedings of the Fifteenth Annual Convention of the Western Federation of Miners, Stenographer's Report, June 10–July 3, 1907*, Denver, Colorado, 107–9. Darrow's bill between May 1906 and March 1907 alone was $14,803.75, an enormous sum for the IWW organization to fund. Money poured in from pockets of wealthy Colorado and Idaho Mine Owners' Associations and other state mining interests to prosecute the men and permanently break the WFM.

29. Martin, *The Corpse on Boomerang Hill*, 311.

30. Clara Stiverson, interview, 91.

31. See "Minutes of the IWW Founding Convention," https://www.iww.org /history/founding.

32. Rabinowitz, *Immigrant Girl*, 123.

33. *Proceedings of the Tenth Convention of the Industrial Workers of the World, Held at Chicago, Illinois, November 20 to December 1, 1916* (Chicago: Industrial Workers of the World, 1917), 141.

34. Kirkpatrick, "Jane Street and Denver's Rebel Housemaids," 45; Kirkpatrick email to author, May 10, 2020.

35. "Here's a Fortune (or Misfortune) for Bill Haywood," *Chicago Tribune*, August 16, 1921; "Haywood Heir to Big Legacy," *Rock Island Argus*, August 16, 1921, p. 3; "Bill Haywood in Way to Get Big Fortune Hidden Romance of I.W.W. Leader," *Belleville News Democrat*, August 16, 1921, p. 2; Foner, *Women and the American Labor Movement*, 402.

36. 1920 United States Federal Census, US Penitentiary, Leavenworth, Kansas, Roll T625_537, Page 6B, Enumeration District 97. There are conflicting records regarding Lambert's naturalization. The 1910 federal census states he naturalized in 1900. The 1920 federal census, based in part on information that the federal penitentiary system provided, states that Lambert arrived in the U.S. in 1906 and never naturalized. The latter is probably true. Charles Lindsay Lambert was born April 14, 1881, in Arbroath, Scotland. Robert Merrill, email to author, November 1, 2018. Merrill is a family member.

37. Charles L. Lambert to Fred Kirby, December 5, 1953.

38. "Synopsis of Minutes of Meeting of General Executive Board, Held June 29th–July 6th, 1917," Bisbee Deportation Legal Papers and Exhibits, Special Collections, AZ114, Box 1, Folder 2, University of Arizona (UA); "I.W.W. Activities," Case #368973:33.

39. Chaplin, *Rough-and-Tumble Story*, 195.

40. "I.W.W. Activities," Case #368973:33.

41. "Housemaids' Union Rents House in Franklin Street," 12.

42. Ibid. See Botkin, *Frank Little*, 292, to see how Wobblies changed their support of Wilson.

43. "Housemaids' Union Rents House in Franklin Street," 12.

44. Mary Shieber, "The Education of Women," *Solidarity*, December 9, 1916, p. 3.

45. Ibid.

46. Kirkpatrick, "Jane Street and Denver's Rebel Housemaids," 45.

47. Street to Mrs. Elmer S. Bruse.

48. Ibid.

49. "I.W.W. Activities," Case #368973:33.

50. Ibid., 10.

51. Street to Mrs. Elmer S. Bruse.

### Chapter 15

1. Two different addresses were given for the last DWIU No. 113 head-quarters. A Bureau of Investigation report records 502 Quincy Building while another report states 419 Quincy Building. "I.W.W. Activities," #368973:23. Ragnar Johansen, lecturer on labor topics, spoke at 419 Quincy Building, 17th and Curtis Streets, under the auspices of the Domestic Workers Union. His subject was "Woman and the Labor Movement." *Denver Rocky Mountain News*, April 5, 1917, p. 3. Jane and Dawn Street moved to 917 10th Street. *1917 US Denver City Directory*, 1718.

2. Street to Mrs. Elmer S. Bruse. In 1976, fifty-nine years later, Daniel T. Hobby discovered the letter and reprinted it in the Winter 1976 issue of *Labor History*. This document has been the sole piece of information regarding Jane Street, her methods of union organization, and the difficulties she faced with the IWW men until now.

3. Ibid.

4. Ibid.

5. Ibid.

6. Ibid.

7. Ibid.

8. Ibid.

9. Ibid.

10. "Synopsis of Minutes."

11. Rabinowitz, *Immigrant Girl*, 121.

12. William D. Haywood, Testimony before U.S. District Court of Illinois, August 12, 1918, transcript available from U.S. vs. Haywood et al., 1917–1918, Series 5: Legal Problems, Trials, and Defense, File 3: 1385–86, Box 117, Subseries B, Walter P. Reuther Library, WSU.

13. Chaplin, *Rough-and-Tumble Story*, 209; "Synopsis of Minutes."

14. Haywood, Testimony, August 12, 1918.

15. Dubofsky, *"Big Bill" Haywood*, 97–98.

16. Quoted from Industrial Worker, in Dubofsky, *"Big Bill" Haywood*, 98.

17. Elizabeth Gurley Flynn, "Do You Believe in Patriotism," *The Masses*, March 1916, https://www.marxists.org/subject/women/authors/flynn/1916/patriotism.htm.

18. Ibid.

19. Ibid. Edith Cavell was a British nurse who was executed in 1915 by a German firing squad for helping soldiers escape a Germany-occupied Belgium.

20. Bill Haywood, George F. Vanderveer, and Frank Knowlton, *Evidence and Cross Examination of William D. Haywood in the Case of the USA vs. Wm. D. Haywood, et al.* (Chicago: General Defense Committee, 1918), 212; Haywood, Testimony, August 12, 1918.

21. Haywood, Vanderveer, and Knowlton, *Evidence and Cross Examination*, 211–12; Haywood, Testimony, August 12, 1918.

22. Haywood, Vanderveer, and Knowlton, *Evidence and Cross Examination*, 211–12; Haywood, Testimony, August 12, 1918.

23. Haywood, Vanderveer, and Knowlton, *Evidence and Cross Examination*, 211–12; Haywood, Testimony, August 12, 1918.

24. Haywood, Testimony, August 12, 1918. Elmer Groves was a local organizer appointed in April 1917. After the IWW roundup on September 5, 1917, Groves managed to avoid arrest until an American Protective League operator turned him in. Still, Groves only had a civil charge brought against him for having a pistol. "Elmer Groves," Case #231308:1–2, Investigative Reports of the Bureau of Investigation 1908–1922, OGF, 1909–1921, FBI Case Files, National Archives Microfilm Publication M1085, NARA, Washington, DC.

25. Haywood, Vanderveer, and Knowlton, *Evidence and Cross Examination*, 213. Haywood, Testimony, August 12, 1918. During World War I, the AFL coordinated with the U.S. government to support the war effort while at the same time helping crush radical organizations, including the IWW and the SPA.

26. Haywood, Vanderveer, and Knowlton, *Evidence and Cross Examination*, 214. Haywood, Testimony, August 12, 1918.

27. "I.W.W. Activities," Case #368973:33.

28. Ibid., 37–38.

29. Ibid., 9.

30. Ibid., 10.

31. Ibid., 9.

32. "Various," Case #373702:17.

## Chapter 16

1. Botkin, *Frank Little*, 70. The Western Federation of Miners begrudgingly changed policy and began organizing Mexicans in 1907, though most of the Mexicans maintained separate locals. Bisbee, Arizona, preserved its white character with mainly American and Western European miners in a closed camp to labor unions for most of its history, up until 1914.

2. For a look at this strike, see ibid., 253–55.

3. "IWW Members Claim They Were Misled by False Promises of the Union Strike Leaders," *Prescott Journal Miner*, May 27, 1917, p. 1; "Sympathy Strike Now in Jerome," *Tombstone Weekly Epitaph*, June 3, 1917, p. 5. The AFL dominated Globe's mining district.

4. "Death Exacts Enormous Toll from Miners, Butte Stands Appalled at Great Sacrifice," *Anaconda Standard*, June 10, 1917, p. 1. For an examination of the Speculator tragedy, see Michael Punke, *Fire and Brimstone* (New York: Hyperion, 2006).

5. A. S. Embree to Grover H. Perry, June 26, 1917, AZ 114, Box 1, Folder 2, Special Collections, UA; Grover H. Perry to the Executive Committee, Bisbee AZ, July 10, 1917, AZ 114, Box 2, Folder 3, Special Collections, UA; Grover Perry, Testimony before U.S. District Court of Illinois, August 8, 1918, transcript available from U.S. vs. Haywood et al., 1917–1918, Series 5: Legal Problems, Trials, and Defense, File 3:10928, Box 116, Subseries B, Walter P. Reuther Library, WSU.

6. "Various," Case #8000–36190:486–87, Investigative Reports of the Bureau of Investigation 1908–1922, Old German Files (OGF), 1909–1921, FBI Case Files, National Archives Microfilm Publication M1085, NARA, Washington, DC. Ben Webb, chairman of the Miners' Union executive committee, was considered to be a most valuable Bisbee witness since he was believed to be working for a mining company while serving on Bisbee's IWW executive, organization, and audit committees. Other valuable Bisbee informants included Bisbee Postmaster L. R. Bailey, Western Union Telegraph operator R. M. Henderson, H. B. Scott, Thomas Mooney, W. H. Minshull, Dave Foster, E. A. Tovres, John Caretto, and H. Howe. The Bureau of Investigation report stated that these people would be "annihilated" if their names were revealed.

7. For a discussion of Frank Little's and Bill Haywood's correspondence and conversations regarding the IWW's stance on war involvement, see Botkin, *Frank Little*, 251–52, 262–63.

8. "'Wobbly Slim' Known Here, Hanged at Butte for Insult to Troops," *Jerome News*, August 3, 1917, p. 1; "Frank Little Is Lynched," *Jerome Sun*, August 1, 1917, p. 1.

9. Joyce L. Kornbluh, ed., *Rebel Voices: An IWW Anthology* (Chicago: Charles H. Kerr, 1988), 295. After being discovered near Watersmeet, Michigan, Frank Little was taken to an undisclosed location in Wisconsin. "Attempts Settlement at Chisholm," *Solidarity*, August 26, 1916, p. 1. An affidavit of his extensive injuries, some clearly from the Michigan kidnapping, was entered into evidence during the Chicago IWW trial of 1918. "Various," Case #8000–36190:189–90.

10. "Frank Little Lynched in Butte," *Solidarity*, August 4, 1917, p. 1.

11. See Botkin, *Frank Little*, 251–53, for a discussion of Frank Little's physical condition.

12. "Butte's Name Tarnished by the Stain of Lynch Law, Frank Little Hanged at Trestle by Unknown Mob," *Anaconda Standard*, August 2, 1917, p. 1.

13. "I.W.W. Activities," #368973:1. The Bureau of Investigation read the June 20, 1919, letter to Harriet Nillson, c/o Room 220, IWW, 224 S. Spring St., Los Angeles, CA, Germain Bldg., from Jane Street in San Diego. It recapped her meeting with Frank Little and the contents of Lambert's report. The letter was resealed and sent on its way.

14. "I.W.W. Activities," #368973:1.

15. Ibid.

16. "IWW Wins in Jerome," *Solidarity*, June 9, 1917, p. 4; "Mining Conditions in Bisbee, Arizona," August 29, 1917, L9791, B62, Pamphlet 15, Special Collections, UA.

17. "Various," Case #8000–36190: 487.

18. "I.W.W. Activities," Case #368973:7; *1917 Denver City Directory*, 1778.

19. "I.W.W. Activities," Case #368973:9; Devlin to Mary Jane Devlin, November 1938, Jack and Kathy Devlin, Devlin Family Collection.

20. Ibid.

21. Devlin to Charles Patrick "Pat" Devlin (David Street), ca. April 1944.

22. Ibid.

23. "I.W.W. Activities," #368973:6.

24. Phillip J. Mellinger, *Race and Labor in Western Copper* (Tucson: University of Arizona Press, 1995), 178–79.

25. "Butte Vigilantes Hang Little, I. W. W. Agitator, at Bridge as a Warning," *El Paso Herald*, August 1, 1917, p. 5.

26. Perry, Testimony, August 8, 1918, 10930.

27. Ibid.; "Recovering from the Auto Accident," *Daily Arizona Silver Belt*, June 20, 1917, p. 1. Joe Oates claimed he would have been with the group but had remained in Bisbee to get his final pay. John Joseph Oates, Testimony before United States District Court of Illinois, August 3, 1918, Transcript available from U.S. vs. Haywood et al., 1917–1918, Legal Problems, Trials, and Defense, File 4: 10036, Box 115, Subseries B, Walter P. Reuther Library, WSU.

28. "Recovering from the Auto Accident," 1; Perry, Testimony, August 8, 1918, 10930. The county hospital was Inspiration Hospital in Miami. Some historical accounts, based on local newspaper reporting, note that Frank Little then "holed up in a miner's cabin" after his auto accident, where he called strikes, and as a result, narrowly missed deportation. This was not true. The newly formed citizens' Loyalty League in Globe and law enforcement officers had no idea that Frank was in Miami for only one night before heading to Chicago, and not organizing a strike in Bisbee.

29. See Botkin, *Frank Little*, 262–63, for a synopsis of this meeting.

30. See Fred Watson's memoirs of the Bisbee Deportation in "Still on Strike! Recollections of a Bisbee Deportee," *Journal of Arizona History* 18 (Summer 1977): 171–84; Gilbert Mere to Robert W. Houston, January 17, 1977, Fred Thompson Collection, Subseries A, Box 8, File 24, Walter P. Reuther Library, WSU.

31. Gilbert Mere to Fred Thompson, June 9, 1976, Fred Thompson Collection, Subseries A, Box 8, File 24, Walter P. Reuther Library, WSU.

32. For historical accounting of the Bisbee Deportation, see Frederick Watson, "A Deportee Deposition," August 30, 1970, in *The Great Bisbee IWW Deportation of July 12, 1917*, by Robert E. Hanson (Montana: Signature Press, 1987). See also James Byrkit, *Forging the Copper Collar* (Tucson: University of Arizona, 1982), 187–215. For contemporary local views see "The Great Wobbly Drive," *Bisbee Daily Review*, July 13, 1917, p. 1, 4.

33. Ray Ewing, "The Big Drive," originally published in *Souvenir of Bisbee*, by a Recycled Miner, 1979, in *The Great Bisbee IWW Deportation of July 12, 1917*, by Robert E. Hanson (Montana: Signature Press, 1987); Gilbert Mere to Fred Thompson, May 25, 1976, Fred Thompson Collection, Subseries A, Box 8 File 23, Walter P. Reuther Library, WSU. On the evening of July 11, 1917, the Local 800 strike committee received a "vague" warning. See Fred Watson's memoirs of the Bisbee Deportation in "Still on Strike!," 171–84.

34. Watson, "A Deportee Deposition"; Byrkit, *Forging the Copper Collar*, 187–215; "The Great Wobbly Drive," p. 1, 4.

35. Watson, "A Deportee Deposition"; Ewing, "The Big Drive." Ray Ewing reported one barrel of water per boxcar, which emptied quickly. See Byrkit, *Forging the Copper Collar*, 210–15, for descriptions of the train ride. See Woodrow Wilson, *Final Address in Support of the League of Nations*, Pueblo, Colorado, September 24, 1919. Instead of speaking directly to Congress, Wilson conducted a series of public "barn-storming" speeches across the West where he emphasized, "I cannot say too often—any man who carries a hyphen about with him carries a dagger that he is ready to plunge into the vitals of this Republic whenever he gets ready." The Immigration Act of 1917 further defined individuals and groups who were undesirable as American citizens. In this case, President Wilson vetoed the act but was overruled.

36. The Law of Necessity is a form of where defendants argue that their actions are necessary to prevent a greater evil. See State of Arizona vs. H. E. Wootton (generally known as the "Bisbee Deportation case"), 1918, as presented in *Law of Necessity as Applied in State of Arizona, Bisbee IWW vs. Deportation Case H. E. Wootton*, document available in Bisbee Deportation Legal Papers and Exhibits, Special Collections, H9791 B621 L41, UA. See State of Arizona, Bisbee I.W.W. vs. Deportation Case H.E. Wootton.

37. See Botkin, *Frank Little*, 279–94, for Frank Little's activities in Butte, Montana, prior to his murder.

38. "Butte's Name Tarnished by the Stain," 1; "Not One Clew as to Lynchers," *Anaconda Standard*, August 4, 1917, p. 2.

39. "Butte's Name Tarnished by the Stain," 1; "Not One Clew as to Lynchers," *Anaconda Standard*, August 4, 1917, p. 2; "Little Inquest Begun Before Coroner Lane and a Jury of Seven Miners," *Butte Daily Post*, August 3, 1917,

p. 12. Testimony concluded that Frank Little had not been dragged down Butte streets, as if to lessen the horrific actions. Yet other witnesses claimed to have seen Frank Little dragged behind the car. In addition, testimony claimed that sand embedded in his bloody knees was evidence of a struggle at the site of the hanging. More likely the sand was from his unconscious body being dropped to the ground at some point. Frank Little Death Certificate, August 1, 1917; Frank Little Coroner's Verdict, August 7, 1917, Butte, Silver Bow County, Montana. All documents relating to the coroner's inquest and its three-day investigation mysteriously disappeared. "Little Executed by Masked Men," *Butte Daily Post*, August 1, 1917, p. 3. No murderers have ever been factually identified in the murder case of Frank H. Little.

## Chapter 17

1. California State Board of Health, County of Los Angeles, City of Los Angeles, No. 8301, Birth Index, 1905–1995. Charles Devlin told his children years later that he and Jane were married, an untruth. Devlin to Mary Jane Devlin, November 1938.

2. Jane was still living with Charles Carroll Devlin when he registered for World War I on September 12, 1918. Devlin had written her last name as Devlin when he registered. The couple lived at 809 N. Hollenbeck Street in Los Angeles. He was working as an elevator operator in the Wright and Callendar Bldg. United States, Selective Service System, *World War I Selective Service System Draft Registration Cards, 1917–1918*, Washington, DC: National Archives and Records Administration, M1509, 4,582 rolls, California, Los Angeles County, Roll 1531195, Draft Board 5.

3. Devlin to Mary Jane Devlin, November 1938; *1917 Long Beach, California, City Directory*, 229. Likely this was on the lots belonging to Balboa Amusement Producing Company, the only movie production company in Long Beach. See http://www.cla.csulb.edu/departments/rgrll/projects/balboaresearch/ for a history of productions at Balboa Entertainment Producing Company.

4. Dubofsky, *"Big Bill" Haywood*, 109.

5. "Government is Probing IWW, Determined to Check Antiwar Activity Headquarters of Organization," *Colorado Springs Gazette*, September 6, 1917, p. 1.

6. "Various," Case #67: 273, Investigative Reports of the Bureau of Investigation 1908–1922, Bureau Section Files (BSF), 1909–1921, FBI Case Files, National Archives Microfilm Publication M1085, Roll 916, NARA, Washington, DC.

7. Dubofsky, *"Big Bill" Haywood*, 109.

8. Dubofsky, *We Shall Be All*, 234–35.

9. Dubofsky, *"Big Bill" Haywood*, 109. Dubofsky claims that agents confiscated over five tons of materials. This surely includes mimeograph and typing machines.

10. See Haywood, Testimony, August 12, 1918, for Haywood's interrogation regarding patriotism.

11. "IWW Activities," Case #368973:1. Only Bertha O'Neill wrote Frank Little before he was murdered.

12. Dubofsky, *We Shall Be All*, 198. A General Recruiting Union office was located at IWW headquarters in Chicago. The Los Angeles recruiting local was possibly No. 602.

13. United States, Selective Service System, *World War I Selective Service System Draft Registration Cards, 1917–1918*, Washington, DC: National Archives and Records Administration, M1509, 4,582 rolls, Colorado, Denver County, Roll 1561844, Draft Board 7.

14. Devlin to Mary Jane Devlin, November 1938.

15. "IWW Found Guilty on First Ballot," *Rockford Daily Register Gazette*, August 19, 1918, p. 2. For Bill Haywood's account of the 1918 IWW trial, see *Bill Haywood's Book*, 313–24.

16. Harvey Duff, *The Silent Defenders: Courts and Capitalism in California* (Chicago: Industrial Workers of the World, 1920), 22. The actual verbiage read, "by demanding stated wages and certain terms from the employers throughout the United States and unless the employers of labor will agree to pay the stated wages and agree to the certain terms demanded, the said defendants and the said persons, with whom said defendants conspired, would refuse to work for or give 'their services to said employers, and would engage in what is known in every day parlance as a strike.'"

17. Steven Parfitt, "IWW History Project," http://depts.washington.edu/iww/index.shtml.

18. Charles Lambert to Fred Kirby, December 25, 1953. Lambert wrote this cover letter to Kirby, attached to his "Open Letter to President Harding," about Judge Landis and the IWW trial and resulting Leavenworth incarceration for IWWs picked up in 1917 and 1918. Since Lambert had no wife or family, the letter was an early Christmas gift to Kirby, who had asked for the letter to be willed to him upon Lambert's death. Robert Merrill, email to author, November 1, 2018.

19. Lambert to Fred Kirby, December 25, 1953.

20. Parfitt, "IWW History Project." The quote is attributed to Melvyn Dubofsky.

21. Devlin to Pat Devlin (son), April 1944, Jack and Kathy Devlin, Devlin Family Papers.

22. Devlin to Mary Jane Devlin, November 1938.

23. "IWW Activities," Case #368973:2.

24. Ibid., 6.

25. Devlin to Mary Jane Devlin, November 1938.

26. "IWW Activities," Case #368973:6.

27. Ibid.

28. Ibid., 9.

29. Ibid.

30. Devlin to Mary Jane Devlin, November 1938.

31. "IWW Activities," Case #368973:7.

32. Ibid., 5.

33. Ibid., 6.

34. Ibid., 33.

35. Ibid., 6, 11. Thomas Whitehead led the provisional GEB.

36. Ibid., 8.

37. Ibid., 8, 9.

38. "I.W.W. Activities," Case #368973:6; "IWW Convention," *Solidarity*, September 27, 1913, p. 1. See *Industrial Worker*, August 14, 1913, for various articles relating to the controversy. "A Critical Period," *Solidarity*, September 27, 1913, p. 2. For complete minutes of the IWW convention, see *Stenographic Report of the Eighth Annual Convention of the Industrial Workers of the World*, September 14–29, 1913 (Chicago: Industrial Workers of the World, 1913). See also Botkin, *Frank Little*, 203–4, for discussion of the decentralization movement at the Eighth Annual Convention of the IWW.

39. "IWW Activities," Case #368973:7.

40. Ibid., 2, 6, 34.

41. Ibid.

42. Ibid.

43. "Various," Case #8000-67171:7, Investigative Reports of the Bureau of Investigation 1908–1922, OGF, 1909–1921, FBI Case Files, National Archives Microfilm Publication M1085, NARA, Washington, DC. The book is actually called *Evidence and Cross Examination of William D. Haywood in the Case of the USA. vs. Wm. D. Haywood, et al.* (Chicago: General Defense Committee, 1918). Haywood's lawyers put the book together shortly after the conclusion of the Chicago trial, likely to defray defense expenses.

44. "Various," Case #8000-67171:7.

45. "IWW Activities," Case #368973:2, 6, 33.

46. Ibid., 2, 6, 57.

47. J. Edgar Hoover renamed the Bureau of Investigation the Federal Bureau of Investigation after being appointed its chief on July 1, 1932.

48. The California Criminal Syndicalism Act, passed directly to deter IWW activities, defined criminal activity as "any doctrine or precept advocating . . . the commission of crime, sabotage . . . or unlawful acts of force and violence . . . as a means of accomplishing a change in industrial ownership or control, or effecting any political change." Anyone knowingly associating with a group that advocated, taught, or abetted criminal syndicalism could be charged with criminal liability under the California statute. This included measures that checked IWW propaganda.

### Chapter 18

1. 1910 Federal Census, Mission, San Diego, California, Roll T624_95, Page 11B, Enumeration District 0129, FHL microfilm 1374108.

2. "IWW Activities," Case #368973:58.

3. Ibid., 2. The Western Costumes Company occupied 908 S. Broadway, Los Angeles, in 1919.

4. Ibid.; Devlin to Mary Jane Street, November 1938.

5. "IWW Activities," Case #368973:14, 54.

6. See State of California, Department of Public Health, Vital Statistics, Standard Certificate of Birth, No. 755.

7. Ibid.

8. Devlin to Mary Jane Street, November 1938.

9. "IWW Activities," Case #368973:5.

10. Ibid., 10.

11. Ibid., 9.

12. Ibid., 10.

13. Ibid.

14. Ibid., 8.

15. Ibid., 11, 20.

16. When Bureau of Investigation agents confiscated Jane Street's letter to Mrs. Elmer Bruse about February 1917, they had no warrant, and their action was profoundly illegal.

17. "Charge He Stole Woman's Overcoat," *Seattle Star*, June 28, 1919, p. 10. C. W. Sellers, using the alias J. W. Burns, was a mechanic employed by a carnival company. "Various," #373702:1, 14; "I.W.W. Activities," #36873:56. In Salt Lake City, a Bureau of Investigation agent reported that Sellers was "quite prominent" in IWW circles and his activities well known to the Bureau office there.

18. Sellers did attend the IWW convention, representing Washington and Arizona. "One Big Union Convention Selects Great Falls for Meeting in Fall," *Great Falls Daily Tribune*, July 9, 1919, p. 1. Sellers, along with A. S. Embree, spoke to delegates at the Montana IWW Convention. See his remarks in *Butte Daily Bulletin*, July 7, 1919, pp. 1, 8.

19. "IWW Activities," Case #368973:8.

20. Ibid., 55.

21. Woodrow C. Whitten, "Criminal Syndicalism and the Law in California: 1919–1927," *Transactions of the American Philosophical Society, New Series* 59, no. 2 (1969): 15. *Criminal syndicalism* has been defined as a doctrine of criminal acts for political, industrial, and social change. These criminal acts include advocation of crime, sabotage, violence, and other unlawful methods of terrorism. "Criminal Syndicalism Law & Legal Definition," *US Legal, Inc.*

22. "IWW Activities," Case #368973:45.

23. Ibid., 4.

24. Ibid., 46.

25. Ibid., 4. Charles Devlin lived at 1000 ½ Main Street in Los Angeles.

26. Ibid., 14, 54.

27. Ibid., 46.

28. Ibid., 55.

29. Ibid., 37.

30. Ibid., 36, 38–39.

31. Dubofsky, *We Shall Be All*, 260. William Stephens served as California's governor from March 15, 1917, until January 8, 1923.

32. Ibid.

33. "IWW Activities," Case #368973:25.

34. Ibid.

35. Ibid.

36. Ibid., 26.

37. Ibid.

38. Ibid., 26.

39. Ibid., 17.

40. Ibid., 26.

41. WWI Draft Registration Card, Colorado, Denver County, Roll 1544476, Draft Board 2.

42. "IWW Activities," Case #368973:27.

43. Ibid.; 1920 Federal Census, San Diego, San Diego, California, Roll T625_130, Page 5A, Enumeration District 234.

44. "IWW Activities," Case #368973:27.

45. Ibid.

46. Ibid., 28, 61.

47. Ibid., 29.

48. Ibid., 40, 58.

49. WWI Draft Registration Card, California, San Diego County, Roll 1543751.

50. "IWW Activities," Case #368973:58.

51. Ibid.

52. Ibid., 59.

53. Ibid., 62.

54. "Take One Prisoner and Seize Lot of IWW Literature," *San Diego Union*, December 23, 1919, p. 1.

55. "IWW Activities," Case #368973:58.

56. "Take One Prisoner and Seize Lot of IWW Literature," 1.

57. "IWW Activities," Case #368973:19.

58. Ibid., 16.

59. Ibid., 17.

60. "Woman Is Held as Member of IWW," *San Diego Evening Tribune*, December 30, 1919, p. 1.

61. Ibid. Dawn Street was taken to a detention home. Pat Devlin stayed with Mrs. Ryan, Jane's landlady. Baby Mary Jane went home with Police Matron Veale.

### Epilogue

1. Marcus Roberts served as Jane's defense attorney. "IWW Activities," Case #368973:15, 60.

2. Ibid., 68.

3. Ibid., 15.

4. Ibid., 31–32. See *California, Voter Registrations, 1900–1968* (database online), Provo, UT, Ancestry.com, for Walter A. Weymouth's politics. "Stand Pat" or "Standpatter" Republicans were a conservative faction of the Republican Party *standing pat* to their core-conservative values, in opposition to their more progressive members.

5. "Fair Practice Board to Meet," *San Diego Evening Tribune*, December 1919, p. 15. By the time Jane's hearing concluded, among businesses being monitored were San Diego's shoe merchants. A public boycott was in progress for "not placing in plain figures upon every pair of shoes, on display or for sale to the general public, the actual net cost after the deduction of all trade discounts, and the addition of cartage and express charges incident to the placing of the shoes upon the shelves." See Editorial, "Fair Price Head Makes Reply to Article," *San Diego Evening Tribune*, February 7, 1920, p. 5.

6. "Various," Case #373702:5, Roll #821, Investigative Reports of the Bureau of Investigation 1908–1922, OGF, 1909–1921, FBI Case Files, National Archives Microfilm Publication M1085, NARA, Washington, DC.

7. "IWW Activities," Case #186701–26:7, Investigative Case Files of the Bureau of Investigation 1908–1922, Bureau Section Files, National Archives Microfilm Publication M1085, NARA, Washington, DC. Jane's second membership card, #166683 in Local 110, was found in an IWW headquarters, in a boarding house, at 1519 Locust Street.

8. Leslie, personal interview, September 28, 2018.

9. E. H. Gamble affidavit.

10. Ibid.

11. Ibid.

12. Kirk Harris sworn affidavit.

13. New York Passenger Lists, 1820–1957, Year 1928, Arrival New York, Microfilm Serial T715, 1897–1957, Microfilm Roll 4325, Line 13, Page 248; Leslie, personal interview, September 28, 2018.

14. Certificate No. 20408, Certificate of Literacy, The University of the State of New York, Education Department, October 28, 1928, Leslie, Jane Street Family Papers.

15. Chihuahua, Mexico, Civil Registration Marriages, 1861–1967.

16. Leslie, personal interview, September 28, 2018.

17. Ancestry.com, *U.S., World War II Army Enlistment Records, 1938–1946* (database online), Provo, UT, Ancestry.com, 2005.

18. Leslie, personal interview, September 28, 2018.

19. Ibid.

20. Ibid.

21. State of California Department of Professional and Vocational Standards Board of Examiners, Psychology Examining Committee, June 1, 1948, Leslie, Jane Street Family Papers.

22. Leslie, personal interview, September 28, 2018.

23. *California Death Index, 1940–1997*; Statement, J. T. Oswald Mortuaries, April 25, 1966, Leslie, Jane Street Family Papers. David Street paid for Jane's cremation. Possibly Mary Jane made the decision to disperse Jane's remains when there was money to pay for it. Jack and Kathy Devlin, Devlin Family Papers.

24. For information, see https://www.domesticworkers.org/. Regarding prior domestic workers' efforts, see Elizabeth Beck, "The National Domestic Workers Union and the War on Poverty," *The Journal of Sociology & Social Welfare* 28, no. 4 (December 2001): Article 11, https://scholarworks.wmich.edu/jssw/vol28/iss4/11.

25. For current activities regarding legislation (2019), see https://onlabor.org/an-explainer-whats-happening-with-domestic-workers-rights/.

26. Former Colorado state treasurer Cary Kennedy (2007–11) made the statement. *Strong Sisters: Elected Women of Colorado*, Documentary.

27. For information about Denver's Women's March, see https://www.womxnsmarchdenver.org/.

28. Adams, "My Association with a Glamourous Man," 15.

29. Fetter, *Colorado's Legendary Lovers*; Morton, Tom, "Louise Sneed Hill and Denver's 'Sacred Thirty-Six,'" *Fairmount Who's Who*, April 23, 2013.

30. Fetter, *Colorado's Legendary Lovers*. Wells's partner, under consultation with Louise, liquidated assets in the First National Bank of Telluride, in which Bulkeley Wells had an interest, and Louise cut off any other monies to him. Adams, "My Association with a Glamourous Man," 15.

31. "Veteran Member of Crawford Hill Household Dies," *Denver Post*, April 28, 1930, p. 3; Frances Wayne, "Member of Household of Mrs. Crawford Hill Paid Honor at Funeral," *Denver Post*, May 7, 1930.

32. Otto Liese to Nathaniel Hill, May 3, 1930.

33. See the Crawford and Louise Sneed Hill Collection, "Cora Cowan," MSS 309, Files 1–2, SHL, for all the letters and financial reports regarding Cora Cowan's unusual estate. One document incorrectly assigns the Hill family plot to Riverside Cemetery. It was, in fact, Fairmount Cemetery. Cora was cremated at Riverside Cemetery.

34. The Smith Act, or Alien Registration Act, of 1940 made it an offense to advocate or belong to a group that advocated the violent overthrow of the government.

35. For more information on Elizabeth Gurley Flynn and Carlo Tresca, see Flynn, *The Rebel Girl: An Autobiography*; and Nunzio Pemicone, *Carlo Tresca: Portrait of a Rebel* (Oakland, CA: AK Press, 2010).

36. Rabinowitz, *Immigrant Girl*, 158, 124, 248–49.

37. Kirkpatrick, "Jane Street and Denver's Rebel Housemaids," 45.

38. Robert Merrill, email to author, November 1, 2018. Merrill is a Lambert family member.

39. Phil Engle, "The Stool Pigeon, a Drama in Two Acts," *Industrial Pioneer* 1, no. 10 (February 1924): 41–42, 44.

40. Rosenberg, email to author, August 26, 2019; Certificate of Death, State of Minnesota, #20420–3327.

41. Rosenberg, email to author, August 26, 2019; Certificate of Death, State of Minnesota, #20420–3327. A photo, #4737, thought to be of Phil Engle's funeral, is filed at the Walter Reuther Library at Wayne State University.

42. See Grace Tuttle's ad in the *Denver Rocky Mountain News*, March 24, 1918, p. 34.

43. Leslie, personal interview, September 28, 2018.

44. "Thompson Mortuary," *Denver Post*, February 12, 1925, p. 27.

45. Washington, Marriage Records, 1854–2013.

46. WWII Draft Registration Card for Albert Kohler, U-523, 4-27-1942. Jane was living at 1600 Maine (Mine?) Street, Philadelphia, PA.

47. "Various," Case #373702:12,19.

48. "Men Who Spurn US Citizenship Led Butte Mobs," *Great Falls Daily Tribune*, May 7, 1920, p. 2.

49. See the Bureau of Investigation's entire case file on Claude Sellers, "Various," Case #373702.

50. "Fire at Tacoma Prison," *Seattle Star*, June 1, 1920, p. 1; "Centralia IWW Accomplice Burns His Way Out of Jail," *East Oregonian*, 1.

51. *Washington, Death Certificates, 1907–1960*, Salt Lake City, Utah, FamilySearch, 2013.

52. "Miscellaneous Files, 1909–1921," Case #18164, 104, Investigative Reports of the Bureau of Investigation 1908–1922, OGF, 1909–1921, FBI Case Files, National Archives Microfilm Publication M1085, NARA, Washington, DC.

53. *1933 St. Louis City Directory*, 1203.

54. Phil Wright, Ancestry.com message to author, September 16, 2018. Wright is Winona Wright's grandson.

55. Ibid.

56. Missouri State Death Certificate #19418.

57. Devlin to Mary Jane, November 1938.

58. Devlin to Charles Patrick "Pat" Devlin (David Street), April 1944.

59. Leslie, personal interview, September 28, 2018.

60. *California Death Index, 1940–1997*.

61. Leslie, personal interview, September 28, 2018.

62. For more information on Hollywood actor David Street, see https://www.imdb.com/name/nm0834070/bio.

63. Leslie, personal interview, September 28, 2018.

# BIBLIOGRAPHY

## *Primary Sources*
## Archives and Manuscript Collections

Bisbee Deportation Legal Papers and Exhibits. Special Collections. University of Arizona (UA).

Center for Public History & Digital Humanities. Department of History and Cleveland State University. Cleveland, OH.

Colorado State Archives (CSA). Denver.

Joseph A. Labadie Collection. Special Collections Library. University of Michigan (UMI). Ann Arbor.

Library of Congress

Missouri State Archives. Jefferson City.

Sophia Smith Collection. Five College Archives & Manuscript Collections. Smith College Archives. Northampton, MA.

   Rhoda Elizabeth McCulloch Papers, 1884–1978

Stephen H. Hart Library and Research Center/History Colorado Center (SHL). Denver.

   Colonial Dames of Colorado Collection

   Crawford and Louise S. Hill Collection

   Denver Women's Club Collection

   Ellis Meredith Collection

   Frederick Bonfils Collection

   Liska Stillman Churchill Collection

   National Society of the Colonial Dames of America in the State of Colorado Collection, 1896–1990

   YWCA Denver Manuscript Collection

Walter P. Reuther Library. Wayne State University (WSU). Detroit.

   Fred Thompson Collection

   Industrial Workers of the World (IWW) Collection

Western History Collection. Denver Public Library (DPL). Denver, CO.

   Caroline Bancroft Collection

   Digital Collection

## Newspapers

*Anaconda Standard* (Butte, MT)

*Arkansas Gazette* (Little Rock)

*Belleville News Democrat* (IL)
*Brooklyn Eagle* (NY)
*Butte Daily Post* (MT)
*Cheyenne Record* (Cheyenne Wells, CO)
*Chicago Day Book*
*Chicago Tribune*
*Cincinnati Post* (OH)
*Colorado Gambler* (Greenwood Village)
*Colorado Golden Transcript*
*Colorado Springs Gazette*
*Daily Arizona Sunbelt* (Globe)
*Daily Illinois State Journal* (Springfield)
*Daily News* (Denver)
*Daily Rocky Mountain News* (Denver)
*Delta Independent* (CO)
*Denver Post*
*Denver Rocky Mountain News*
*Denver Times*
*Duluth News Tribune*
*El Paso Herald*
*Evening Star* (Washington, DC)
*Great Falls Daily Tribune* (MT)
*Greeley Tribune* (CO)
*Illinois State Journal* (Springfield)
*Indianapolis Journal*
*Jerome Sun* (AZ)
*Jersey City Evening Journal* (NJ)
*Kansas City Star* (MO)
*New York Daily Tribune*
*Ordway New Era* (CO)
*Plain Dealer* (Cleveland)
*Prescott Journal Miner* (AZ)
*Riverside Daily Press* (CA)
*Rock Island Argus* (IL)
*Sacramento Bee*
*Sacramento Union*
*San Diego Evening Tribune*
*San Diego Union*
*San Francisco Call*
*San Francisco Chronicle*
*Seattle Star*
*Ski-Zette* (Camp Hale, CO)
*Telluride Journal* (CO)

*Tombstone Weekly Epitaph* (AZ)
*Topeka State Journal*
*Washington Post*
*Washington Times* (Washington, DC)

## Labor and Radical Periodicals

*Butte Daily Bulletin* (MT)
*Cleveland Socialist*
*Industrial Pioneer* (Chicago)
*Industrial Worker* (Spokane and Seattle, 1909–17)
*International Socialist Review*
*IWW Songs to Fan the Flames of Discontent, 1916*
*New York Call* (Socialist Party of America)
*One Big Union Monthly* (IWW)
*Solidarity* (Chicago and Cleveland)

## Family Documents, Photographs, Personal Correspondence, and Other Papers Privately Held

Cowan Family Papers (includes family interviews).

Devlin, Jack and Kathy. Devlin Family Papers (includes family interviews).

Engle Correspondence.

Huysman Family Papers (includes family interviews).

Lambert, Charles Lindsay. Charles Lindsay Lambert to Fred Kirby, December 5, 1953.

Leslie, Guy. Jane Street Family Papers (includes family interviews).

Street, Jane. Jane Street to Mrs. Elmer S. Bruse, 1917, https://archive.iww.org /history/library/Street/letter/.

Wright, Phil. Wright Family Papers.

## Government Documents and Collections

"100 Years of Marriage and Divorce Statistics in the United States." U.S. Department of Health, Education, and Welfare. National Vital Statistics System, Series 21, No. 24, December 1973.

Arkansas County Marriages, 1838–1957.

Arkansas Death Index, 1914–1923.

California Death Index, 1940–1997.

California, Department of Public Health, Vital Statistics.

California Great Register of Voters, 1900–1968.

California Voter Registration, Sacramento County, CA, 1912–1914.

Chihuahua, Mexico. Civil Registration Marriages, 1861–1967.

City of St. Louis, Missouri. Registry of Births.

Indexes to the Carded Records of Soldiers Who Served in Volunteer Organizations During the Spanish-American War, compiled 1899–1927, documenting the period 1898–1903. National Archives and Records Administration (NARA), Washington, DC.

Investigative Reports of the Bureau of Investigation 1908–22. FBI Case Files. National Archives and Records Administration (NARA), Washington, DC.

    Bureau Section Files, 1909–21.

    Old German Files (OGF), 1909–21.

Kansas State Census Collection, 1855–1925.

*The Military Occupation of the Colorado National Guard, 1913–1914.* Denver: Press of the Smith-Brooks Printing Company, 1914.

Minnesota Death Certificates.

Missouri State Archives, Marriage Records.

Missouri State Death Certificates, 1910–1962.

Neill, Charles Patrick. *United States Bureau of Labor, Report on Condition of Woman and Child Wage Earners in the United States.* 19 Volumes. Washington, DC: Government Printing Office, 1910–13.

*Official Register of the United States, Civil, Military, Service, 1937.* NARA, Washington, DC.

*Passenger and Crew Lists of Vessels Arriving at New York, New York, 1897–1957.* Microfilm Publication T715, 8892 rolls. NAI: 300346. Records of the Immigration and Naturalization Service; National Archives at Washington, DC.

Passport Applications. January 2, 1906–March 31, 1925. NARA, Washington, DC.

*Registers of Enlistments in the United States Army, 1798–1914.* NARA, Washington, DC.

*Report of the Adjutant General of the Arkansas State Guard.* U.S., Adjutant General Military Records of Arkansas, 1631–1976.

Stigler, George J. *Domestic Servants in the United States, 1900–1940.* National Bureau of Economic Research, Occasional Paper 24, April 1946, New York.

United States Federal Census.

United States Federal Slave Schedules.

Washington State Death Certificates 1907–1960. Salt Lake City, UT: FamilySearch, 2013.

World War I Selective Service System Draft Registration Cards, 1917–1918. NARA, Washington, DC.

## Memoirs and Oral Histories

Adams, E. B. "My Association with a Glamourous Man, Bulkeley Wells." Privately published, 1961.

Addams, Jane. *Twenty Years at Hull-House.* Chicago: Addams Publications, 2011.

Chaplin, Ralph. *The Rough-and-Tumble Story of an American Radical.* Chicago: University of Chicago Press, 1948.

Devlin, Charles. "Memoirs." Devlin Family Collection, n.d.

Ewing, Ray. "The Big Drive." Originally published in *Souvenir of Bisbee*, by a Recycled Miner, 1979. In *The Great Bisbee IWW Deportation of July 12, 1917*, by Robert E. Hanson. Montana: Signature Press, 1987.

Flynn, Elizabeth Gurley. *The Rebel Girl: An Autobiography*. Revised edition. New York: International Publishers, 1994. First published 1973.

Foner, Philip. *Fellow Workers and Friends: IWW Free-Speech Fights as Told by Participants*. Westport, CT: Greenwood Press, 1981.

Haywood, William D. *Bill Haywood's Book: Autobiography of Big Bill Haywood*. New York: International Publishers, 1929.

Langdon, Emma Florence. *The Cripple Creek Strike 1903–1904*. Victor, CO, 1904.

Rabinowitz, Matilda. *Immigrant Girl, Radical Woman*. Ithaca: Cornell University Press, 2017.

Rosen, Ellen Doree. *A Wobbly Life: IWW Organizer E. F. Doree*. Detroit: Wayne State University Press, 2004.

Steel, Edward M. *The Correspondence of Mother Jones*. Pittsburgh: University of Pittsburgh Press, 1985.

Stiverson, Clara, interview by Elizabeth Jameson, July 29, 1975. As quoted in Elizabeth Jameson, "Imperfect Unions, Class, and Gender." *Frontiers: A Journal of Women Studies* 1, no. 2 (Spring 1976): 91.

Street, Jane. "Something Like the Big House." Jane Street Family Papers.

Watson, Fred. "A Deportee Deposition," August 30, 1970. In *The Great Bisbee IWW Deportation of July 12, 1917*, by Robert E. Hanson. Montana: Signature Press, 1987.

———. "Still on Strike! Recollections of a Bisbee Deportee." *Journal of Arizona History* 18 (Summer 1977): 171–84.

### Books, Documents, and Pamphlets

Brissenden, Paul Frederick. *The IWW: A Study of American Syndicalism*. New York: Columbia University, 1919.

"Domestic Workers, Fight for Your Rights!" Chicago: Industrial Workers of the World, n.d.

Fink, Walter H. *The Ludlow Massacre*. United Mine Workers Association, 1914.

Flynn, Elizabeth Gurley. "Sabotage." Originally published as "Sabotage, the Conscious Withdrawal of Industrial Efficiency," October 1916. www.iww.org/history/library/Flynn/Sabotage.

Green, Archie, David Roediger, Franklin Rosemont, and Salvatore Salerno, eds. *The Big Red Songbook*. Oakland: PM Press, 2016.

Haywood, Bill, George F. Vanderveer, and Frank Knowlton. *Evidence and Cross Examination of William D. Haywood in the Case of the USA vs. Wm. D. Haywood, et al.* Chicago: General Defense Committee, 1918.

Hill, Joe. "The Rebel Girl." *IWW Songs to Fan the Flames of Discontent*. 9th ed. Joe Hill Memorial Edition. Cleveland: IWW Publishing Bureau, 1916.

*Industrial Workers of the World Constitution.*

Kornbluh, Joyce L., ed. *Rebel Voices: An IWW Anthology.* Chicago: Charles H. Kerr, 1988.

Frank Little, Coroner's Verdict. August 7, 1917. Butte, Silver Bow County, Montana.

Frank Little, Death Certificate. August 1, 1917. Butte, Silver Bow County, Montana.

*Official Proceedings of the Fifteenth Annual Convention of the Western Federation of Miners, Stenographer's Report, June 10–July 3, 1907.* Denver, Colorado.

*Proceedings of the Second Industrial Workers of the World Convention, September 17 to October 3, 1906.* Chicago: Industrial Workers of the World, 1906.

*Proceedings of the Tenth Convention of the Industrial Workers of the World, Held at Chicago, Illinois, November 20 to December 1, 1916.* Chicago: Industrial Workers of the World, 1917.

*Stenographic Report of the Eighth Annual Convention of the Industrial Workers of the World,* September 14–29, 1913. Chicago: Industrial Workers of the World, 1913.

Thompson, Fred W., and Patrick Murfin. *The I. W. W.: Its First Seventy Years 1905–1975.* Chicago: Industrial Workers of the World, 1976.

*The Truth about the IWW Prisoners.* New York: American Civil Liberties Bureau, 1922.

## Directories

*Ballen and Richards Denver City Directory, Denver, CO,* 1902.

*Dayton, Ohio, City Directory,* 1887.

*Denver City Directory, Denver, CO,* 1909, 1910, 1912, 1915, 1916, 1918, 1920.

*Hot Springs, Arkansas, City Directory,* 1903, 1906, 1908, 1909, 1910.

*Leavenworth City Directory,* 1896, 1898.

*St. Louis City Directory,* 1933.

*Terre Haute, Indiana, City Directory,* 1904.

## Articles and Chapters

Cannon, James. "The Champion from Far Away." In *Notebook of An Agitator,* 163–69. New York: Pathfinder Press, 1958. First published in *Labor Action,* January 16, 1937.

Flynn, Elizabeth Gurley. "Do You Believe in Patriotism." *The Masses* 8, no. 5 (March 1916). https://www.marxists.org/subject/women/authors/flynn/1916/patriotism.htm.

Goldman, Emma. "Marriage and Love." In *Anarchism and Other Essays.* New York: Mother Earth Publishing, 1910. https://www.marxists.org/reference/archive/goldman/works/1914/marriage-love.htm.

## Court Cases

Haywood, William D. Testimony before U.S. District Court of Illinois, August 12, 1918. Transcript available from U.S. vs. Haywood et al., 1917–1918. Series 5: Legal Problems, Trials, and Defense, File 3, pages 11359–11376, Box 117, Subseries B. Walter P. Reuther Library, WSU.

Moyer, Charles H. Plaintiff in Error, v. James H. Peabody, Sherman M. Bell, and Bulkeley Wells, 212 U.S. 78 (1909).

Oates, John Joseph. Testimony before United States District Court of Illinois, August 3, 1918. Transcript available from U.S. vs. Haywood et al., 1917–1918, Series 5: Legal Problems, Trials, and Defense, File 4: 10036, Box 115, Subseries B, Walter P. Reuther Library, WSU.

Perry, Grover. Testimony before U.S. District Court of Illinois, August 8, 1918. Transcript available from U.S. vs. Haywood et al., 1917–1918, Series 5: Legal Problems, Trials, and Defense, File 3:10928, Box 116, Subseries B, Walter P. Reuther Library, WSU.

State of Arizona vs. H. E. Wootton (generally known as the "Bisbee Deportation case"), 1918, as presented in *Law of Necessity as Applied in State of Arizona, Bisbee IWW vs. Deportation Case H. E. Wootton.* Document available in Bisbee Deportation Legal Papers and Exhibits, Special Collections, H9791 B621 L41, UA.

## Other Histories and Pamphlets

*Central Reformed Church, Members, 1850–1874.* Hope College. Thiel Research Center. Holland, Michigan.

"Information Concerning Denver's Most Superb and Charming Residence Addition, New Capitol Hill." New Capitol Hill Realty Co., Denver, 1900. Colorado Historical Society 978.81 C172.

Leonard, John William, ed. *Woman's Who's Who of America, 1914–1915.* New York: American Commonwealth, 1914.

National Civil Liberties Bureau. *War-Time Prosecutions and Mob Violence, Involving the Rights of Free Speech, Free Press, and Peaceful Assemblage.* 1919. Reprint, Amsterdam: Fredonia Books, 2004.

*Representative Women of Colorado.* Denver: Alexander Art, 1911.

Runnette, Mabel Mann. *A History of the Monday Literary Club, 1881–1939.* 2 Vols. (January 1939). SHL.

Stone, Wilbur Fiske. *History of Colorado.* Chicago: S. J. Clarke, 1918.

## Speeches

Sanger, Margaret. "Voluntary Motherhood." National Birth Control League, March 1917.

Wilson, Woodrow. *Final Address in Support of the League of Nations.* Pueblo, Colorado. September 24, 1919.

## Databases

Ancestry.com. *U.S., World War II Army Enlistment Records, 1938–1946* (database online). Provo, UT, 2005.

*California, Voter Registrations, 1900–1968* (database online). Provo, UT, Ancestry.com.

"IWW History Project." University of Washington. http://depts.washington.edu/iww/map_locals.shtml.

*U.S., Find A Grave Index, 1600s-Current* (database online). Provo, UT, Ancestry.com, 2012.

## *Secondary Sources*
## Dissertations, Theses, and Unpublished Material

Bartram, James K. "I Can't Speak: Social Control and the IWW Free Speech Movement." Master's thesis, California State University, 2018.

Goldstein, Marcia Tremmel. "Breaking Down Barriers: Black and White Women's Visions of Integration—The Young Women's Christian Association in Denver and the Phyllis Wheatley Branch, 1915–1964." Master's thesis, University of Colorado at Denver, 1995.

Kirkpatrick, David. "Jane Street and Denver's Rebel Housemaids: The Gender of Radicalism in the Industrial Workers of the World." Master's thesis, Princeton University, 1992.

Mark, Kaite. "Domestic Workers: An Ongoing Fight for Human Rights, Respect, and Dignity at the Workplace." http://archives.evergreen.edu/webpages/curricular/2010-2011/ageofirony/aoizine/kaite.html.

Martin, Taylor. "The Fight for Industrial Democracy and Domestic Prosperity: Working Class and Prominent Women's Participation in the Colorado Coal Field Strike, 1913–15." Master's thesis, University of Colorado at Boulder, 2015.

## Books

Adler, William M. *The Man Who Never Died.* New York: Bloomsbury, 2012.

Armitage, Susan, and Elizabeth Jameson. *The Women's West.* Norman: University of Oklahoma Press, 1987.

Asbaugh, Carolyn. *Lucy Parsons: An American Revolutionary.* Chicago: Haymarket Press, 1976.

Bancroft, Caroline. *Gulch of Gold: A History of Central City, Colorado.* Denver: Sage Books, 1958.

Baron, Ava, ed. *Work Engendered Toward a New History of American Labor.* Ithaca: Cornell University Press, 1991.

Beaton, Gail M. *Colorado Women: A History.* Boulder: University Press of Colorado, 2012.

Berman, David R. *Radicalism in the Mountain West, 1890–1920.* Boulder: University Press of Colorado, 2007.

Berson, Robin K. *Jane Addams: A Biography*. Westport, CT: Greenwood Press, 2004.

Blevins, Tim, Chris Nicholl, and Calvin P. Otto, eds. *The Colorado Labor Wars 1903–1904*. Colorado Springs: Pikes Peak Library District, 2006.

Botkin, Jane Little. *Frank Little and the IWW: The Blood That Stained an American Family*. Norman: University of Oklahoma Press, 2017.

Brundage, David Thomas. *The Making of Labor Radicalism: Denver's Organized Workers, 1878–1905*.

Burg, William. *Sacramento's K Street: Where Our City Was Born*. Charleston: History Press, 2012.

Crutchfield, James A. *It Happened in Colorado*. Helena, MT: Two Dot Press, 2008.

Davis, John W. *Wyoming Range War: The Infamous Invasion of Johnson County*. Norman: University of Oklahoma Press, 2010.

Dubofsky, Melvyn. *"Big Bill" Haywood*. New York: St. Martin's Press, 1987.

———. *We Shall Be All: A History of the Industrial Workers of the World*. Abridged ed. Edited by Joseph A. McCartin. Urbana: University of Illinois Press, 2000.

Dumenil, Lynn. *The Second Line of Defense: American Women and World War I*. Chapel Hill: University of North Carolina Press, 2017.

Elshtain, Jean Bethke. *Jane Addams and the Dream of American Democracy*. New York: Basic Books, 2002.

Faulkner, Debra B. *Ladies of the Brown: A Woman's History of Denver's Most Elegant Hotel*. Charleston: History Press, 2010.

Fetter, Rosemary. *Colorado's Legendary Lovers*. Golden, CO: Fulcrum, 2004.

Foner, Philip S. *Women and the American Labor Movement: From Colonial Times to the Eve of WWI*. New York: Free Press, 1979.

Gitelman, Harvey N. *The Legacy of Ludlow*. Reprint edition. Philadelphia: University of Pennsylvania Press, 2016.

Goldstein, Marcia Tremmel. *Denver Women in Their Places: A Guide to Women's History Sites*. Denver: Historic Denver, 2002.

Goodstein, Phil. *The Ghosts of Denver: Capitol Hill*. Denver: New Social Publications, 1996.

Grinstead, Leigh A. *Molly Brown's Capitol Hill Neighborhood*. Denver: Historic Denver, 2002.

Hayden, Dolores. *The Grand Domestic Revolution: A History of Feminist Designs for American Homes, Neighborhoods, and Cities*. Cambridge: MIT Press, 1981.

Hurst, James W. *Pancho Villa and Black Jack Pershing: The Punitive Expedition in Mexico*. Westport, CT: Praeger, 2007.

Jensen, Vernon H. *Heritage of Conflict*. Ithaca, NY: Cornell University Press, 1950.

Katzman, David. *Seven Days a Week: Women and Domestic Service in Industrializing America*. Champaign: University of Illinois Press, 1981.

Knight, Louise W. *Spirit in Action*. New York: W. W. Norton & Company, 2010.

Martin, MaryJoy. *The Corpse on Boomerang Hill*. Montrose, CO: Western Reflections, 2004.

Mayer, Heather. *Beyond the Rebel Girl*. Corvallis: Oregon State University, 2018.

Mellinger, Phillip J. *Race and Labor in Western Copper*. Tucson: University of Arizona Press, 1995.

Mercer, A. S. *The Banditti of the Plains*. Norman: University of Oklahoma Press, 1954.

Milkman, Ruth. *On Gender, Labor, and Inequality*. Chicago: University of Illinois, 2016.

Milkman, Ruth, ed. *Women, Work, and Protest*. New York: Routledge, 1985.

Noel, Thomas J., and Barbara S. Norgren. *Denver: The City Beautiful*. Denver: Historic Colorado, 1993.

Palmer, Phyllis. *Domesticity and Dirt*. Philadelphia: Temple University Press, 1989.

Pemicone, Nunzio. *Carlo Tresca: Portrait of a Rebel*. Oakland, CA: AK Press, 2010.

Preston, William, Jr. *Aliens and Dissenters: Federal Suppression of Radicals, 1903–1933*. 2nd ed. Chicago: University of Illinois Press, 1994.

Punke, Michael. *Fire and Brimstone*. New York: Hyperion, 2006.

Renshaw, Patrick. *The Wobblies: The Story of the IWW and Syndicalism in the United States*. Updated edition. Chicago: Ivan R. Dee, 1999.

Riley, Marilyn Griggs. *High Altitude Attitudes: Six Savvy Colorado Women*. Johnson Books, 2006.

Scott, Joan Wallach. *Gender and the Politics of History*. New York: Columbia University Press, 1999.

Sellars, Nigel A. *Oil, Wheat & Wobblies*. Norman: University of Oklahoma Press, 1998.

Suggs, George. *Colorado's War on Militant Unionism: James H. Peabody and the Western Federation of Miners*. Norman: University of Oklahoma Press, 1991.

Tax, Meredith. *The Rising of Women: Feminist Solidarity and Class Conflict, 1880–1917*. Chicago: University of Illinois Press, 2001.

Van Raaphorst, Donna L. *Union Maids Not Wanted: Organizing Domestic Workers, 1870–1940*. New York: Praeger, 1988.

Wallach, Joan Scott. *Gender and the Politics of History*. New York: Columbia University, 1999.

### Articles, Chapters, and Pamphlets

Barbour, Charlotte A. "Vanished Neighborhood on Capitol Hill, Denver." *Colorado Magazine* 37, no. 4 (October 1960): 254–61.

Beck, Elizabeth. "The National Domestic Workers Union and the War on Poverty." *Journal of Sociology and Social Welfare* 28, no. 4 (December 2001): Article 11. https://scholarworks.wmich.edu/jssw/vol28/iss4/11.

Boris, Eileen, and Premilla Nadasen. "Domestic Workers Organize." *Working USA: The Journal of Labor and Society* 11, no. 4 (December 2008): 413–37.

Byrkit, James. *Forging the Copper Collar*, 187–215. Tucson: University of Arizona, 1982.

Cameron, Ardis. "Bread and Roses Revisited: Women's Culture and Working-Class Activism in the Lawrence Strike of 1912." In *Women, Work & Protest*, edited by Ruth Milkman, 43–46. New York: Routledge, 1985.

Crain, Caleb. "There Was Blood." *New Yorker*. January 19, 2009.

Eleff, Robert M. "The 1916 Minnesota Miners' Strike against U.S. Steel." *Minnesota History* 51, no. 2 (Summer 1988): 63–74.

England, Kim, and Kate Boyer. "Women's Work: The Feminization and Shifting Meanings of Clerical Work." *Journal of Social History* 43, no. 2 (Winter 2009): 307–40.

Feldberg, Roslyn L. "'Union Fever': Organizing Among Clerical Workers, 1900–1930." In *Workers' Struggles, Past and Present*, edited by James Green, 151–67. Philadelphia: Temple University Press, 1983.

Goldin, Claudio L. "The Work and Wages of Single Women, 1870–1920." *Journal of Economic History* 40, no. 1 (March 1980): 81–88.

Goodfriend, Joyce D., and Dona K. Flory. "Women in Colorado." *Colorado Magazine* 53, no. 3 (Summer 1976): 201–28.

Greguras, Fred. "1916 State Mobilization Camps." Revised June 2015. https://dmna.ny.gov/historic/reghist/wwi/.

"High Society and the Mining Hall of Fame." *Colorado Central Magazine*, September 1, 2005. https://coloradocentralmagazine.com/high-society-and-the-mining-hall-of-fame/.

Hobby, Daniel T., ed. "We Have Got Results: A Document on the Organization of Domestics in the Progressive Era." *Labor History* 17 (Winter 1976): 103–8.

Kessler-Harris, Alice. "Where Are the Organized Women Workers," *Feminist Studies* 3, no. 112 (Fall 1975): 92–110.

Larson, Thomas. "The Good Shoemaker and the Poor Fish Peddler." *San Diego Reader*, August 5, 2005. https://thomaslarson.com/publications/san-diego-reader/62-the-good-shoemaker.html.

Laskey, Hadar. "The Rise of Women in the Workforce in the 19th and 20th Century." https://historicalgeographiesofthecity581.wordpress.com/2017/10/30/the-rise-of-women-in-the-workforce-in-the-19th-and-20th-century.

Masich, Matt. "The Colorado Coalfield War and the Children of Ludlow." *Colorado Life Magazine*. N.d. http://www.coloradolifemagazine.com/The-Colorado-Coalfield-War-and-the-Children-of-Ludlow/.

Mattina, Anne F. "Corporate Tools and Time-Serving Slaves: Class and Gender in the Rhetoric of Antebellum Labor Reform." *Howard Journal of Communications* 7 (1996): 151–68.

———. "'Yours for Industrial Freedom': Women of the IWW, 1905–1930." *Women's Studies* 43 (2014): 170–201.

Peace, Samuel Thomas. "Zeb's Black Baby," In *Vance County, North Carolina: A Short History*, 216. Henderson, NC: Seeman Printery, 1955.

Shah, Hinah, and Marci Seville. "Domestic Worker Organizing: Building a Contemporary Movement for Dignity and Power." *Albany Law Review* 75, no. 413 (2012).

Shor, Francis. "'Virile Syndicalism' in Comparative Perspective: A Gender Analysis of the IWW in the United States and Australia," March 14, 1998. https://www.iww.org/history/library/misc/Shor1998#notes.

Terborg-Oenn, Rosalyn. "Survival Strategies Among African-American Women." In *Women, Work & Protest*, edited by Ruth Milkman, 140–41. New York: Routledge, 1985.

Tracy, Natalicia, Tim Sieber, and Susan Moir. "Invisible No More: Domestic Workers Organizing in Massachusetts and Beyond." Brazilian Immigrant Center and the Labor Resource Center. University of Massachusetts, Boston, MA, October 2014.

White, Ahmed A. "The Crime of Economic Radicalism: Criminal Syndicalism Laws and the Industrial Workers of the World, 1917–1927." *Oregon Law Review* 85, no. 3 (2006): 649–769.

Whitten, Woodrow C. "Criminal Syndicalism and the Law in California: 1919–1927." *Transactions of the American Philosophical Society, New Series* 59, no. 2 (1969): 3–73.

## Websites

"Chicago Fire of 1871." *History.* https://www.history.com/topics/19th-century/great-chicago-fire.

Circus Historical Society. https://circushistory.org/.

Industrial Workers of the World. https://www.iww.org/.

"IWW History Project." University of Washington. http://depts.washington.edu/iww/.

Jane Addams Hull House. https://janeaddamshullhouse.org.

Morton, Tom. "Louise Sneed Hill and Denver's 'Sacred Thirty-Six,'" Fairmount Foundation. April 23, 2013. http://fairmountheritagefoundation.org/louise-sneed-hill-and-denvers-sacred-thirty-six/.

National Domestic Workers Alliance. https://www.domesticworkers.org/.

## Documentaries, Radio, and Television

Klocksin, Katie. "Tensions and Torches after the Great Chicago Fire." WBEZ 91.5. Chicago. https://www.wbez.org/shows/curious-city/tensions-and-torches -after-the-great-chicago-fire/23056033-9387-4d4b-a398-ab0431419279.

*Strong Sisters: Elected Women of Colorado.* Documentary. Directed by Laura Hoeppne and Meg Froelich. StrongSisters.org. 2016. http://www.strongsisters .org/ and https://www.youtube.com/watch?v=kgtaICe0Wvg&feature=youtu.be.

## Music

Judge, Jack, and Harry Williams. "The Maids' Defiance." Sheet Music.

# INDEX